Power and Sustainability of the Chinese State

Since the start of the twenty-first century China has risen to the status of an important world power. This book examines Chinese power, focusing in particular, although not exclusively, on its economic capabilities, and considering how this is likely to develop in the future. It provides a detailed assessment of the key facets of Chinese power today, including GDP, growth, multinationals, and technological and scientific innovation. It identifies the key trends in these areas, compares China's experience with other important global powers such as the US, and considers how this is viewed by the Chinese themselves, including through the lens of their popular culture and mass media. It goes on to identify the foremost problems facing China and the Chinese state today, including fiscal management and public finance, poverty, inequality and rural development, and considers whether China is capable of overcoming these challenges and continuing its remarkable economic development. It addresses crucial questions such as the impact of globalization on Chinese power, and whether Communist Party rule is sustainable for the foreseeable future.

Keun Lee is the Director of the Institute for China Studies, and a Professor of Economics at the Seoul National University, Korea. His main research topic is the economics of catch-up applied in the context of corporate governance and growth, industrial policy, and innovation and technology policy in Korea and China.

Joon-Han Kim is currently President of the POSRI (Posco Research Institute). Previously, he was a Senior Fellow at the Daegu-Gyeongbuk Development Institute, the Construction & Economy Research Institute of Korea (CERIK), the Korea Institute for Industrial Economics and Trade (KIET), and also taught at the Hanyang University. His main areas of research are public finance and industrial economics.

Wing Thye Woo holds the New Century Chair in International Trade and Economics at the Brookings Institution (Washington, DC). He is also Professor at the University of California (Davis), the Yangtze River (Zhang Jiang) Professor at the Central University of Finance and Economics (Beijing), and the Director of the East Asia Program in the Earth Institute, Columbia University.

China policy series

Series editor

Zheng Yongnian, China Policy Institute, University of Nottingham, UK

1. China and the New International Order
Edited by Wang Gungwu and Zheng Yongnian

2. China's Opening Society
The non-state sector and governance
Edited by Zheng Yongnian and Joseph Fewsmith

3. Zhao Ziyang and China's Political Future
Edited by Guoguang Wu and Helen Lansdowne

4. Hainan – State, Society, and Business in a Chinese Province
Kjeld Erik Brodsgaard

5. Non-Governmental Organizations in China
The rise of dependent autonomy
Yiyi Lu

6. Power and Sustainability of the Chinese State
Edited by Keun Lee, Joon-Han Kim and Wing Thye Woo

Power and Sustainability of the Chinese State

Edited by
Keun Lee, Joon-Han Kim and Wing Thye Woo

Routledge
Taylor & Francis Group
LONDON AND NEW YORK

First published 2009 by Routledge
2 Park Square, Milton Park, Abingdon, Oxon OX14 4RN

Simultaneously published in the USA and Canada
by Routledge
270 Madison Avenue, New York, NY 10016

Routledge is an imprint of the Taylor & Francis Group, an informa business

Typeset in Times New Roman by Keyword Group Ltd.
Printed by the MPG Books Group in the UK

British Library Cataloguing in Publication Data
A catalogue record for this book is available from the British Library

Library of Congress Cataloging in Publication Data
Power and sustainability of the Chinese state / edited by Keun Lee, Joon-Han Kim and Wing Thye Woo.
p. cm. -- (China policy series)
Includes bibliographical references and index.
1. China--Economic conditions--2000- 2. Economic forecasting--China. 3. China--Economic policy--2000- I. Lee, Keun, 1960- II. Kim, Joon-Han, 1952- III. Woo, Wing Thye.

HC427.95.P69 2008
330.951--dc22 2008027780

ISBN10: 0-415-46939-2 (hbk)
ISBN10: 0-203-88452-3 (ebk)

ISBN13: 978-0-415-46939-5 (hbk)
ISBN13: 978-0-203-88452-2 (ebk)

Contents

List of tables vii
List of figures ix
List of contributors xi

1 The diverse dimensions, capabilities and sustainability of China's power: An introduction 1
KEUN LEE, JOON-HAN KIM AND WING THYE WOO

PART 1
Perceiving and measuring the power of China **9**

2 Reflections on China's power 11
KWANG OK KIM

3 Quantitative assessment of China's economic power and science and technology power in a comparative perspective 31
ANGANG HU

4 Assessing the tacit dimension of China's science and technology power 47
JONG-HAK EUN

PART 2
Assessing the capabilities of the Chinese state **73**

5 Assessing China's capability to manage the high-probability risks to economic growth: fiscal, governance and ecological problems 75
WING THYE WOO

6 Assessing the fiscal power of the Chinese state: assessing the central government's capacity to implement national policies 100
CHRISTINE WONG

PART 3
Assessing the international dimension of China's power 117

7 Assessing China's power reflected in foreign trade 119
WEI ZHANG

8 Assessing the diplomatic power of China 146
ZHONGYING PANG

PART 4
Party-state-society relations and sustainability 167

9 Globalization and the state power in China 169
ALVIN Y. SO

10 Can the Communist Party sustain its rule in China? 186
YONGNIAN ZHENG

Index *211*

Tables

3.1 GDP and industrial output growth in the rise period 32
3.2 Ratio of GDP (market exchange rate) of country to world total (% 1980–2005) 34
3.3 Ratio of GDP (PPP) of country to world total (% 1980–2003) 35
3.4 Sources of China's economic growth (annual growth, % 1978–2020) 35
3.5 Indicators to assess S&T power 37
3.6 S&T power to world total (% 1980–2004) 37
3.7 Forecasts for China's GDP growth (% 2005–2020) 39
3.8 China's economic perspective (2005–2020) 41
3.9 Rank of main indicators of China in world (1978–2020) 42
3.10 China's marginal contribution to the world GDP growth by period (%) 43
Annex 3.1 S&T indicators to world total in major countries (% 1980–2004) 46
4.1 China's ranking in scientific publications 50
4.2 Major research fields of Chinese scholars 50
4.3 China's patent grant for indigenous and foreign entities 51
4.4 International patent applications (through PCT) 52
4.5 Corporate R&D: Indigenous vs. foreign firms 63
4.6 Indigenous firms' technology import and assimilation 66
4.7 Technology import and assimilation by different types of firms (2005) 67
5.1 Comparative perspective on the size of the national debt (as a percentage of GDP) 94
6.1 Growing disparities in per capita budgetary expenditures by province 105
6.2 Fiscal trends differ for subnational governments 106
6.3 Key new programs for rural education and health 108
6.4 Cost estimates for a start-up HSP 111
7.1 GDP growth of China (1978–2005) 120
7.2 Exports (1978–2005) 121

7.3 Imports (1978–2005) 122
7.4 China's GDP and export shares in the world total (1978–2005) 123
7.5 Export by trading forms (2006) 126
7.6 Top 10 export product group in SITC 127
7.7 China's export country concentration (2005) 128
7.8 China's import country concentration (2005) 129
7.9 Minimum wage comparison in selected countries 131
7.10 TFP growth in industrial sectors (%) 134
7.11 Labour productivity in industry in selected countries (1995 US$) 136
7.12 Export by enterprise types (2006) 137
7.13 Total FDI in China (1979–2005) 138
7.14 Economic indicators of 54 NETDZs (2005) 139
8.1 China's global network of diplomatic missions (diplomatic machinery of government) 151
8.2 China institutions of research and education in diplomacy or international studies 153
8.3 China's memberships in inter-regional, sub-regional and regional institutions 156

Figures

3.1	Relative GDP per capita to U.S. in China, Japan and Korea	41
4.1	Increasing R&D expenditure propelled by corporate R&D	48
4.2	International comparison of R&D expenditure: PPP vs. MER (2004)	49
4.3	Increasing number of scientific publications by Chinese scholars	50
4.4	University graduates and entrants by field of study in China	53
4.5	Unbalanced attention of the traditional approach	56
4.6	A broader perspective on the technological power building mechanism	58
4.7	Industrial production in China	60
4.8	Share of foreign-invested firms in Chinese high-technology industries (by industrial production)	60
4.9	Share of foreign-invested firms in Chinese high-technology exports	61
4.10	Increasing share of wholly owned foreign companies	62
6.1	Trends in budgetary revenues and expenditures	102
6.2	Central revenues as a share of GDP	102
6.3	Central government share of revenues total and net of tax rebates	103
6.4	Trends in central revenues and transfers	103
6.5	Fiscal resources by province 2004 (Yuan per capita)	105
6.6	Hierarchical delegation in China	111
7.1	Ratio of exports to GDP (1978–2005)	123
7.2	China's GDP and export shares in the world	124
7.3	Balance of international trade (1978–2005)	124
7.4	Changes in export structure	125
7.5	Changes in import structure	126
7.6	Depreciation of RMB (1985–2005)	136
10.1	CCP's membership since 1997	193
10.2	Professions of CCP members, 2005	194

List of contributors

Jong-Hak Eun, Professor, Kookmin University, Korea

Angang Hu, Professor, Tsinghua University, China

Joon-Han Kim, President of POSRI (Posco Research Institute), Seoul, Korea

Kwang Ok Kim, Professor of Anthropology, Seoul National University, Korea

Keun Lee, Director, Institute of China Studies; Professor of Economics, Seoul National University, Korea

Zhongying Pang, Professor, Renmin University of China

Alvin Y. So, Professor, University of Science and Technology, Hong Kong

Christine Wong, Professor, Oxford University, UK

Wing Thye Woo, Senior Fellow, Brookings Institution; Professor, University of California at Davis, USA

Wei Zhang, Professor, Cambridge University, UK

Yongnian Zheng, Professor, University of Nottingham, UK

1 The diverse dimensions, capabilities and sustainability of China's power:

An introduction

Keun Lee, Joon-Han Kim and Wing Thye Woo

The intellectual context of this book

It is becoming more and more common to read that China will rise in the twenty-first century to become the most important power in the world.[1] Increasingly, people everywhere on earth are talking about China; especially how China is affecting their countries and lives, what they can (or cannot) do with or without China, and what will happen to China in the future (Chung 2006). It is therefore timely for us to ask what are the sources of China's power, what can China do and how long can China sustain its power? These are the subjects that this book seeks to explore.

This book organises the discussions into four parts. Part 1 focuses on the perception and measurement of China's power by investigating how China's power is perceived by the ordinary Chinese people, and how it is reflected in their popular culture and mass media; and by measuring the power of China with explicit indicators (e.g. GDP growth) and tacit indicators (e.g. who are the actual innovators, foreign or domestic companies?). Part 2 assesses the capability of the Chinese state in terms of what it has achieved so far; and, more importantly, what are the problems it is facing now, how it is dealing with them, and what are the reasons that the efforts of the Chinese state are meeting only limited success? Part 3 considers the international dimension of China's power by looking at China as a trading power and China as a diplomatic power. Part 4 zeroes in on the sustainability of China's power in three aspects: whether China can manage the internal conflicts from rising inequality and other social problems; what is the impact of globalisation on the Chinese power and capabilities; and whether the Chinese Communist Party can sustain its rule in China.

Perceiving and measuring the power of China

In *Reflections on China's Power* (see Chapter 2), Professor Kwang Ok Kim perceives the Chinese government to have launched a special project to shape the national emotion and public sentiments toward the revival of the historical glory of the great Chinese empire. By appropriating the national emotion through successful manipulation of people's collective memories of time and space, the Chinese Communist Party has obtained the people's consent to exercise patriarchal authority and absolute power over the social space.

Through the newly moulded collective memories, people now have a new perspective on their own civilisation and cultural tradition. The past history is seen as a struggle between the barbarous West and Chinese civilization. It is now the time to restore China's traditional position in the world and to keep the world under Chinese civilisation so that the idea of *tianxia* is realised. Professor Kim proposes that a new concept of nationhood is being invented in the name of *zhonghua* minzu (the Great Chinese nation).

Professor Kim observes that this new version of a China-centric world view has created a populist nationalism in China that has led to conflicts between China and its neighbours. Among the young people of China, Korea, and Japan, for example, there are serious disputes and mutual attacks through the internet which are violent enough to be called 'war on the internet'. The young people in these three nations usually appear to lack any political interest related with national issues and enjoy cross-border flow of popular culture. But whenever they feel that their national pride is attacked, their collective memories of the past would immediately cause them to undertake very aggressive counter-attacks. The 'petit nationalism' of this kind is deeply rooted in China's younger generations, and the resulting nationalistic violence is allowed and even politically encouraged in the name of patriotism and the rhetoric of national greatness.

At the present stage, the Chinese mass media has successfully mobilised national emotion and public sentiment to drive people to pledge their full support for the state. Despite the existence of disconcerted voices within different sectors of society, people as a whole understand the internal problems and external affairs within the imagination of China as a great nation and thus within the framework of China's uniqueness. Professor Kim concludes his reflections on China's power by questioning the Chinese people's accommodative calibre of global standard of morality and cultural diversity of the world.

The evolution of the economic power and the science and technology (S&T) power of China is put into comparative perspective by Professor Angang Hu in *Assessing China's Economic Power and Science and Technology Power in Comparative Perspective* (see Chapter 3). Using actual exchange rates, China's share of global GDP increased from 1 per cent in 1980 to 5 per cent in 2005, raising China from the tenth largest economy in the world to the fourth largest (after the US, Japan and Germany). By 2020, China's share of world GDP will rise from 10.2 per cent to 15.8 per cent; and China would have been the biggest contributor to the increase in world GDP between 2005 and 2020 by being responsible for 20 per cent to 35 per cent of the increase.

When Professor Hu repeated the calculations using PPP exchange rates instead, China's share of global GDP had declined from 4.9 per cent in 1978 and increased to approximately 15.1 per cent in 2005;[2] which meant that China had overtaken Japan as the world's second biggest economy in 1992. China's share would rise to over 20 per cent by 2020, and the increase in China's GDP between 2005 to 2020 growth would have accounted for over 30 per cent of the increase in world GDP.

Professor Hu also analyses the transformation of China's scientific and technical (S&T) power by using five indicators:

- the number of international scientific and technical journal articles written by resident Chinese researchers
- the number of innovation patent applications received
- the number of personal computers
- the number of internet users
- the level of research and development expenditure.

China's S&T power was already ranked number two in the world in 2000.

Professor Jong-Hak Eun criticises the traditional neo-classical practice of using only the *codified* part of S&T knowledge to measure China's S&T power (see Chapter 4). Using a new conceptual framework that allows him to include the *tacit* part of S&T knowledge in measuring S&T power, Professor Eun concludes that the conventional ranking of present S&T power of China should be depreciated to a certain degree. He also argues that the further enhancement of China's S&T power would depend not only on the economic situation but also on the socio-political policies and conditions in China.

Assessing the capabilities of the Chinese state

At the 6th Plenum of the 16th Central Committee of the Chinese Communist Party (CCP) in October 2006, the foremost task of CCP was not identified as usual (since December 1978) to be 'economic construction' but was identified instead to be 'the establishment of a harmonious society by 2020.' This change, according to Professor Wing Thye Woo in *Assessing China's Capability to Manage the High-Probability Risks to Economic Growth: Fiscal, Governance and Ecological Problems* (see Chapter 5) has the obvious implication that the present major social, economic and political trends are not leading to a harmonious society or, at least, not leading to a harmonious society fast enough. Professor Woo depicts the Chinese economy as a speeding car, facing the possibility of three classes of failures that could result in a car crash.

Specifically, a *hardware failure* refers to a breakdown in an *economic mechanism*, a development that is analogous to the collapse of the chassis of the car; e.g. a banking crisis that dislocates production economy-wide; a budget crisis that necessitates reductions in important infrastructure and social expenditure. A *software failure* refers to a flaw in *governance* that creates frequent widespread social disorders that disrupt production and lower investment, a situation similar to a car crash caused by a fight among the passengers within the speeding car, e.g. severe social disorders from either the high-growth strategy creating too much inequality and corruption or from the state not being able to meet the rising social expectations about governance issues. A *power supply failure* refers to the economy being unable to move forward because it hits either *a natural limit or an externally imposed limit*, a situation that is akin to the car running out of gas or having its engine switched off because an outsider reached in and pulled out the ignition key, e.g. an environmental collapse; and a collapse in China's exports because of a trade war.

Within each class of failure, Professor Woo identifies the highest probability event to be, respectively, the weakening of China's fiscal position, social disorder, and water shortage; and he ranks these three specific negative events, in descending order of probability, to be social disorder caused by outmoded governance, water shortage as a result of inept environmental management, and a fiscal crisis generated by the repeated recapitalisation of the state banks and the rapid aging of the population.

Professor Woo is very cautiously optimistic that China would succeed in establishing a harmonious society. His considerable caution comes from, one, the new major reforms being technically difficult to implement (e.g. setting up social safety nets), and having few, if any, successful precedents in the world to draw upon (e.g. designing market-compatible environmental regulation); and, two, the possibility that the many potential losers from these major reforms could successfully organise to resist meaningful implementation of the reforms.

China's power is fundamentally linked to its fiscal power, and this is the focus of Professor Christine Wong in *Assessing the Fiscal Power of the Chinese State* (see Chapter 6). How the government raises money, how much it can raise, how the money is spent, and how allocation decisions undertaken have critical effects on economic, political, and social outcomes like the GDP growth rate and the distribution of income. Professor Wong observes that from the start of its transition to a decentralised, market-oriented economy, China has gone through some hard times in public finance terms. The dismantling of the planning apparatus had led quickly to an erosion of the government's main revenue mechanism – SOE profits, and government revenues went into a steep decline, from more than 30 per cent of GDP in the late 1970s, to a low of only 11 per cent in the mid-1990s; and that at the nadir, the central government controlled a budget of only 3 per cent of GDP.

In Professor Wong's historical overview of the fiscal system and its reform in China, from the introduction of the Tax Sharing System in 1994 to other diverse reform measures including the changes to the budgeting and treasury management processes introduced in the late 1990s, she notes that some critical reforms have yet to be undertaken, most notably, in central-local fiscal relations, and in the clarification of the public role in the new economy. In her opinion, China's fiscal system has not yet been adequately transformed into one that is capable of supporting the country's emergence as an economic powerhouse in the twenty-first century. She take as an illustration the new Harmonious Society paradigm introduced by the administration led by Hu Jintao and Wen Jiabao to detail the many difficulties the government will face in efforts to implement the new pro-poor, pro-rural policies.

Assessing the international dimensions of China's power

China's international trade has witnessed rapid growth and radical structural changes in the past three decades. In *Assessing China's Power Reflected in*

Foreign Trade (see Chapter 7), Professor Wei Zhang analyses the several factors and their interactions responsible for the rise of China as a trade power: China's low-cost labour, its market-oriented economic reforms promoted productivity, and state policies attracted a large surge of foreign investment inflow. He notes that this trade expansion has been accompanied by a serious imbalance between its export and import since 1994, the radical shift in export composition from primary-goods intensive to manufacturing-goods intensive, and the very high market concentration of both export and import. He attributes the growth and composition shifts in China's trade to the realisation of its comparative advantages.

However, Professor Zhang emphasises that the further expansion of China's international trade is facing some serious constraints and challenges. For example, China's imbalanced trade structure and high market concentration, have caused tensions between China and its main trade partners. In Professor Zhang's assessment, the most important constraints on the expansion of China's trade power will come from environmental degradation within China, the intertwined macroeconomic relationship between internal imbalance and external imbalance, and the new challenges due to China's WTO obligation. All those factors will put pressures on China to increase investment in environmental protection and social welfare systems, therefore inevitably increasing the cost of production and export. The termination of state subsidies to foreign-invested export-oriented firms will also slow down the speed of expanding China's trade share in the world.

While trade power is only one aspect of the international dimensions of China power, diplomatic power is another important aspect. Professor Zhongying Pang analyses China's diplomatic power from the following perspectives: 'hard power', 'soft power', 'relational power' and 'structural power' in *Assessing the Diplomatic Power of China* (see Chapter 8). He also discusses the quality of China's diplomacy.

Professor Pang points out that China's diplomacy has mainly concentrated on 'economic diplomacy' since the late 1970s. He argues that the element of multinational companies (MNCs) should be included in understanding the linkage between China's diplomacy and its power; and that while China's diplomatic power has been rising very quickly, the limits of its diplomatic power are apparent. He concludes that the future of China's diplomatic power depends on where China makes fundamental reforms in its economy and polity, and whether China could improve its foreign policy decision-making and implementation.

Party-state-society relations and sustainability

The aim of *Globalization and the State Power in China* (see Chapter 9) by Professor Alvin So is to examine how the forces of globalisation have transformed the Chinese state. Professor So finds that the Chinese mode of governance has shifted '*upward*' to suprastate organisations when it joins such organisations as the WTO and WHO, has shifted '*downward*' to substate organisations when it carried out fiscal decentralisation, has shifted '*sideways*' to border governments when subregion economies have sprung up along the coast, and shifted '*outward*' to market and society when it carried out neo-liberal policies to download welfare obligations.

Professor So argues that China has handled the globalisation challenges very well. For the '*upward*' challenge, China is able to seize the opportunity to expand its power and influence in suprastate organisations, to learn how to play the rules of games to its advantage, and even able to initiate its own macro-regional organisations, like SCO and ASEAN+1. For the '*downward*' and '*sideways*' challenges, China is able to turn them into effective forces of economic development while still maintaining full control over the substates and the border governments. For the '*outward*' challenge, China is also able to re-regulate the market and contain the harms done by it. His conclusion is that the Chinese state has managed the globalisation process extremely competently. China has not been threatened by globalisation and is definitely not a victim of the forces of globalisation.

Professor Yongnian Zheng addresses the intriguing question asked by his chapter *Can the Communist Party Sustain its Rule in China?* (see Chapter 10) by elaborating the various sources that legitimatise, and thus sustain, the rule of the CCP. There are cultural roots of authoritarianism in China, and more than anything else, the CCP is the personification of a modern emperor. Unlike the traditional highly decentralised emperorship, this modern emperorship is highly centralised. The engagement in socio-economic transformation by the CCP is the source of the legitimacy of its rule.

Professor Zheng observes that CCP's engagement in socio-economic transformation has in turn transformed the CCP. In order to cope with the rapid speed of socio-economic transformation, the party has been relentlessly searching for a feasible solution to the problem of rationalising its relations with the state and with different social actors. Professor Zheng uses the expression of 'rigid flexibility' to describe the overall evolution of the CCP: the overall structure remains intact while its content consistently undergoes changes. It is important to see the sustainability of the CCP in the light of these content changes, despite a seemingly unchanged one-party structure. On the question of the impacts of globalisation on the CCP and its rule in China, he recognises opposite impacts from global capitalism on the sustainability of CCP rule.

Professor Zheng's overall conclusions are that a rigid CCP is not sustainable, and that China's experience in the past three decades shows that the CCP is open to change, albeit a slow pace of change. The answer to the question of whether CCP rule is sustainable depends both on whether it can continue to transform itself and how it is transformed.

Can China sustain its power?

China certainly seems to be on track to emerge as a new super power in the twenty-first century. As many Chinese emphasise nowadays, it is actually the re-emergence of China. As noted by Angang Hu (see Chapter 3), China's GDP was almost one third of world GDP in 1820, it declined to 4.6 per cent in 1950 and then increased to 15.1 per cent in 2005. Measuring China power by such output-based indicators can be misleading however when a large portion of high value-added production activities based on advanced S&T are in the hands of multinational corporations (MNCs). Jong-Hak Eun (see Chapter 4) observes that the recent Chinese achievements in attracting R&D centres of MNCs also could have a crowding-out effect if it were to lead to the indigenous companies losing their best talents to foreign-owned companies.

In this sense, China's power might be better assessed if it is looked at in terms of China's ability to solve the problems that appear (the hardware, software and power supply failures identified by Wing Thye Woo in Chapter 5). This approach is also taken in several other chapters in of this book: how to handle fiscal weakness by Christine Wong (see Chapter 6), trade conflicts by Wei Zhang (see Chapter 7), and political modernisation by Yongnian Zheng (see Chapter 10). These analyses show that China is showing only limited success in these areas. For example, while the bulk of fiscal resources are in the hands of the lower levels of the Chinese state (e.g. provincial and county levels), these lower levels of government are not really accountable for their responsibilities in areas like education and health (which affect public welfare directly). Such fiscal weakness is not new but the central government has not been able to solve the problem despite the two decades of efforts. These cases reveal clearly the limitations of China's capabilities and its exercise of power.

This book's answer to the question of whether China can sustain its power is that it depends upon China's ability to handle the following tasks. On the domestic front, China has to manage its fiscal weakness, multidimensional (regional and sectoral) inequalities, and social conflicts better. On the external front, China's high economic growth depends upon continued access to the American markets and thus adept handling with economic relations with the US is vital. China also faces substantial challenges in the area of international politics because China has yet to learn how to play as a key international actor, a change from its traditional role as a low key player, as noted by Zhongying Pang (see Chapter 8). While Alvin So is optimistic about China's ability to cope with globalisation (see Chapter 9), Yongnian Zheng (see Chapter 10) points out that globalisation could also be a potential barrier to the flexible transformation of the CCP.

While Yongnian Zheng notes the CCP has a good record in continually changing itself, one cannot be sure of its success in the future. As Wing Thye Woo notes, the past success does not mean it will succeed in the future because the Chinese will be facing totally new challenges that have never been present in the past in terms of both their nature and scale. Given the huge and ever increasing impact of China on the rest of the world, it can be said, as by Angang Hu, that China's success is the world's success and that China's failure is also the world's failure. This means that the sustainability of China's power depends not only on whether China could build the so-called 'harmonious society' within China but also on whether China could keep harmonious relations with the rest of the world.

We are not assured about whether China could maintain its harmony with the world, however. Kwang Ok Kim (see Chapter 2) notes the rising nationalist tone in Chinese folk culture and the mass-media, where people are re-defining their national emotion and imagination toward the revival of the glorious Chinese Empire as the political, economic, and cultural centre of the world. The Chinese state has produced TV dramas and documents to re-shape the hidden desires of its people. Out of this state encouragement of a new 'national emotion', the Chinese public is now increasingly publicising its yearning for China to become a real super power to vie with the USA on the world stage.

Given all of the above considerations, the questions about the exercise of power by China, and the sustainability of China's power, remain to be answered by the Chinese people themselves. We hope that the enlightened self-interests of the Chinese people will determine the making of state policies and the evolution of the political culture within China and the Chinese Communist Party.

Notes

1 Recent examples are in Lampton (2008).
2 China's share had fallen from almost one-third of the world total in 1820 to 4.6 per cent in 1950.

References

Chung, Jae Ho (ed.) (2006) *Charting China's Future: Political, Social, and International Dimensions*. Lanham, Maryland: Rowman & Littlefield Publishers.

Lampton, David (2008) *Three Faces of Chinese Power*. California: University of California Press.

Part 1

Perceiving and measuring the power of China

2 Reflections on China's power[1]

Kwang Ok Kim

If one can control memory, one can control people.

(M. Foucault)

Without imagination, it is impossible to have desire.

(J. Lacan)

Introduction

At the beginning of the new era of China opening up in the early 1980s, a television documentary 'River Elegy' (*heshang*) swept the nation. In 2006, almost two decades later, CCTV aired a super documentary series 'The Rise of a Great Nation' (*daguojueqi*) which was accompanied by mounting heated debates among the people of PRC, including the Chinese living overseas.

Both the 'River Elegy' and the 'Rise of a Great Nation' originally started from the same questions of why China had lost her glory and how she can be revived as a great nation in the world. The former gave people a message that China had lost her glory and remained backward because her old culture and civilization caused China to fail in achieving modernity. Soon after the Tiananmen Square incident, however, the documentary became a target of official and public criticism. It was branded as anti-revolutionary and unpatriotic. The production team of the film was accused of blindly following the Western imperialist-centered version of history without a sense of national dignity. The film was also under suspicion for attempting to criticize Mao's reign of China. The whole process of intellectual discourse waxed and waned around the film, echoing the hot debates between the Westernization movement (*yangwu yundong*) after the May Fourth Movement (1919) and its counter intellectual movement (*dongfang xuepai*), to discover a modernization drive from Chinese civilization and cultural tradition.

The *Rise of a Great Nation* was a series of documentaries focusing on such countries as Spain, Portugal, Great Britain, Germany, France, Russia, the USA, the Netherlands, and Japan. It examined how these nations achieved great (imperial) power.[2] The series ended with a concluding narration about the great Chinese empire being humiliated at the turn of the century, the 50 years of PRC as a period of unprecedented and ever increasing development and prosperity, which would lead spectators to imagine that China is being revived as a great world power. The film was enthusiastically acclaimed. There was a series of heated public discussions that national wealth and strong military power (*fuguo qiangbing*) are the very basis on which the dream of Great China (*dazhonghua* or *daguo*) can be realized. Many were stimulated by the rousing message that a Great China is imminent.

The film *Daguo Jueqi* has now become a new classic text for all intellectuals in their discussion of China's future. During the past couple of years, various spectacular movies, television dramas and documentaries were produced to rewrite the history of China, from ancient times to the present. Print mass media also induced an expectation among people of a Great China, thereby encouraging popular patriotism and a new sense of pride and self-assurance about being Chinese. From this popular nationalism, people in their everyday conversations express unbridled protectionism against the approaching foreign powers. An upsurge of public debates began in 2007, following the *Daguo Jueqi*, on the issues of China launching into international competition in the manufacture of super-sized aircraft and carrier ships, the development of high-tech missiles, and the promotion of space industries. If anyone showed a negative or reluctant attitude toward these issues, then he or she would be criticized as lacking national pride and patriotism.

It is not unusual in China to see television dramas and documentaries, and even special popular cultural programs on national commemoration days and seasonal festivals, to be designed and broadcast in relation to certain socio-political campaigns. When we talk of China's power, in this context, it is necessary to evaluate not only the size of the economy and political voice in the world order system, but also the fashion of national culture which is shaped through interaction between the state and people. We will tentatively call it, for the purpose of this discussion, 'national emotion' or 'public emotion'. As public emotion is recognized, and even encouraged by the state, it can also be called 'national emotion'. 'National emotion' is a form of flexible cultural fashion because it is the process of making and re-making. It deals with people's ideology, worldview, ideas and attitudes toward the state and nation, and politically correct sentiment officially defined in the name of the nation. This set of emotions and sentiments produces specific images of past history as well as of the national future.

If we accept Anderson's theory that a nation is an imagined community (Anderson 1983), we would accede that China is regarded as a multi-imagined community. There is a high degree of internal differentiation and ethnic and cultural heterogeneity. The most vital question is, therefore, not how to solve inequality of power and wealth among people, but how to make people believe that they are members of a (national) community sharing the same culture and historical destiny. Politics, in this regard, is a very cultural process manufacturing a national emotion by which people construct their imagined community (Cohen 1988).

In the study of contemporary China, the state-society relationship has been the key theoretical perspective. China, since the socialist revolution, has been perceived to be the most distinctive case of the state imposing and penetrating its power and authority into the private sphere of people's day-to-day life (Shue 1988). Such subjects as political elites, CCP, system of unit (*danwei*), social identity of a person (*hukou*), and official record of a person (*dang-an*) have been exploited in understanding the state's domination over the people's private sphere. In this context, it has been the central concern of study to discover the growing possibility of civil society to cope with the ever expanding state power.

Inspired by such scholars as J. Scott (1985, 1990) and M. de Certeau (1984), who elaborated on the theory of arts of resistance of the weak in their everyday life situations, many scholars of Chinese studies have focused on people's strategic responses to the state. This is in order to deal with contemporary phenomena in the context of conflict and competition between the state and (civil) society (see Perry and Selden 2005, 2000).

It is true that people sometimes voice complaints and criticisms against the government when state policies affect the conditions of material life. Sometimes, they organize demonstrations to demand their rights. We need to consider the cultural system and historical background of China, however, in order to discuss the question of whether people's complaints about some of the government's policies can be branded as challenge and conflict between the state and society. For the Chinese, the state is an absolute entity, a powerful entity conceived only through imagination.

Confucianism being so deeply embedded in their worldview, the Chinese in general have a strong tendency to believe that the state and society are not two separate entities opposing each other but are interrelated to make one conclusive system. Therefore, people are allowed to attempt their collective act of resistance in accordance with regulation within the state framework. Despite a general prediction that economic prosperity will bring more space for civil society, in contemporary China, the expansion of state space seems to be far exceeding the growth of civilian space. The state and society, in this regard, do not stand in a zero-sum relationship. China, through a very long history of state, has constructed a multi-ethnic nation with its typically complicated cultural heterogeneity and regional varieties. Reflecting this multi-national reality, the government has developed special policies to deal with relationships among nationalities. However, when talking about China as a nation-state, both Chinese, especially the Han Chinese, and foreigners usually disregard the existence of the other 55 ethnic groups. They treat China as an ethnically and culturally homogeneous national community of the Han. This leads us to reconsider the Chinese concept of the state, and that of the state-society relationship, which might be different from concept in the Western tradition.

It should also be pointed out that resistance or challenge against the state does not necessarily occur as an inevitable response to the reality of a social 'crack'. Experiences of oppression, alienation, poverty, exploitation, or even of being uprooted, do not necessarily lead to a violent revolutionary challenge to the state. In other words, what people are really concerned with is a proper explanation of their lived experience in real life situations. People are willing to endure their contemporary life situation and even support the state, if they are given an acceptable explanation. Therefore, it is far more important for the state to control people's emotion and sentiment through various cultural policies and programs. People define their life and evaluate the meaning of their existence through the politically produced 'national emotion'. Despite its importance, however, the idea of 'national emotion' has not been fully considered in understanding real society. This is because scholars do not make an effort to do a long-term participant-observation within people's everyday life situations. Also, social scientists have a tendency to neglect it because it cannot be digitalized as scientific data, while relying heavily upon official documents and statistics and political rhetoric.

There have been many studies on how social or collective memories are made among different social forces within a national community (Johnson *et al.* 1982; Connerton 1989; Fentress, and Wickham 1992). Scholars have also analysed cases of contest between official and private memories in socialist states (see Watson 1994). However, these studies overlook the fact that, in the case of contemporary China, the state exercises its absolute control over mass media. It produces and controls people's collective memories and imaginations.

In China, mass media, especially television and movies, are the most effective and powerful instruments to link people with the state across regional, ethnic, class, and generational differences. All mass media programs are under the firm control of the General Bureau of Radio and Television (*guangdian congju*) in the Ministry of Culture. Any major product should be designed and produced in accordance with the guidelines and supervision of the state. Passing through the state's strict censorship procedure, the final version of a product has to wait for the state's permit before its release to the public (see Kang and Zhou 1992).

This chapter therefore attempts to describe what type of imagination and emotion the Chinese state and people produce for the contemporary issue of 'China as a Great Nation' (*Da Guo*), based on a personal observation of cultural practices and popular discourses as they appeared in television programs, movies, and popular magazines.

Background of producing public imagination and national emotion

Despite unprecedented prosperity, the radical transformation of society during the past 20 years has produced many new socio-political problems in China, i.e., corruption, social injustice, and an ever expanding gap between classes, regions, and social sectors. It has also led to the demise of ecology, the problems with water and food safety, a poor public healthcare system, institutional inefficiency, and so on. Scholars point out that the existence of such problems, as a whole, is seriously threatening national integration. Ordinary people would also raise critical questions concerning uneven development among sectors, a bubble economy, and governmental blue prints for the national future. Focusing on CCP's caliber to cope with these mountains of problems, some political scientists raise a question of governance deficit (see Pei 2006; Howell 2004), while other scholars take a positive stance of emphasizing the progressive attitude of the Party and government in dealing with the problems (Naughton and Yang 2004; Cho 2006; Guthrie 2006). While political scientists lean more on the Party and government, sociologists tend to adopt a broader and more inclusive perspective on society. They are mainly concerned with the question of socio-economic differentiation among members of the national community and the increasing gap between classes (see Li *et al.* 2004). Some scholars are even serious enough to diagnose the contemporary Chinese society to be 'cracked' (*duanlie*) (see Sun 2003).

Nonetheless, we see that the government is well aware of these problems and is therefore making great efforts to seek practical measures to cope with them. Institutional reform is continuously carried out. Legal institutions and laws on economy and industry are also being reformed to meet international standards. Strict legal measures are being taken against serious cases of corruption and violations. Government officials and party cadres are recruited, through the examination system, among young professionals with higher educational backgrounds. These efforts and changes indicate that the Party and government have enhanced their capability to rule the nation. Evaluating CCP's internal reform and success to gain people's support in the midst of indispensable negative outcomes of the rapid economy-centered growth, political scientists would define the status quo with such phrases as 'fragile stability' (Dickson 2000), 'stable unrest' (Whyte 2000), or 'stable instability' (Chung 2006).

It should be noted that the Party has made an enormous effort to cope with unwanted but radical changes in the social landscape. As people began to show indifference toward socialism or socialist ideology as an aftermath of the Great Cultural Revolution, the state popularized such catchphrases as 'Chinese market economy' to implement the Reform and Opening-up Policy. It also launched several cultural programs of 'Patriotism Education' instead of 'socialism education' in the early 1990s. At the 15th Congress of CCP in 2002, the delegates amended the CCP constitution and defined the Party not only as the vanguard of the workers but also as the vanguard of the people (*zhonggou renmin*) and the Nation of China (*zhonghua minzu*). Here, we note the word 'people' instead of a specific class of 'worker', on the one hand, and that of a newly invented category '*zhonghua minzu*', beyond a specific nationality or ethnic group, on the other. The CCP, in this way, began again with multiple and inclusive identities not as a party of workers but as a party of all people, and not a party for class struggle but a party for a new universal Nation of China. The government ventured to rebuild, re-construct, innovate, restore, and excavate many archaeological sites and historical relics and heritage, most of which were destroyed during the Great Cultural Revolution. Under the banner of 'Raising Up and Spreading the Great Chinese Cultural Tradition' (*hongyang zhonghua wenhua*), the government designated these restored historical and cultural relics as the material cultural properties (*wenwu danwei*) of the state or local government. These historical sites and constructions also became bases for patriotism education (*aiguo jiayu jidi*), wherein students and workers of a unit were encouraged to organize group pilgrim tours as part of their outdoor educational activity. Through this, the Party and government came to establish their image as the protector of the history and culture of the people and the nation (Kim 1993, 2000). Through the appropriation of patriotism and cultural nationalism, CCP appealed to the people and overseas Chinese for their support.

China needed international recognition and support for entering and positioning in the international stage, e.g. hosting the Asian Games in 1993, bidding for the Olympic Games, getting membership to international organizations such as WTO, and securing influence in world politics. For this, the government made its great effort to revive and propagate the greatness of Chinese culture and civilization. In order to purge the shadowy memories of the Great Cultural Revolution and the nightmare of the Tiananmen Square incident, on the one hand, and stimulated by their achievement of economic development which freed people from poverty and hunger, on the other, CCP and the government came to design a politics of culture to let people have a new image on past history as well as the future of the nation.

The present government created, as a new ideological principle to cure social and cultural cracks, the cultural agenda of 'harmonious society' (*hexie shehui*). It issued a list of values in the name of Eight Virtues and Eight Shames (*barong-bachi*) as another version of Socialist Spiritual Civilization to control people's minds and behavior. It is easy to understand that the ideology is based on Confucian ethics, emphasizing the absolute value of the state and social orderliness as the base of harmonious society beyond all forms of differentiation. Institutes for Confucian Studies were established at various higher educational and research institutions under governmental auspice. Confucian culture is officially re-evaluated as the proud tradition of Chinese civilization. It may also be noted that, unlike during Mao's period, knowledge and education are highly regarded. Of the social orderliness and harmony, people are strongly encouraged to try harmonious compromise, mutual understanding and cooperation instead of dispute and conflict. Practice of civilization (*jiang wenming*) is emphasized as the very basis of public security. Mass media is also advised to be patriotic enough to lead the public with positive and productive reports in order to construct a 'healthy' nation.

Under the collective system and the planned economy system during the Maoist period, the people's space became cellularized under the directorship of the state. The government has attempted to minimize any possible voice of the people on the issue of the state's power to occupy people's private spheres, emphasizing the intimacy between the state and society. Here we see the infiltration of the state into people's everyday life spheres. Through the agency of local cadres, the state managed its body politics with such systems as *duanwei* and *hukou*, and the state ownership of land to control people's time, space, imagination, and emotion. Now, in the post-Mao era as mentioned earlier, a proliferation of private spaces came to challenge state authority so that national integration became one of the most serious issues within the political field.

The main current within the discussions among social scientists in China concern the question of how to strengthen the institutional efficiency and how to expand the state space. As a result, this type of interpretation has served the expansion of state power and authority. Here we see that the traditional Confucian thought is reconsidered by the government. Authorities would point out that peasants are improperly civilized so that they should be cared for by the state rationale and by enlightened bureaucrats. It is remarkably interesting to see that, even during Mao's period, the government reproduced its image with patriarchal authority and defined the state-people relationship in terms of the parent-child relationship. Many political campaigns meanwhile severely attacked Confucianism as anti-revolutionary and a feudal legacy. In this regard, we can say that the state implanted the Confucian image of state among the ordinary people, while it tried to crush other Confucian values through political movements like 'Down with Four Olds' or the Great Culture Revolution.

In the Confucian frame of state-society (people) relationships, leaders of state are conceived in the image of the Enlightened Prince; while ordinary people are described as not properly civilized and always in need of guidance and protection by the state rationale. Hence, public discourses are deemed to attribute social problems to people's poor character. Since the mid-1990s, the socialist spiritual civilization movement switched its emphasis from the 'reform of folk custom' (*minsu gaige*) to the 'development of personal quality' (*suzi tigao*). It means one is required to realize one's responsibility for social problems, and asked to try to cultivate one's quality to serve the state as an exemplary citizen. For example, problems such as AIDS and environmental pollution are usually explained as being caused by people's egoism, lack of scientific knowledge, unhealthy lifestyle, cultural backwardness, and so on.

Public discourses, therefore, repeat the agenda of the socialist spiritual civilization movement, which emphasizes that people eliminate their traditional culture and upgrade their level of character. In this context, it is highly recommended to find solutions on the basis of voluntary activities rather than publicly criticizing or blaming the lack of proper administration of the public healthcare system. Poverty, disease, and pollution are interrelated, as we find many cases of socially undesirable reality in the poor sector of society. Yet scholars are encouraged to find the main reason for this, not from the structural and systemic problem but, from the people themselves. Only a high ranking official in charge of the matter is entitled to publicize that subject, arguing that the government tries to fulfill its responsibility for society. However, it proves the people's voice comes only through the body of government.

In this regard, it is then natural to emphasize the importance of the state in the study of China. The state attempts to control people's worldview through remaking collective historical memories, with a revival of Confucianism as a political cultural resource. During the past couple of years, the Chinese government has developed 'mass media politics' to enhance people's mass patriotism and popular nationalism. The proliferation of television history dramas leads people to imagine the expansionism and conquer dynamics of the Han empire; the rise of Tang as the largest empire in the world; the prosperity and refined culture of the Sung dynasty; globalization (Zheng His Sea Expedition) and the Confucian civilization of the Ming dynasty, etc. Various documentaries also led people to be retrospective about their historical experiences of Western imperialist invasion, the turmoil of the late period of Qing, and the corrupted KMT government. As a whole, these teach people that they should be alert and civilized to protect their nation.

Producing national emotion, collective memory and imagination of Great China

For cultural projects to revive Great China, the past history of losing sovereignty to Western power is revived in various popular culture genres. These contribute to a development of mass patriotism as well as antagonism against the 'imperialist' Others. Television series and films are effective tools for making collective historical memories and public discourses for patriotism, especially among the young generation. There are three modes of popular or mass culture practiced in contemporary China.

1) Making collective memory of the CCP

Since the beginning of PRC, the majority of films and (later) television dramas for the masses have been on stories composed of the corruption and anti-nationalistic attitudes of KMT, the ideological superiority and patriotism of the Red Army and CCP, and the ruthless and inhumane Japanese army. To commemorate the 85th anniversary of the CCP in 2006, various programs for symbolic experience of the history of revolution and the birth of PRC were produced and covered by the nationwide television networks. 'Red Memories' (*hongshe jiyi*) and a pilgrim activity called 'My Long March' (*wode changcheng*), among others, were broadcast through the years 2006 and 2007.

'Red Memories' is a special program with the format of 'today in history'. It gives the Red Army's geographical movement or victory until the establishment of PRC in 1949 for the particular date. The program is composed of pieces of documentary films and parts of movie dramas of battles between the Red Army and the KMT Army's pictures of national leaders, interviews with retired soldiers, officers and generals, together with explanations by historians.

'My Long March' was made by voluntary participants from various parts of the nation and abroad. Overseas Chinese and national minorities also participated. These participants, male and female, vary in age, occupation, health condition, and social and regional background. They symbolize that the March was made by all the people of China. Starting at Ruijin, Jiangxi Province on 1st May, May Day, 2006, the March lasted for eight months and was completed by arriving at Yan'an on 1st January, New Year's Day, 2007. CCTV aired special reports on their progress, everyday during the March. From January 2007, at 7 pm every evening following the news, CCTV began to broadcast special editions and various forms of after-meetings related to the March.

Several moving stories were visualized. Following the original route of the Red Army's march, they visited historical places and sites and also met local old men who had participated in the original March. They passed by poor and backward villages in remote valleys and survived hunger and cold, with meager food and shabby shelter. Though exhausted and demoralized, they did not give up nor did they complain about the hardships they confronted. A high school student, who already had a problem with his foot, turned down the senior leader's suggestion to rest. He continued walking in the cold winter night, and walked till 1.50 a.m. to complete his original plan to hike 103 km a day. In front of a wild and cold river, a group of young people performed a commemoration rite, offering wine to the souls of soldiers who died attempting to cross the river. A young middle school boy continued to walk all night in the snow-covered mountains in the 'spirit of the long march'. A 40-year-old man broke his leg but rejected advice to be hospitalized, and so junior colleagues carried him on a cart they made. A 54-year-old woman was on the edge of collapse, but she managed to complete the course. On the unpaved hilly road, she stood up supported by a colleague to see the spectacular scene of snow-covered wild mountains under her feet. She received a call on her cell phone from her husband and daughter in Beijing, both shouting '*jiayou jiayou*' to encourage her. At that very moment the large screen showed her face in tears, all the participant-spectators at the television station also burst into tears and applauded. A group of participants from Ninghua, Fujian Province recalled at Xiang River the tragic fate of the 34th Battalion. Dubbed as Ninghua Battalion, as it was composed of people from the region, 13,707 out of 20,000 soldiers of the 34th Battalion died in the battle. The battle of Xiang River was the fiercest and most cruel one in the history of war. In order to pay special homage to their dead fathers and uncles, the young men came all the way from Fujian to march in front of the beautiful but wild river of Xiang. Old Sister Yang arrived at the famous *Ludingqiao* (Luding Bridge) at the dawn of the 4th of December after 18 hours of hard walking for 101km. She recalled that, when she completed 80km, she almost collapsed from pain and exhaustion. She could not bear the pain and burst into tears, but she kept walking. Her father's story was related to the bridge, she said. Under a rain of gun fire from the KMT army, a group of 20 Red Army soldiers vigorously attempted to cross the bridge but all were killed – except her father. As the participants shared historical memories of the battle, spectators were deeply moved. They praised her saying that her successful march to the Luding Bridge symbolizes the spirit of the Red Army, which will live forever.

Every evening, 'My Long March' ended with a moving conclusion of the participants all waving large red flags. They all shout in tears: 'Without CCP there can be no New China (*meiyou goncandang jo meiyou xinjungguo*)' and 'Without our predecessors' blood and sweat, we cannot enjoy today's prosperity and pride (*meiyou womende quanbeide xue he han, women meiyou xiangshou jintiande fanrong he jaoao*)'. The program was filled with words like fatherland (*zuguo*), splendid glory (*huihuangde guanrong*), greatness of China (*zhongguo weida*), red army spirit (*hongjun jingshen*), CCP (*gongchandang*), patriotism (*aiguo*), blood and sweat (*xiehan*), sacrificial spirit (*xisheng jingshen*), responsibility and moral duty toward the state (*dui guojiade zhiren he lunlidaode*), invincible and fearless will (*bupa er bujiede izhi*), endurance and patience toward all types of bitterness (*neungchiku*), etc. Participants of the march would say: 'At this very moment (or through the whole course of the long march), I was born again as the proud son/daughter of our Great China (*weidade zhongguo*)'.

It is also interesting to note that recent films, about anti-Japanese war and the communist revolutionary struggle, begin to include handsome intellectuals of wealthy family backgrounds as the patriotic revolutionary figures. In films made previously, only peasants and Red Army soldiers were shown as patriotic and revolutionary fighters. Urban wealthy intellectuals and KMT supporters were described as anti-revolutionary and un-nationalistic traitors collaborating with the imperialist Japanese (*han-gan*). A recently-released television series tells a moving story of cooperation between soldiers of the Red Army and the KMT Army in order to fight against the Japanese army. A love affair is also inserted to tell the story of how a beautiful young lady, coming from an elite family with KMT connections, fell in love with a highly educated, intellectual Red Army officer.

Repeatedly watching these types of television dramas and documentaries leads people to a re-written collective memory of the history of CCP's PRC. Television programs change the meaning and symbols of the socialist revolution of China, from one of class struggle to a national yearning. The revolution, the birth of PRC, is the dream-and-reality of the entire nation – consisting of KMT, capitalists, intellectuals, the Taiwanese, the people of Hong Kong (British colonial subjects), overseas Chinese, ethnic minorities, and so on.

2) The Chinese version of occidentalism

Television documentaries concerning the invasion by Western imperialists and the decline of Qing China are also very popular. Of these, films about the *Opium War* dating back 100 years are pivotal in the mass education of patriotism. They depict how the British imperialists poisoned the whole of China with opium and how they robbed China of Hong Kong. A new television documentary, *Summer Palace* (*Yuanmingyuan*) was released. It featured a contrast between China and the West in terms of civilization and barbarianism. According to the narration, the Summer Palace was the most beautiful and elaborate construction in the world and the proudest treasure of all human civilization and art. More splendid and refined than Versailles Palace in France, *Yuanmingyuan* was the fusion of civilization and art of the East and the West, until it was completely uprooted and destroyed by barbarous British and French soldiers. The ruins of *Yuanmingyuan* were previously used as a material space to prove feudal exploitation and the historical inevitability of CCP's revolution against it. It was also a shameful reminder of history that, once, Great China became a paper tiger plundered by a Western power. Now, memories embedded in the ruins of *Yuanmingyuan* are reinvented to disparage the Western Others. The film depicts the West as the savage, while China is the symbol of human civilization. These films end with comments on Britain finally surrendering its rule of Hong Kong to the PRC, to symbolize the revival of Great China and her victory over the Western imperial power.

By juxtaposing China and the West in terms of civilization and barbarism, these series of films and documentaries re-write the collective historical memory of the past and encourage Chinese spectators to have a sense of cultural and moral superiority to the Western world. It also leaves an insight that China should consolidate her strength, tough enough to protect herself from a possible second invasion of the neo-capitalist imperialists of the West. In this context, it is understood that the government invested a substantial amount of money to renovate *Yuanmingyuan*, which had been previously left almost deserted, in order to make it the national center for patriotism education.

3) Tianxia and revival of the Great Tang Empire

Films and documentaries based on historical novels have become popular. Also enjoying great success are films concerning the process of founding Qin, Han, and Tang. Among the highly acclaimed works are: Director Zhang Yimou's movie *Hero (yingxiong)*, a story about the Emperor Qin (*Qinshihuang*); the television series *Zhenguanzhiqi*, about the process of founding the Tang Empire by emperor Taizhong Li Shimin; and a documentary on the Ming dynasty's Zheng He, who made a global voyage before Columbus discovered America. They succeed in proving the pride of China as a Great Nation. Zhang Yimou was celebrated in the West through his films, such as *Judou* and *Honggaoliang*, which depicted peasant life in the traditional and backward world symbolized by yellow soil (*huangtu*). Now, he is supported by the government with a huge amount of money to make large-scale film spectaculars, such as the recently released *Mancengjindai Huangjinjia*. He appears preoccupied with his ambition to maximize the greatness of China through his popular visual art productions.

Hero gives a message of national unification (*tianxia tongyi*) under the Emperor who was sent from Heaven to unify the world. Hence, the people's challenge against the emperor is an act of destruction of the order of the whole universe against the Heavenly Will. The Emperor cannot be judged by ordinary people's morality or justice code. He was born, and he acted, only to accomplish Heavenly mandate to keep the world united and civilized, *tianxia*. There are also films about the history of territorial expansion under the Han Empire. The television series *Woxin Xiangtan* (Sleeping on the Straw and Tasting the Bitterness of Bear's Ulcer) was also broadcast nationwide. It is a story of King Gouchien of Yue who finally conquered King Fucha of Wu and, revenged the humiliation he and his people had suffered from the Wu Kingdom. He made a long-term plan and invited many wise men and loyal bureaucrats to accumulate national wealth and military strength while he kept a low profile, living a humble life in order to cover his ambition while maintaining his alertness.

Zhenguanzichi is the television series which has enjoyed the most enduring popularity. It is a spectacular production depicting the life of Li Shimin, the founder of Tang, who is regarded as the greatest emperor. He is depicted to possess all the caliber and virtue required of an ideal emperor, i.e. wisdom, leadership, ambition, perspective, patriarchal authority, love of people, literal knowledge, military capability, courage, generosity, fairness and justice, morality and manners, and right judgment, along with being decisive, accommodating, and so on. He consolidated the very basis of the Great Tang period, which as the center of the world, enjoyed prosperity, power, and civilization, as it accommodated a variety of ethnic groups and their cultures. Such television dramas and movies as *Woxin Xiangtan*, *Yingxiong*, *Zhenguanzichi*, create a popular imagination of how Great China was built in ancient times. They also symbolically tell the history of contemporary PRC. People usually enjoy talking about analogous interpretations between leaders of contemporary PRC and the equivalent figures in history dramas.

Rise of a Great Nation (*Daguo Jueqi*)

As television debates are broadcast repeatedly by the national networks, people cannot miss them. There was a program, shown once in February and, again, in March 2007, in which six discussants were invited to debate on whether or not China should launch her ambitious project to build up carrier ships to protect the sea. The debate continued for one and a half hours. Of the six guest discussants, only one, an old history professor, opined that the contemporary should be cooled down, and the public should retain rational thinking and be reasonable in dealing with this issue. He argued that economic prosperity and the leveling up of people's quality of life should precede the strengthening of military power. The other discussants – a retired admiral, an expert in international strategies, and also one in national security, a very talkative television talent, and an expert in the history of war – then attacked the old historian. The five criticized and even ridiculed the historian, citing he lacked patriotism and was naively reiterating the Western perspective in order to mis-interpret and distort historical truth. They insisted that priority should be given to superior military power (*qangbing*) before national wealth (*fuguo*).

In order to support the majority opinion, the program showed pictures of the Opium War, with narrations explaining how the Great Nation of China was defeated by such a small nation as Britain because China failed to modernize her military equipment. The 'five eagles' in the television program repeatedly emphasized their contention that a nation can be protected only with real superior military power of its own. They mentioned that the Japanese are increasing military power, which is threatening the security of China and other Asian countries. As it is China's responsibility to protect as well as to keep peace and common prosperity in the region, these discussants insisted, it is inevitable for China to have her own carrier ship. College students, who were seated behind as spectator-juries, mostly expressed support for those five eagles by waving flags. The old history professor tried to persuade the participants by citing that the reason for China's defeat in the Opium War was, not so much of the backward military power but more so, the weakness in internal integrity and China's incapability of adapting to the world situation. However, the other discussants laughed at him and criticized his idea as old fashioned explanation. The debate finished with the chairperson's comment: 'It seems to me that the majority of people support the standpoint that a great nation with superior military power should precede a wealthy nation.'

These series of popular (or mass) media culture continuously re-invent national historical memories and the collective images of Great China. They also reinvent patriotism, by which they foster a suspicious gaze to the approaching foreign capitalist power. These mass cultural products serve as a basis for stimulating people's support for the national project to promote a super military power. People are also induced into an imagination where the world order system is under a process of restructuring, with China at its center. More than anything else, people strongly believe that China is revived as the Great Nation. Intellectuals criticize this type of fashionable belief with words like 'television politics' or the 'politics of history drama'. Through these films, spectators make a pilgrim journey into the imagined world of Great China in the remote past so that they can transplant their dream of revival of the Great Nation. It is a form of secularized ritual of the ghost dance belief. At the same time, people learn the importance of relationship between greatness of national leadership and moral duty of the subject people. These films, more importantly, produce the metaphor of power, leadership, national integration under absolute state authority, and the harmonious relationship between the leader and the people as the basis of a great nation like China.

Nationalization of folk culture and locality

Folk custom, *minsu,* has been basically one of the main targets of the socialist scientific revolution project. Peasant tradition has been denounced as a feudal legacy, anti-revolutionary, superstitious, and an irrational illusion. During the 1980s and 1990s, the government launched the socialist spiritual civilization movement targeting folk custom. Especially conspicuous consumption at weddings and funerals, as well as folk beliefs and their related rituals, were strongly criticized and victimized by the state authority (Kim 2000).

Recently, however, we see the very active and competitive revival, and even invention, of folk custom in the name of national cultural heritage. This proliferation of folk custom is understood in its connection with the local tourist industry and with establishing networks with overseas Chinese. Later, it developed into a form of political investment in that people began to say the greatness of Chinese culture is embedded not only in elite culture but also in folk custom. Many international festivals of folk custom are organized, and overseas Chinese are invited under the name of 'search for roots.' (*xungen yundong*). Taiwanese, Singaporeans, and many overseas Chinese (*huaqiao* and *huayi*), situated in various parts of the world, organize tour groups to re-visit their ancestral places. Through the expansion of historical connection, they renew their ethnic identity as Chinese.

Traditional peasant music, dance, ritual, and material cultures became popular subjects of television culture programs. The yellow earth plateau *(huangtu gaoyuan)* of Shanxi, the remote villages of old stone houses in Anhui, and the vast desert-mountain wilderness of Xinjiang have been chosen as favorite film locations for the narrative of China's long history of culture and civilization, and the pure antiquity of the nation. The color yellow was used, in the documentary *River Elegy*, as a symbol of the feudal age and backwardness of China. Now, together with the color of red, it has become the most distinctively representative color for Great China.

Since 2005 especially, China has enthusiastically operated activities to register as many items as possible of Chinese folk culture to the World Non-material Cultural Heritage (*sijie feiwuzi wenhua yuchan*) Chapter under UNESCO. UNESCO is the UN organization for education, science, and culture, and the government regards the registration itself to be related to the national face. It therefore became involved in the movement. In this way, folk custom as a venue for folk's private and informal life has become an official space. It is legitimized only when approved by the state. Knowledge of folk custom has now become special curricula to cultivate official patriotism among young people.

At a class in an elementary school in Shandong Province, a teacher was emphasizing the importance of keeping and finding folk custom. She told her pupils: 'If we cannot keep our great cultural heritage and civilization, we will lose them to others.' As an example, the teacher mentioned the '*Kangneung Dano Rites*' of Korea, which is registered as World Cultural Heritage. The teacher was misled, however, and misled her pupils, too, by saying the Koreans had stolen China's seasonal Festival of *Duanwu* and registered it as part of Korea's cultural heritage.

On a personal note, I have traveled widely in China and have come across similar comments from various people of different backgrounds. They would approach and ask me to bluntly criticize or protest against the matter. Regardless of educational background and age level, from small children to PhD students and university professors, people have been misled to believe this story of stolen cultural heritage. I usually correct them by saying it is not the Duanwu Day. It is a special form of folk festival practiced for over several hundred years in a specific small town of Gangneung. An anthropologist at Peking University participated in the internet debate, citing that nobody can claim an exclusive ownership over a cultural item. Culture flows transnationally and is mutually adopted, he added, as he even proposed that the Chinese should be generous enough to share culture with other nations, and accommodate other cultures as well. He was immediately assailed by the Chinese 'netizens' who accused him of being a traitor. On the website, they hurled attacks on the professor, such as: 'How could a traitor like this guy be given the position of a professor at such a prestigious national university?'

Initially, the movement to register folk cultural items as non-material cultural heritage began as a non-governmental civil movement. Professor Wu, a leading senior folklorist of China, wrote an article in a Chinese newspaper accusing the Koreans of having stolen China's cultural heritage of the Duanwu festival. Having been invited several times to Korea as an expert in the study of folk culture, he knew very well that the Gangneung Danoje is different from Danwu of the fifth day of the fifth month in the lunar calendar. He also knows the entire process of the Korean's effort to register it under UNESCO's Non-material Cultural Heritage Chapter. However, he intentionally distorted the story at the cost of denigrating the Koreans and the Korean government. Born of his ambition or even nationalism, he intended to show the government and the people the importance of national cultural tradition, which had been deserted by 'scientific socialism'. An artist in Tianjin, inflamed by this story, then initiated the movement on a voluntary basis to re-discover and register China's folk culture. The government soon became involved. Instead of '*minjian wenhua*' (folk culture), the cultural heritage began to be called '*minzu wenhua*' (national culture). In this way, local culture became national culture under state authority. Local people, in turn, were happy to have their locality recognized as national property and here, we can see the politics of folk culture. Although their folk culture is separated from the people's own space of practice and comes to belong to the nation, people do not regard it as if their tradition was lost to government ownership. In their eyes, the state is not separated from their world but is actually part of it.

Temple festivals (*miaohui*) provide many examples to consider the contested terrain between state and people's tradition. Recently, local and district governments have revived or reinvented various forms of local temple festivals. These are aimed at developing national cultural properties to be registered as world non-material culture. Unlike during the Mao period, people are now encouraged to express their patriotism by consciously reproducing their traditional cultural properties. Provincial governments compete with each other in registering with UNESCO's World Cultural Heritage Chapter their natural places of special environmental merit, archaeological sites, historic heritages, and traditional folk festivals. Oftentimes, conflicts occur between government and local people over the hegemony of the festival concerned.

In a fishing community in Shandong, for example, people organized their own traditional local festival for Mazu. The local government, however, once prohibited the festival in the name of the socialist spiritual civilization movement. It instead organized another festival in Mazu temple, but the local people's participation turned out to be very small. Tension was resolved when they finally agreed to allow the local people to continue holding their traditional festival on Mazu's birthday. Meanwhile, the local government organized an International Fishers' Festival on *guyu* day, a different day, in order to avoid any possible conflict. The people and the government thus came to a compromise.

In Yixian, Hebei, there are approximately 40 shrines to Empress Houtu, the goddess of Earth. People pay homage to the goddess each year, on the 15th day of the third month in the lunar calendar. More than 400,000 people come from all over, in order to participate in the festival. In 2005, as it was so crowded, which also means good business, the local government tried to organize it in the name of local cultural heritage. The people resisted the plan. As a result, the local government built a temple and participated in the festival organized by the local people.

Behind the revival of folk customs, there are actually folklorists who try to get the government's recognition of and support for the importance of peasant culture. They seek to posit the locality of a set of folk cultures in the national context. Folklorists, local people, and government, in this way, conspire to 'elevate' the status of a local culture to the level of national culture. People, therefore, do not stick to their tradition in order to resist the state. On the contrary, there is negotiation and compromise between the government and the local people on the ownership of 'people's' tradition. This is because the state wants to occupy people's culture in the name of the nation. Nationally oriented scholars and academicians developed the concept of 'national study' (*guoxue*), in which folklore is also included.

It is important to see that sports are also becoming one of the most efficient genres to produce and invent national identity and patriotism, in violent and dramatic ways. When Beijing was chosen as the host city of the 2008 Olympiad, people flooded into the streets everywhere in China, and in tears. They fanatically marched waving the national flag and also carried writings of 'We've won!' (*women yingle*). Now, even in a small remote mountain village, we can see the local people's daily life carried out according to the schedule of preparation for the Olympics. This was established by the central government at the national level. In this regard, we can say that a sport event, especially the Olympics, puts all ethnic differences, local varieties, socio-economic class differences, and the urban-rural gap into a single national system of integrity. State-centered discourse, worldviews, values, and so on, are made routine in daily life as a discipline. To carry out the Olympics successfully is the absolute duty and responsibility of the people as citizens of China.

Unity in diversity or diversity in unity

Among the people, inevitably, there are disconcerted responses to the flood of productions of history dramas and documentaries. People within the intellectual community split into different stances toward the contents or underlying political messages of the product concerned. Many highly educated intellectuals even show their intentional indifference toward these. Some 'leftist' journals and intellectuals have raised criticisms on how the new fashions of nationalism and popular patriotism are being molded.[3]

Intellectuals branded the fashion as 'politics through TV drama' (*shijui zhenhqi*).[4] They raised suspicion of the proliferation of television history drama having a connection to any hidden intention of the government. Some serious professors of history and outspoken intellectuals would express their warnings that interpretation of history should be based only on scientific analysis and should not be distorted for any political purpose.[5] Just as the spectacular films and documentaries produced by governmental support such as Zhang Yimou's *Hero* (*Yingxiong*) and CCTV's *The Rise of a Great Nation* (*Daguo Jueqi*), films of counter discourses have also appeared and, in fact, are popular among young intellectuals. For example, while Zhang Yimou's *Yingxiong* focuses on the greatness of political power to achieve a great nation, Jia Zhangke's film *Still Life* (*Sanxia Haoren*) depicts stories of ordinary people victimized by the state initiated projects geared toward a Great Nation of China. From time to time, some magazines issue special editions to raise critical questions about current social problems.

These types of criticism, made within the limited boundary of the intellectual community, means the majority of people who lack diversified sources of past times do not have any choice but to watch television programs, which are released all year round through the nationwide networks of public media. The emotion and sentiment people experience, through this cultural encounter in their daily lives, encourages them to have a new collective memory of China's history. The 'national emotion' and historical memory are combined with the imagined reality of the expansion of China's power. These are visualized by unprecedented transformation of the landscape, as well as materialized sovereignty in the field of international politics. Along with these huge buildings, enormous construction projects, economic prosperity, and enriched consumer life, people witness China's entry into international organizations and China's hosting of many world conventions such as the Beijing Olympiad of 2008 and the Shanghai Expo of 2010, as well as China's central role in various international matters including the Six-Party Talks to deal with the North Korean nuclear problem. People now have an imagination that the present territory of China, including Tibet, Xinjiang, Inner Mongolia, and the three provinces of the Northeast, remains unchanged since ancient times. They also believe that those 55 minority ethnic groups have been the component members of the Chinese national community since ancient times. The booming phenomena, in which central and local governments organize various forms of events in the name of the nation, have been phrased by some as 'politics of events'. Others call it a 'festive state', implying the exploitation of race, ethnicity, and nationalism as cultural performance (Guss 2000).

The 'national emotion' produced by these cultural experiences is enough to lead people to express their 'underlying desire' for redefining being Chinese. It creates imagination toward the revival of the once glorious Chinese Empire as the political, economic, and cultural center of the world. In other words, the state produces television dramas and documentaries in order to meet people's hidden desire and yearning. From this publicly recognized 'national emotion', people now publicize their desire and yearning toward a real superpower to vie against the U.S.A. They now use the term '*tianxia*', world under the Heaven, instead of the concept of empire, which means the world under Chinese civilization and leadership.

As a response to globalization, however, it is interesting to see the official mass media, or mass media under state guidance, vigorously produce history documentaries to renew collective memories of glories of a Great China, along with those memories of losing the greatness of China. In this context, the West is portrayed to be another barbarous Other who devastated civilized China at the turn of the last century. It is understandable, therefore, that the Chinese would express their suspicion of any possible recycling of history in contemporary time. Popular journals issue special editions to raise questions about whether foreign businesses take unfair benefit from low-wage labor and cheap resources in China. Ordinary people would be reluctant to admit that the foreign businesses bring capital investment, provide employment opportunities, and transfer advanced high technology to their Chinese counterparts, etc. Popular journals and magazines also produce negative images of foreign businesses. These publications stimulate Chinese readers to have enough self-assurance to be outraged by any unfairness and injustice in their everyday life.[6] From this, people demand that their government take some form of protectionist measure against the evil-minded foreign investment. The government is therefore conceived to protect the nation on behalf of the people. Hence, imagination of external threat is politically necessary for the government to ensure the people's support.

It should be noted here that the Chinese government is sensitive to any symptom of making a crack in the integration of the state community. For that reason, it develops institutional measures to cope with such a possibility. The state, at this juncture, is allowed to control people's time, space, and emotion, and maximizes its efficiency to rule the national community. However, this is practiced at the cost of people's private space. When the state is concerned only with economy-centered development policies, there might appear serious cracks in the field of society and culture, and these cracks will eventually lead to the critical problem of social disintegration.

Conclusion

China is currently facing both the need to consolidate state power to achieve national integration and the international expectation to be an open and responsible superpower in global politics. As the cultural basis for a great nation, the government has launched a special project to shape the national emotion directed toward the ambition to revive the historical glory of the Great Empire. There appear to be politically serious social problems, though. A possible tension or conflict between the state and society is compromised or buffered by the cultural space where people's imagination of a Great Nation is visualized. By appropriating the national emotion through successful manipulation of people's collective memories of time and space, the Party obtained recognition to exercise patriarchal authority and absolute power of the state over the social space.

People now come to have a new perspective, through the newly molded collective memories, on their own civilization and cultural tradition. Past history is seen as a struggle between the barbarous West and the Chinese civilization. It is time to launch the ambitious dream of reviving a civilized China and keeping the world under Chinese civilization, so that the idea of *tianxia* is realized. It is also noted that, in addition to the popular patriotism, a new idea of nation is being invented, in the name of *zhonghua minzu,* conceptually.

The new version of a China-centered world view and popular nationalism, however, inevitably produces conflicts between nations around China. Among the young people of China, Korea, and Japan, for example, there are serious disputes and mutual attacks through the internet which is violent enough to be called 'war on the internet' or 'online war'. The people of the young generation of these three nations usually appear to lack any political interest related to nation, and enjoy a cross-boundary flow of popular consuming culture. However, once they feel that their national face or pride is attacked, they immediately turn very aggressive and make counterattacks, out of collective memories of the past. This type of 'petit nationalism' is deeply rooted in the younger generations and, quite unexpectedly, turns to a nationalistic violence. Practice of this type of nationalistic violence is allowed, and even politically encouraged, in the name of patriotism and the rhetoric of national greatness.

The mass media, at present, are successfully producing and ruling over national emotion and public sentiment to drive people to express their fully-pledged support to the state. Despite the disconcerted voices among different sectors of society, as a whole, people understand the internal problems and external affairs within the imagination of China as a Great Nation and within the framework of China's uniqueness. This inevitably leads to the question of the Chinese people's accommodating caliber of a global standard of morality and the cultural diversity of the world.

For a proper evaluation of China as a great nation, in this regard, it is necessary to understand the nature of relationship between the state and society through analysis of the political practice of culture between the two. It is also necessary to understand how 'national emotion' is shaped and reshaped through changing relationships between the state and society.

Notes

1 This is part of my research on contemporary China, supported by the Research Abroad Program 2006–2007 of the Korea Research Foundation.
2 At an interview with CCTV, a senior professor of Chinese Academy of Social Sciences pointed out that it was a mistake of the production team to omit Italy.
3 It is quite interesting to note the words 'Rightist' and 'Leftist' in China, where people have a vivid memory of the anti-rightist movement. Previously, an intellectual was branded as a rightist if he/she had a tendency to be critical against the socialist ideology. But now the word is used vice versa.
4 See a special edition of *Nanfengchang* (Window of South Wind) 1.3.2007.
5 Some foreign observers would regard this type of criticism as an example of conflict between the state and society, and an evidence of China's moving toward civil society.
6 See the special issue of *Renwu Zougan (Weekly on People)* 15.3.2007.

References

Anderson, B. (1983) *Imagined Communities*. London: Verso.
Cohen, A. (1988) *Symbolic Construction of Community*. London: Tavistock.
Certeau de, M. (1984) *The Practice of Everyday Life*. Berkeley: University of California Press.
Cho, Y.N. (2006) *Chinese Politics under Hu Jintao*. Seoul: Naman (in Korean).
Chung, J.H. (ed.) (2006) *Charting China's Future: Political, Social, and International Dimensions*. Lanham, Maryland: Rowman & Littlefield Publishers.
Connerton, P. (1989) *How Societies Remember*. Cambridge: Cambridge University Press.
Dickson, B. (2000) 'Political Instability at the Middle and Lower Levels: Signs of a Decaying CCP, Corruption, and Political Dissent', D. Shambaugh (ed.), pp. 40–56.
Fentress, J. and Wickham, C. (1992) *Social Memory: New Perspectives on the Past*. Oxford: Blackwell.
Guss, D. (2000) *The Festive State: Race, Ethnicity, and Nationalism as Cultural Performance*. Berkeley: University of California Press.
Guthrie, D. (2006) *China and Globalization: The Social, Economic, and Political Transformation of Chinese Society*. London: Routledge.

Howell, J. (ed.) (2004) *Governance in China*. Lanham, Maryland: Rowman & Littlefield Publishers.

Johnson, R., McLennan, G., Schwarz, B. and Sutton, D. (eds) (1982) *Making Histories: Studies in History Writing and Politics*. Minneapolis: University of Minnesota Press.

Kang, H.D. and Zhou F. (1992) 'History of China's Radio and Television Broadcast', H. Kang ed. *History of Broadcasting in the World*. Seoul: Naman, pp. 255–324 (in Korean).

Kim, K.O. (2000) *Chinese Peasants in Revolution and Reform*. Seoul: Jipmundang (in Korean).

Kim, K.O. (1993) 'Socialist Spiritual Civilization and Resurgence of Folk Tradition in Contemporary China', *Cross-Cultural Studies of Culture,* No. 1 (in Korean).

Li, P., Li, Q., Sun, L. *et al.* (2004) *Zhongguoshehuifencheng: (Social Stratification in China's Today)*. Beijing: Shehuikexue Wenxian Chubanshe (Social Sciences Documentation Publishing House).

Naughton, B. and Yang, D. (eds) (2004) *Holding China Together: Diversity and National Integration in the Post-Deng Era*. Cambridge: Cambridge University Press.

Perry, E. and Selden, M. (eds) (2005) *Chinese Society: Change, Conflict and Resistance*. London: Routledge.

Pei, M.(2006) *China's Trapped Transition: The Limits of Developmental Autocracy*. Cambridge, Massachusetts: Harvard University Press.

Scott, J. (1985) *Weapons of the Weak: Everyday Forms of Peasant Resistance.* New Haven: Yale University Press.

Scott, J. (1990) *Domination and the Arts of Resistance: Hidden Transcripts*. New Haven: Yale University Press.

Shambaugh, D. (ed.) (2000) *Is China Unstable? Assessing the Factors*. Armonk, New York: M.E. Sharp.

Shue, V. (1988) *The Reach of the State: Sketches of the Chinese Body Politic*. Stanford: Stanford University Press.

Sun, L. (2003) *Duanlie (Crack): Chinese Society since 20th Century*. Beijing: Social Science Material Publishing Co.

Watson, R. (ed.) (1994) *Memory, History, and Opposition under State Socialism*. Santa Fe: School of American Research Press.

Whyte, M. (2000) 'Chinese Social Trends: Stability or Chaos?', D. Shambaugh (ed.), pp. 143–63.

3 Quantitative assessment of China's economic power and science and technology power in a comparative perspective

Angang Hu

Introduction

One of the biggest events that have taken place over the past 30 years in the world economy is the rapid rise of China as an economic power. This has gone far beyond the conventional anticipation of international experts, and even beyond the anticipation of the Chinese government. The 1987 13th National Party Congress visualized for 2000 a GNP growth quadruple that of 1980 (Zhao 1987), but in fact it reached 6.55 times of 1980's GNP (State Statistical Bureau 2007a). The 1997 15th National Party Congress visualized a GDP growth double that of 2000, for the first decade of the twenty-first century (Jiang 1997). The 2002 16th Party Congress put forward the 2020 GDP goal of quadruple that of 2000, averaging an annual growth of 7.2 per cent (Jiang 2002). However, the actual GDP growth by 2006 was 74.9 per cent more than the 2000 GDP, averaging an annual growth of 9.8 per cent (State Statistical Bureau 2007a). Signs indicate that China will maintain a sustained and accelerated growth in the next 15 years. It could be called the China miracle (Overholt 1994; Lin *et al.* 1994). There had been a British miracle, an American miracle, a German miracle, a Japanese miracle, and the four Asian dragon miracles in the past 250 years. Now, the world is paying attention to the China miracle, as well as the Indian miracle.

In its economic takeoff, China has created a historical world record in economic growth and population size. International comparison (see Table 3.1) shows that, during the 43 years which span the years 1870 to 1913, the GDP of the UK, Germany, and the United States increased 2.24, 3.32, and 5.26 times, respectively, while during the 23 years from 1950 to 1973, Japan's GDP grew 7.7 times. Breaking the 9.3 per cent record created by Japan, China's GDP grew 13.4 times in the 28 years, from 1978 to 2006, averaging an annual growth of 9.7 per cent. It is probable that, by 2020 when its GDP will be increased 42 times in just 42 years (1978–2020), China will replace the time record for sustainable high growth created by the UK, Germany, and the USA. It is important to mention that when the UK, Germany, and USA effected economic take-off in 1870, their populations were 31.39 million, 39.23 million, and 40.24 million respectively (Maddison 2001). Japan had a population of 83.81 million when it began its economic take off in 1950. In contrast, China had more than 20 times the population of the above

Table 3.1 GDP and industrial output growth in the rise period

	GDP			*Industrial output*		
Country	*Period*	*Growth index (time)*	*Annual growth (%)*	*Period*	*Growth index (time)*	*Annual growth (%)*
U.K.	1870–1913 (43 years)	2.24	1.90	1876–1913	1.85	1.7
U.S.	1870–1913 (43 years)	5.26	3.94	1874–1913	7.37	5.4
Germany	1870–1913 (43 years)	3.32	2.83	1875–1913	3.53	3.5
Japan	1950–1973 (23 years)	7.70	9.29	1947–1975	11.3	9.1
China	1978–2006 (28 years)	13.4	9.71	1978–2006	21.1	11.5
China	1978–2020 (42 years)	42	9.31			

Source: Angus Maddison (2001) *The World Economy: A Millennial Perspective,* Paris: OECD.
Mandel, E. (1998) *Long Waves of Capitalist Development, Chinese edition,* translated by the International Economics Institute of Nankai University: Commercial Press, China's data (1978–2006).
National Bureau of Statistics (2007) *China Statistics Abstract 2007*, China Statistical Press, p. 33.

four countries, with a 962.59 million population in 1978, when its economy began to take off.

What is an economic miracle? Why are there miracles? When and where do miracles appear? What are the basic reasons of economic miracles? Are there homologies or heterogeneities of miracles in different countries? What are the characteristics of the China miracle? How does it appear? How do we create the China miracle? How does it succeed? How do we assess the rise of China? What indicators should be used to measure China's power in the economy and in science and technology?

This author has defined the rise of a country as the sustained rise of major indicators (for economy and science and technology) in the world's total. Conversely, a sustained drop means the decline of a country. Both rise and decline are measured covering a period of at least dozens of years (more than 25 years). The author has evolved a simple method to measure the national power in economy and in science and technology, by calculating the proportion of major indicators in the world's total (which form a dimensionless data series) and then using it for international comparison. This method directly reflects the power of a country in the realms of the economy and science and technology, as well as its roles and influence in the world.

The paper is divided into five parts: section 2 calculates and analyzes the sources of China's economic power and growth. Section 3 is devoted to China's power in science and technology and its driving force; Section 4 examines the future trend of China's economic development and the changes in its economic power in the period 2005–2020; Section 5 gives an analysis of China's influence and its roles in the world economic growth; Section 6 presents the author's brief conclusions.

This author observes China's power both in economy and in science and technology from the historical perspective. The relative changes in China and in some leading developed countries (USA, Japan and Germany) are also compared, from the international perspective since 1980, in terms of economic power and power in science and technology.

China's economic power and its growth source

There is no commonly accepted international definition and computation method regarding the economic power of a country. This paper defines the national economic power of a country as the comprehensive capacity to pursue its economic strategic goal with purposeful action – that is, its capacity to create economic resources worldwide.

There are two simple methods to assess the national economic power of a country. One is the absolute economic power – namely, its economic growth and size based on a relative base period. The economic power is in direct proportion to the economic size of the base period, and is also in exponential relationship with the economic growth rate. The other is the relative economic power – that is, the economic growth and size during a given period, relative to the economic growth and size of other countries. The relative economic power is in direct proportion to the economic size of other countries during the base period, and also in exponential relationship with the economic growth speed.

A principal method to calculate the relative economic power of a country is by recognizing that the following: the proportion of the economic aggregate (GDP) and the economic power of the country is indirectly related to its relative proportion in the world economic aggregate during the base period. This means the bigger the proportion in the base period, the greater the economic power. It indicates the important impact of the initial conditions, which is correlated with the ratio of its economic growth to the world economic growth. It also shows that the higher the economic growth as compared with the world economy, the bigger the proportion. The method is superior to the previous and the latter methods. It does not only study the changes in the economic aggregate of a county, relative to other countries. More so, it stresses the study of the changes in the country's relative position in the world economic pattern, in the context of economic globalization. As mentioned above, the rise of a country's economic power refers to the sustained rise, for at least 25 years, in proportion to its economic aggregate in the world's total.

At present, two different methods are used to measure the economic aggregate of the world and the specific countries. One is the exchange rate method, converting the base currency into US dollars according to the current value. This uses the three-year average to offset short-term fluctuations. The other is Purchasing Power Parity (PPP), converting GDP into US dollars (World Bank 2007). Both the World Bank and the International Monetary Fund (IMF) publish these two statistics of the world and various countries. Each method has its advantages and disadvantages. This paper uses the two methods to estimate the economic power of the world and a few large countries.

The first method has been used to compute the proportion of China's GDP to the world's total based on the year 2000 constant dollar price from 1980–2005, with major data coming from the World Bank's world development indicators. In terms of the proportion of GDP to the world's total, China ranks 10th in the world, with 1.04 per cent in 1980. It rose to 1.86 per cent in 1990 and, by 2000, rose again to 3.78 per cent, ranking 6th in the world. By 2005, the figure was 5.02 per cent, (see Table 3.2), placing China just behind the United States, Japan, and Germany, with a rank of being 4th in the world.

The second method, PPP, has been used to compute the proportion of China's GDP to the world's total, based on Maddison's data and the 1990 international dollar price. It is necessary to point out that in 2007, Maddison modified this data series based on China's 2004 economic survey data (Maddison 2003). China's economic aggregate accounted for 5.19 per cent by 1980. It sustained its rise until it reached 15.1 per cent by 2003, for over a period of 25 years (see Table 3.2). If computed based on World Bank data, using PPP, China's GNI in 2005 would be 14.2 per cent of the world's total. If calculated based on the CIA data, in 2006, it would have accounted for 15.4 per cent of the world's total (CIA 2007). Hence, China's GDP in the world's total range is 1/7–1/6.

The relative gap in economic power between the United States and China has narrowed year by year. In 1950, the United States and China were 5.94 times apart in economic power. This difference dropped to 4.14 times by 1980, and dropped further to 1.36 times by 2003 (see Table 3.3). If calculated by the World Bank's PPP, the U.S. GNI would be 1.44 times that of China in 2005. If calculated based on CIA data, the U.S. GDP would be 1.30 times that of China in 2006. Hence, the economic power gap between China and the United States has persistently decreased.

The main sources of China's high speed growth are total factor productivity (TFP) and capital input. In 1978–2005, TFP increased 4.7 per cent a year on average and contributed 49 per cent to GDP growth. Capital input increased 9.5 per cent a year on average and contributed 36 per cent to GDP growth, followed by a 3.8 per cent. TFP. The input of human capital, whose annual growth was 2.1 per cent, has contributed 7 per cent to GDP growth. Last, there is labor input,

Table 3.2 Ratio of GDP (market exchange rate) of country to world total (% 1980–2005)

Country	*1980*	*1985*	*1990*	*1995*	*2000*	*2005*
China	1.04	1.52	1.86	2.95	3.78	5.02
United States	29.11	30.01	29.46	29.63	30.76	28.06
Japan	15.93	16.31	17.25	16.56	14.95	10.15
Germany	6.98	6.51	6.45	6.39	5.99	6.27
France	4.77	4.63	4.51	4.28	4.18	4.75
United Kingdom	4.95	4.81	4.73	4.57	4.53	4.94
India	0.87	0.99	1.12	1.28	1.44	1.77

Note: The unit of GDP is constant 2000 U.S. dollars.
Source: World Bank, World Development Indicators 2007, CD-ROM.

Table 3.3 Ratio of GDP (PPP) of country to world total (% 1980–2003)

Country	*1980*	*1985*	*1990*	*1995*	*2000*	*2003*
China	5.19	6.94	7.83	11.15	11.77	15.12
U.S.A.	21.11	21.48	21.39	21.19	21.85	20.61
Japan	7.83	8.05	8.57	8.11	7.29	6.64
Germany	4.06	3.81	3.79	3.55	3.46	3.24
France	5.51	5.11	4.67	4.57	4.27	3.88
U.K.	3.63	3.49	3.49	3.32	3.28	3.15
India	3.18	3.54	4.05	4.62	5.19	5.58
U.S.A./China (time)	4.14	3.10	2.73	1.90	1.86	1.36

Note: GDP unit is 1990 million International Geary-Khamis dollars. East Asia contains 16 countries (regions) which are China, India, Indonesia, Japan, Philippines, South Korea, Thailand, China Taiwan, Bangladesh, Burma, Hong Kong SAR, Malaysia, Nepal, Pakistan, Singapore and Sri Lanka.
Source: Angus Maddison, *World Population, GDP and Per Capita GDP, 1–2003 AD*, http://www.ggdc.net/maddison/, March, 2007.

growing at an annual average of 1.9 per cent, and contributing 6 per cent to GDP growth (see Table 3.4).

There are five major factors stimulating China's economic growth. These effects are mutually associated and mutual-acting, as the sustainable high growth since reforms has its "speed effect." The five major effects are:

1. Catch up effect: that is, the economic growth of a country lagging in industrialization is, during a given period of time, significantly higher than industrialized countries;
2. Structural effect: that is, during a given period of time, the structural indicators of an industrially lagging country change faster than industrialized countries;
3. Open-up effect: that is, an industrially lagging country is faster than industrialized countries in its involvement in the global economic integration;

Table 3.4 Sources of China's economic growth (annual growth, % 1978–2020)

	1978–2005	*2005–2020*
GDP	9.6 (100)	8.5 (100)
Capital	9.5 (36)	10.0 (47)
Labor	1.9 (6)	0.3 (1)
Human Resource	2.1 (7)	2.0 (7)
TFP	4.7 (49)	3.8 (45)

Note: TFP stands for total factor productivity.
Parenthesis shows the factor's contribution to GDP growth.
A situation: weight for capital is 0.4, labor is 0.3 and human resource is 0.3.
Source: Author calculation and simulation.

4. Institutional effect: that is, an industrially lagging country has acquired a higher level of market economy and the economic operation is based on the market mechanism;
5. Technology catch-up effect: that is, an industrially lagging country moves faster in technology diffusion and innovation than technologically leading countries (Hu and Wang 2006).

China's power in science and technology and its driving force

To date, there is no commonly accepted definition and computing method with regard to the power in science and technology. This paper defines the national strength in science and technology and its capacity to utilize scientific and technical resources worldwide. It can be computed by the weighted average proportion of the country's major indicators for science and technology to the world's total.

The first indicator is the scientific innovative capacity – which is expressed by the number of papers published that cover physics, biology, chemistry, mathematics, clinical medicine, biomedical research, engineering and technology, and earth and space sciences. The data, spanning the years 1980–2004, come from the world development indicators of the World Bank.

The second indicator is the technical innovative capacity, which is best expressed by the number of applications for invention patents by its citizens. This includes patent applications or grants in which the first applicant or assignee is a citizen of the state or territory. The data, covering the years 1980–2005, come from the databank of the World Intellectual Property Right Organization.

The third indicator is the capacity to apply new technologies. This is expressed by the number of personal computers in use, those which are self-contained and designed for personal use by individuals. The data, inclusive of all figures from 1990–2004, come from the world development indicators of the World Bank.

The fourth indicator is the capacity to use global information. This is expressed by the number of the internet users or people who have access to the worldwide web. Data covering the years 1990–2004, likewise come from the world development indicators of the World Bank.

The fifth indicator is the potential for future development. This is expressed by the proportion of GDP spending in science and technology, as well as the monetary and capital expenditures on creative work. This refers to expenses undertaken systematically to increase knowledge, including knowledge in such areas as humanity, culture and society, and the application of such knowledge in new areas. Data covering the years 1980–2004 are taken from the world development indicators of the World Bank (see Table 3.5).

The weighted average of the above five major indicators is equivalent to the national power of a country in science and technology. As all the indicators are dimensionless, the weighted average method can be used (in which the weight for each indicator is 0.2). It is necessary to point out that the relative gap in science and technology between China and the U.S. and between China and Japan is a gap in terms of power in science and technology. This does not refer to the level of

Table 3.5 Indicators to assess S&T power

	Period	*Weight*	*Data source*
Academic papers	1980–2004	0.2	WDI 2006
Innovation patent applications (resident)	1980–2005	0.2	WIPO
Personal computers	1990–2004	0.2	WDI 2006
Internet users	1990–2004	0.2	WDI 2006
R&D expenditure	1980–2004	0.2	WDI 2006

science and technology of the country. Study shows the proportion of China's national power in science and technology to the world's total has been steadily rising. This sustained rise can be divided into several stages (see Table 3.6).

The first stage is covered by the years 1980–1990. As a newcomer in the world of science and technology development, China obtained just 0.53 per cent–0.82 per cent in the world's total. The relative gap with the United States was 30.11–48.90 times, and between Japan and China was 18.65–30.50 times. One of the major reasons for these large gaps is the unsound patent system. What merits attention is that China began to prepare to establish a patent system in 1978. The State Patent Office was opened in 1980. The patent law was adopted by the standing committee of the National People's Congress in March 1984, and began to take effect only on April 1, 1985.

The second stage is from 1990–2000. This period marked a rapid development, so rapid that it catapulted China into the world arena as an emerging power in science and technology. China's proportion increased to 3.97 per cent, ranking fourth in the world's total. By 2000, its gaps with the United States and Japan were narrowed to 7.09 and 4.11 times, respectively.

The third stage, covering the years at the start of the new century, marked a continued rapid development in science and technology. This made China a new power, and a new center, in the development of science and technology. Up to 2004, its proportion in the world's total was 7.67 per cent. Overtaking Germany to become the third largest power in terms of science and technology, China has

Table 3.6 S&T power to world total (% 1980–2004)

Country	*1980*	*1985*	*1990*	*1995*	*2000*	*2004*
China	0.53	0.84	0.82	1.34	3.97	7.67
Japan	16.06	20.37	15.24	15.97	16.31	14.52
Germany	6.27	6.01	5.01	5.46	6.06	5.24
U.S.A.	25.76	25.23	39.13	34.97	28.17	24.45
4 Countries total	48.62	52.45	60.2	57.73	54.51	51.88
U.S.A./China (time)	48.9	30.11	47.87	26.19	7.09	3.19
Japan/China (time)	30.5	24.31	18.65	11.96	4.11	1.89

Note: sub-category see annex table.
Source: World Bank, World Development Indicators 2006, CD-ROM; Statistical database, WIPO.

come even closer to the United States and Japan. Thus, the relative gaps in science and technology with the United States and Japan were narrowed to 3.19 and 1.89 times, respectively.

Meanwhile, there are three main driving forces behind the rapid growth in China's national power in science and technology. The first is economic globalization. It has brought China's science and technology development in line with the world, enabling it to share what has been achieved in world science and technology, participate in international research activities, and train personnel offering global services. Technically, China has obtained international technology mainly from two major channels. One is direct technology import. In 1990, China's high-tech import volume made up 2.0 per cent of GDP. The proportion rose to 4.47 per cent by 2000 and to 9.4 per cent by 2006 (State Statistical Bureau 2007a). The other channel is FDI, by making the most of the spillover and positive externality of advanced technologies. The total FDI inflow by 2006 reached 691.9 billion dollars, accounting for 26.3 per cent of GDP (State Statistical Bureau 2006). According to statistics from UNCTAD, China's 1982 FDI inflow made up 0.2 per cent of world total, rising to 1.1 per cent by 1990 and to 5.1 per cent by 2007 (UNCTAD 2008).

The second driving force is market, which has greatly improved the environment for science and technology development; it provided the chance for the application and innovation of scientific and technical achievements. Enterprises have become the main investors in R&D, and the main producers of research and development as well. In 2000, enterprises' spending on research and development was 56 per cent of national funding in this area. Up to 2005, the percentage rose to 65.5 per cent (State Statistical Bureau 2006). In 1995, the number of invention patent applications by Chinese enterprises made up 10.8 per cent of the total. The percentage rose to 32.8 per cent by 2000, and to 43.0 per cent by 2005. The volume of transactions in the technology market in 1995 was 0.44 per cent of GDP. After over 10 years, the percentage rose to 0.87 per cent by 2006 (State Statistical Bureau 2007a).

The third driving force is government guidance and promotion in setting goals for different periods, thus subsequently providing good policies and extensive funding. In March 1978, the first National Science and Technology Conference (NSTC) clearly made science and technology a part of the four modernization points, the basic conditions to build a powerful and modernized socialist country. The conference also called to further absorb advanced foreign technologies (Deng 1984). In 1985, the second NSTC made a number of important decisions concerning the reform of the science and technology system. This ushered in an all-round reform of the system. It also called for opening up to the outside world and winning a reputable status in the world. It represents a long-term basic national policy regarding science and technology development (CPC 1985).

The third NSTC in 1995 decided to launch the strategy of invigorating the nation by developing science and education. The fourth NSTC in 2006 came out with the Outlined Medium- and Long-Term Science & Technology Development Program (2006–2020), setting the goal for 2020, which will bring input in research and development to 2.5 per cent of GDP and will increase the contributions of technical progress to development to over 60 per cent. It will also lower the foreign technology dependence rate to below 30 per cent. Moreover, it will bring China to rank in the world's top five in terms of the number of Chinese citizens' invention patent grants and papers quoted internationally.

China is a successful case in science and technology development among developing countries. Attributed to the mutual action of the three driving forces mentioned above, China has realized a leap forward in its science and technology development, thus shortening the gaps with developed countries. China's research and development spending, since the beginning of 1995, has been growing at an annual rate of over 20 per cent (21.4 per cent in 1995–2006) (State Statistical Bureau 2007a). During this period, the percentage for the United States was 6 per cent while that of Japan and the EU, 5 per cent. China's research and development spending was only one-tenth that of the United States, one-seventh that of the EU, and one quarter that of Japan in 1995. By 2005, the figure became one-third that of the Untied States, half that of the EU, and higher than that of Japan (Hudson Institute 2006).

Future trend of development (2005–2020)

It is very difficult to forecast China's future economic growth. In reviewing the forecasts by Chinese experts and scholars over the past 12 years, the author has found few of them to be accurate enough. In this chapter, the estimate for the country's future economic growth and its economic power has been based more on the long-term point of view than on the simple forecast of specific growth and specific figures. As most predictions are far apart from actual figures, this author deems these to be under-forecasting China's potential future growth, thereby repeating the mistakes of the last 20 years (World Bank 1997). Following are some forecasts for China's economic growth in 2005–2020 which show that they are between 5.5 and 7.4 per cent (see Table 3.7).

Table 3.7 Forecasts for China's GDP Growth (% 2005–2020)

Period	*Global Insight (2006)*	*Economic Intelligence Unit (2006)*	*Goldman Sachs (2005)*	*JCER (2007)*	*World Bank (2007)*
2005–2010	8.6	8.0	7.1		
2010–2015	7.2	5.5	5.8		
2015–2020	6.4	4.4	5.0		
2005–2020	7.4	6.0	6.0	5.5	6.6

Source: *Global Insight* (2006) China Forecast, May; *EIU*, Country Data.

Goldman Sachs (2005) *China's Ascent: Can the Middle Kingdom Meet its Dreams*, *Global Economics Paper*, No. 133, November 11.

Elwell, C.K., Labonte, M. and Morrison, W.M. (2007) *Is China A Threat to the U.S. Economy?* CRS Report for Congress, Order Code RL 33604, http://www.fas.org/sgp/crs/row/RL33604.pdf.

Japan Center for Economic Research (JCER) (2007) *Long-term Forecast of Global Economy and Population 2006–2050: Demographic Change and the Asian Economy*, March.

Winters, A. and Yusuf, S. (2007) *Dancing with Giants: China, India and the Global Economy*, Washington, D.C.: The World Bank.

China's future economic development trend: GDP is expected to grow at an annual rate of about 8 per cent in 2005–2020. This is lower than the potential growth rate (9.3 per cent–9.5 per cent) since 1978, considering the greater the size of GDP, the lower the potential growth would be. On the other hand, GDP is 13 times that of 1978 according to constant prices and 5 times that of 1990.

In 2005–2020, one of the sources of China's high speed growth is TFP, at 3.8 per cent a year on average and contributing 47 per cent to GDP growth. Capital input has remained at a high level of growth, and is likely to reach about 10 per cent. This is because the domestic savings rates are high, above 40 per cent; the domestic investment rate is also high, at over 40 per cent. The growth is capital-driven, comprising of industrial capital, private housing investment, and government public investment especially in infrastructure. The human capital input has also increased rapidly, at about 2 per cent growth rate. This can be ascribed to higher and intermediate education received by the population (especially people at the senior secondary level). The labor input, meanwhile, is at a low-speed development stage. It might enter into a zero-growth stage after 2015 (growth <0.2 per cent) (see Table 3.4).

Economic policies also affect growth and stability. First, the Chinese government has strengthened its macroeconomic control capacity. It is keeping inflation at a fairly low level, making economic fluctuation coefficients small, and maintaining low deficits – factors conducive to the steady growth of the economy. Second, China will set up an incentive mechanism to provide an impetus to the growth of all types of organizations in creating wealth. In 2000–2006, the juristic person units increased 29 per cent, from 4.37 million to 5.65 million (State Statistical Bureau 2007b). Their contributions to GDP growth reached nearly 39 per cent in the period. In addition, good governance and human capital investment, especially the movement of agricultural labor to non-agricultural activities with high productivity, will also raise TFP.

From the international perspective, China as a less developed country has a large gap with developed countries. Thus, China has a late-development advantage with a convergent trend among developed countries. From 1950–1990, Japan caught up with the U.S. at a convergent rate of 3.55 per cent; from 1965–2003, Korea caught up with the U.S. at a rate of 4.36 per cent. The rate for China, in 1978–2003, was 4.64 per cent, higher than both Japan and Korea. Notably, it was 16.5 per cent for China relative to the United States' GDP per capita (it was similar to the situation of Korea in 1973). Therefore, there is potential growth for China to catch up with the U.S. until the GDP per capita reaches Korea's 2003 level, which is at least 42 years from 1978–2020 (see Figure 3.1).

China's economic power will continue its upward trend. This author has used the databank 'World Development Indicators' of the World Bank, employing three different methods to forecast the economic growth for 2020 (see Table 3.8).

Through the exchange rate method, with the GDP of China and the world as the base, China's GDP and that of the world are 8 per cent and 3 per cent, respectively. China's 2005 GDP made up 5.0 per cent of the world's total. By 2020, China's ratio will rise to 10.2 per cent (Winters and Yusuf 2007).

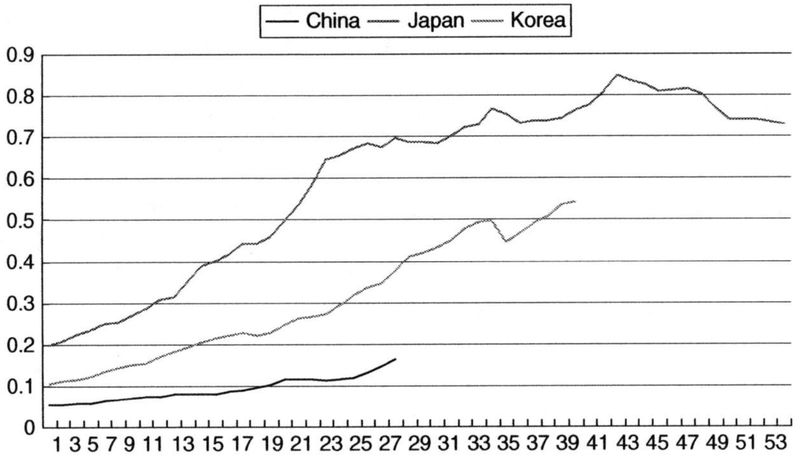

Figure 3.1 Relative GDP per capita to U.S. in China, Japan and Korea.
Note: U.S. GDP per capita = 1.0, the period for Japan is 1950 to 2003, Korea is 1965 to 2003, and China is 1978 to 2003.
Source: Angus Maddison, *World Population, GDP and Per Capita GDP, 1–2003 AD*, http://www.ggdc.net/maddison/.

Again, through the exchange rate method, considering an appreciation of RMB, it will be 3 per cent when the economic growth is 8 per cent. This method puts the proportion of China's GDP by 2020 at 15.8 per cent, higher than the estimate by the first method.

Meanwhile, through the PPP method, taking China's GDP growth as 8 per cent and the world's GDP growth as 3 per cent, the ratio of China's GDP in the world's total would be above one-fifth by 2020.

Whichever method is used, the rise of China's economic power is apparent, and the proportion of China's GDP to the world's total will continue to increase.

Table 3.8 China's economic perspective (2005–2020)

	Exchange rate A	*Exchange rate B*	*PPP*
Assumption: world growth	0.03	0.03	0.03
Assumption: China growth	0.08	0.08+0.03 (3% in RMB value)	0.08
Ratio of China's GDP to world total (2005)	5	5	14.2
Ratio of China's GDP to world total (2020)	10.2	15.8	above1/5

Note: Data in 2020 were simulated by author. Exchange rate A excludes the prospect of RMB increasing in value; exchange rate B includes the prospect of RMB increasing in value.
Source: World Bank (2006) World Development Indicators 2006, CD-ROM, Washington D.C.: World Bank.
World Bank (2007) *World Development Report 2007*, Washington D.C.: World Bank.

In the book, *Roadmap of China's Rising* (Hu 2007), likewise written by this author, the summary judgment on the future development trend of the world economy pointed out that the GDP proportion of both Western Europe and Japan will assume a downward trend. The author cited China and India to assume an upward trend in their respective GDP proportions. That of the United States will remain unchanged before it begins to drop. By 2020, China will outshine the United States in economic scale (PPP) and India will outstrip Japan. By then, the pattern of the five biggest economies will take shape – that is, by order of the size of economic scale: China, the United States, Western Europe, India, and Japan. These will make up about 60 per cent of the world's economic aggregate (Hu 2007).

The trajectory of China's rising economic power is very clear. Based on the analysis of historical data and the forecast for future trends, it is feasible to make a judgment as to its world ranking in terms of all major economic and social indicators (see Table 3.9). Following are the reasons.

First, the GDP calculated by the exchange rate method will rise from tenth place in 1978 to fourth place by 2005; and will climb further up to second place by 2020, after the United States. In 1978, as a typical low-income country, China was ranked 175th place among the 188 countries in terms of per capita GNI. It rose in 2005 to 110th place among the 180 countries, elevating it to become a middle-income country. By 2020, China's per capita GNI will climb to 80th place to become an upper-middle income country.

Second, the GDP calculated by PPP will rise from fourth place in 1978 to second place in 2005, and will rank first in the world by 2020. In 2005, China's per capita GDP was placed 72nd place among 162 countries, inching closer to a middle-income level.

Third, foreign trade is one of the key factors in rapidly stimulating China's economic power. Its ranking in foreign trade shot up from 27th place in 1978 to third in 2005. By 2020, China will become the world's second largest trading country, next to the United States.

Table 3.9 Rank of main indicators of China in the world (1978–2020)

	1978	*1990*	*2000*	*2005*	*2010*	*2020*
GDP	10	11	6	4	3	2
GDP (PPP)	4	3	2	2	2	1
GNI per capita	175 (188)	178 (200)	141 (207)	110 (180)	99 (180)	80 (180)
GDP per capita (PPP)		110 (162)	84 (162)	72 (162)		
HDI	74 (113)	88 (121)	85 (173)	85 (177)	75 (177)	60 (177)
Foreign trade	27	16	8	3	2	2
S&T power			4	3	3	2
Comprehensive national power	5	3	2	2	2	2

Note: Parenthesis shows country's number among ranking.
Source: Hu, A. (2007) *China Rising and Openness*, Manuscript, May.

Fourth, it is important to note the rapid improvement in the social development level, the strength in science and technology and in integrated national power. China's human development index will rise from 74th among 113 countries in 1978 to 60th among 177 countries by 2020. The strength in science and technology will rise from third in 2005 to second by 2020. In its integrated national power, China rose from fifth in 1978 to second by 2000 and will continue to escalate into 2020, further narrowing the relative gap with the United States.

The impact of China's economic growth on the rest of the world

China's rise as an economic power is not only a matter of vital importance to the 1.3 billion Chinese people, but also a matter of great influence and significance for the people of other countries (Hu 2007). China is creating a new world record in economic growth. From 1978 to 2006, China's average GDP growth reached 9.7 per cent and its annual average total industrial output reached 11.5 per cent (State Statistical Bureau 2007a). The rapid increase in China's economic strength is reflected not only in the growth rate and the proportion of GDP in the world's total, but also in the steady rise of the proportion of GDP increment in the world This can be called the constant growth of marginal contributions to the growth of the world economy.

Calculation by the exchange rate method, based on the World Bank database, shows the contributions of China's GDP increment to the world's GDP increment as follows: 4.1 per cent in 1980–1990, 9.7 per cent in 1990–2000, and 15.3 per cent in 2000–2005. China's contributions will continue to exceed one-fifth in 2006–2020. If calculated by PPP, an upward trend has been assumed, rising from 11.5 per cent in 1980–1990 up to 26.1 per cent in 1990–2000 and further up to 29.6 per cent in 2000–2005. China's contributions will account for almost one-third of the world's total increment in 2006–2020 (see Table 3.10).

According to Dollar's 2007 study, China's contributions to the world's GDP (PPP) growth was 28.14 per cent from 1990–2005. This is the biggest among all countries and major economies, even higher than the 19.31 per cent of the United States and also higher than the 18.33 per cent of 22 combined high-income countries,

Table 3.10 China's marginal contribution to the world GDP growth by period (%)

Period	*Exchange rate (Constant 2000)*	*PPP (International 2000)*
1980–1990	4.1	11.5
1990–2000	9.7	26.1
2000–2005	15.3	29.6
2005–2020	20	33

Source: Data (in 1980–2005): World Bank, *World Development Indicators 2006*, CD-ROM.World Bank, *World Development Report 2007*.
Data (in 2005–2020) were simulated by the author.

excluding the United States and Japan. Undoubtedly, a pattern is taking shape with China as a new pole in the world economic growth. According to Dollar's forecast of the contributions of all countries and economies from 2006–2020, China's contributions will continue to grow and is expected to exceed one-third (36.6 per cent). The shares of the United States and Japan in the GDP increment will continue to drop, at 16.2 per cent and 1.9 per cent, respectively, while the shares of other countries and economies, except India (which is rising from 9.46 per cent to 11.9 per cent), would be very small and would even assume a downward trend (Dollar 2007).

Concluding remarks

In the past three decades, the trajectory of China's strength in economy and science and technology is very clear in its sustained rise. Also rising steadily is China's marginal input to the proportion of major economic and science and technology indicators in the world. China has become a new center for the world's economic growth and science and technology development. The position of such a regional center will continue to be strengthened in the long run. In the process of development, China would be facing both opportunities and challenges. The key lies in how to seize the opportunities and how to deal with the challenges, turning bad situations into good ones, and converting disadvantages into advantages, so as to bring about long-term prosperity.

The twenty-first century is a period for the Chinese nation to stand aloft in the forest of nations. It is also a century for it to become a world super power. China's path to modernization is a path of constant exploration for Chinese leaders, a path of innovation in all areas, a path of collective learning and sharing by the 1.3 billion people, and finally a path of studying while 'doing by learning' and 'learning by doing'. China's road to modernization is the road toward progress. It is also a road that will change China and its influence on the world (Hu 2007). As it is, China already exerts growing influence in the world, with its rising economic strength and science and technology development. As spillover and externality of this development, China is also giving emergent contributions to the development of the world's economy and science and technology. China's success is the success of the world. China's failure is the failure of the world.

References

CIA (2007) *World Fact Table*. https://www.cia.gov/library/publications/the-world-factbook/index.html.

CPC (1985) *Central Committee on the Reform of Science & Technology System*. In Selected Important Literature since the 12th National Party Congress (II). Beijing: People's Publishing House.

CPC (2006) China's Outlined Program for the Medium- and Long-Term Development in Science & Technology. Beijing: People's Publishing House.

Deng, Xiaoping (1984) *Selected Works of Deng Xiaoping* (Volume II). Beijing: People's Publishing House.

Dollar, David (2007) 'Asian Century or Multi-polar Century?', Paper prepared for "The Rise of Asia?", the Global Development Network Annual Conference, Beijing, January 13–14.

Hu, Angang (2007) *Roadmap of China's Rising*. Beijing: Beijing University Press.

Hu, Angang and Wang, Yahua (2006) National Conditions and Development: Development of Five Major Capitals in China (1980–2003) and Long-term Development Strategy. Beijing: Tsinghua University Press.

Hudson Institute (2006) China's New Great Leap Forward: High Technology and Military Power in the Next Half-Century. In National Conditions Report.

Jiang, Zemin (2002) *Build a well-off Society in Every Aspect and Break New Ground for the Cause of Socialism with Chinese Characteristics*. In CPC Central Literature Research Office, eds. Selected Documents Since the 16th Party Congress (I). Beijing: People's Publishing House.

Jiang, Zemin (1997) Hold High the Great Banner of Deng Xiaoping Theory and bring the Cause of Building Socialism with Chinese Characteristics into the 21st Century. In CPC Central Literature Research Office eds. Selected Documents since the 15th Party Congress (I). Beijing: People's Publishing House.

Lin, Justin, Fang, Cai, and Li, Zhou (1994) *China Miracle: Development Strategy and Economic Reform*. Shanghai: Shanghai People Press.

Maddison, Angus (2003) *The world economy: a millennial perspective*. Beijing: Beijing University Press.

Maddison, Angus (2001) Development Centre Studies The World Economy: A Millennial Perspective. Paris: OECD.

Maddison, Angus (2007) World Population, GDP and Per Capita GDP, 1–2003 AD, http://www.ggdc.net/maddison.march.

Overholt, William (1994) The Rise of China: How Economic Reform Is Creating a New Superpower. New York: W. W. Norton & Company.

State Statistical Bureau (2006) *China Statistical Abstract 2006*. Beijing: China Statistics Press.

State Statistical Bureau (2007a) *China Statistical Abstract 2007*. Beijing: China Statistics Press.

State Statistical Bureau (2007b) Statistical Bulletin of the People's Republic of China on National Economic and Social Development in 2006.

UNCTAD (2008) World Investment Report 2008, website:http://www.unctad.org/Templates/webflyer.asp?docid=10502&intItemID=2068&lang=1&mode=toc.

Winters, Alan and Yusuf, Shahid (eds) (2007) *Dancing with Giants: China, India and the Global Economy*. Washington D.C.: The World Bank.

World Bank (1985) *China: Problems and Schemes of Long-Term Development*. Beijing: China Economic and Financial.

World Bank (1997) *China 2020: Development Challenges in the New Century*. Washington D.C.: The World Bank.

World Bank (2007) *World Development Report 2007*. Beijing: Tsinghua University Press.

World Intellectual Property Organization. World Patent 1883–2005, website:http://www.wipo.int/ipdl/en/.

Zhao, Ziyang (1987) *March along the Road to Socialism with Chinese Characteristics*. Beijing: People's Publishing House.

Annex Table 3.1 S&T indicators to world total in major countries (% 1980–2004)

	1980	*1985*	*1990*	*1995*	*2000*	*2004*
Academic papers						
China	0.33	0.54	1.12	1.42	2.21	4.18
Japan	7.47	8.31	8.14	9.04	9.05	8.6
Germany	7.99	7.66	6.35	6.56	6.89	6.34
U.S.A.	39.37	38.64	40.46	32.68	30.93	30.23
4 countries total	55.16	55.15	56.07	49.7	49.08	49.35
Innovation patent applications (resident)						
China	0	0.63	0.88	1.44	2.96	9.87
Japan	31.73	42.79	50.05	47.89	44.9	38.09
Germany	5.49	5.02	4.62	5.47	6.01	5.04
U.S.A.	11.89	9.93	13.63	17.79	18.91	21.49
4 countries total	49.11	58.37	69.17	72.58	72.77	74.49
Personal computers						
China			0.37	1.14	4.24	6.42
Japan			5.56	6.28	8.44	8.38
Germany			4.96	6.13	5.72	5.61
U.S.A,			40.67	35.91	34.76	26.64
4 countries total			51.56	49.46	53.16	47.05
Internet users						
China			0.05	0.15	5.76	10.69
Japan			0.95	5.05	9.73	8.53
Germany			3.79	3.79	6.35	4.69
U.S.A.			75.75	63.18	31.73	21.05
4 countries total			80.54	72.18	53.57	44.97
R&D expenditure						
China	1.25	1.34	1.67	2.53	4.69	7.18
Japan	8.99	10.02	11.51	11.59	9.44	9.01
Germany				5.34	5.34	4.52
U.S.A.	26.01	27.12	25.12	25.27	24.5	22.85
4 countries total				44.73	43.97	43.56

Note: Innovation patent application (resident) in 2004 is 2005 data, Statistical database, WIPO. Personal computers in 1995 is 1996 data.

Source: World Bank (2006) *World Development Indicators 2006*, CD-ROM, Washington D.C.: World Bank.

4 Assessing the tacit dimension of China's science and technology power

Jong-Hak Eun

1. Introduction

'Technology' is widely acknowledged as the pivotal factor that makes economic growth sustainable in the long run. Furthermore, as the concepts of 'knowledge-based economy' (OECD 1996; Dahlman and Aubert 2001; Rooney *et al.* 2005) and 'learning economy' (Lundvall and Johnson 1994; Lundvall 2004; Eun 2005) indicate, economic growth is becoming more dependent upon active production, dissemination, and exploitation of scientific and technological data. In the same vein, the future growth of China, which has achieved a remarkable economic growth (above 9 per cent in terms of annual GDP growth rate) for the last two decades, largely dependent upon the cheap labor and land, would be better decided by the technological capability built in the country. Therefore, the technological power of China is in many people's interests.

Furthermore, recent statistics on science and technology (S&T) activities in China show that China is achieving quite a lot even in S&T. For instance, a recent report of the OECD (2006) argued that China has overtaken Japan and ranked second (after the United States) in the world in terms of research and development (R&D) expenditure in 2006. This news, while reproduced globally (e.g. *Financial Times* 4.12.2006, 5.1.2007; *Joongang Ilbo* 5.12.2006; *Korean Economic Daily* 5.12.2006), seemed to have impressed most people and even frightened quite a few, reinforcing the already-popular opinion of 'China threat.'

However, the assessment of the technological power of China in the existing discussion often falls short of sense of balance and, consequently, accuracy. That might be due to the ignorance of the characteristics of technology, which is often but not always based on well-documented scientific knowledge. Therefore, this chapter aims to assess the technological power of China in a more balanced way taking into account some important factors missing in the existing studies. More specifically, I will try to answer whether we should accept the S&T statistical figures of China simply as they look, or if we should attune (i.e. appreciate or depreciate) them to understand the true image of the technological power of China.

The remainder of this chapter is organized as follows: In Section 2, I provide a quick review of frequently cited recent Chinese S&T statistics and address some *technical* issues that emerge in interpreting and handling those statistical figures.

In Section 3, I raise more *fundamental* issues in the existing discussions and provide a conceptual framework that could be helpful in assessing the technological power of a country in a more balanced manner. In Section 4, I revisit the technological power of China under the guidance of the new framework developed in Section 3. Section 5 is the conclusion of the study.

2. Review of the Chinese S&T indicators and technical issues

China's annual growth rate of R&D expenditure is as high as 21.5 per cent, thanks to the rapid increase of the corporate R&D during 1995–2005 (see Figure 4.1), which surpasses, by a wide margin, its annual GDP growth rate during the same period. As a result, China has ranked fourth in the world in terms of the scale of R&D expenses by the end of 2006. Moreover, China's international ranking has moved further up to the world's second when we use the Purchasing Power Parity (PPP) exchange rate rather than the traditional Market Exchange Rate (MER) (see Figure 4.2).

China's enhanced technological power is not only detected in the S&T input variables (e.g. R&D expenditure) but also in S&T output variables such as scientific publication, patent applications, etc. The number of scientific articles produced by the Chinese has more than quadrupled in less than ten years (see Figure 4.3). Consequently, China's ranking in scientific publications has been heightened from fifteenth in 1995 to fourth in 2005 (see Table 4.1). Although we have recognized that there remains skepticism about the quality of those papers newly expanded by Chinese scholars, it is worth noting that China has become a major producer of knowledge both in basic sciences such as physics and chemistry, and also in

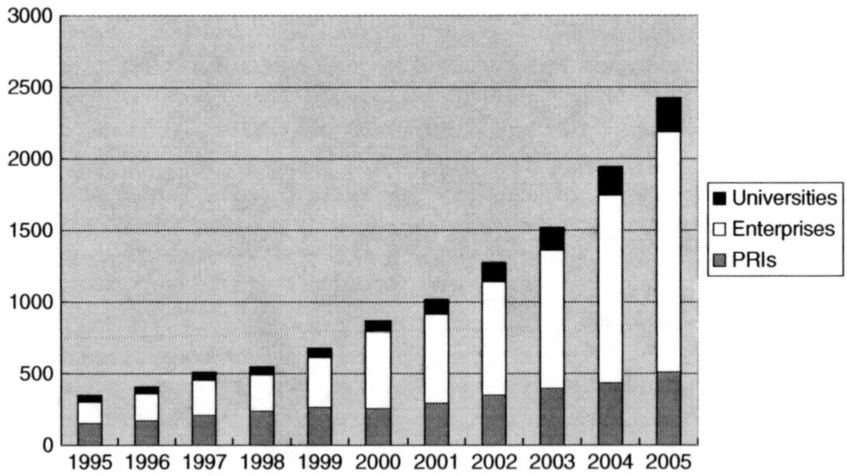

Figure 4.1 Increasing R&D expenditure propelled by corporate R&D.
Source: Calculated from NBS & MOST (2006: 7).

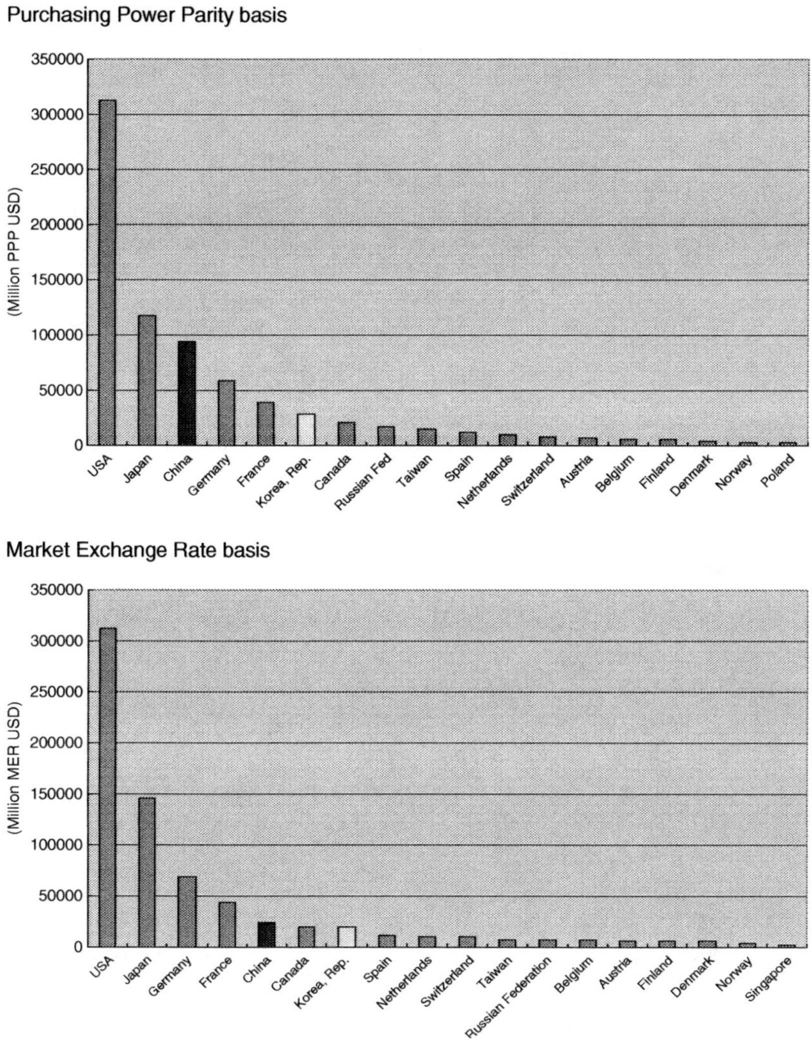

Figure 4.2 International comparison of R&D expenditure: PPP vs. MER (2004).
Source: OECD (2006: 208).
Calculated using R&D data in NBS & MOST (2006: 345–6) and Exchange Rate data in UN WDI 2006 and PWT 6.2.

more applied engineering fields such as electronics, communication, automation, material science, and computer science (see Table 4.2). Zhou and Leydesdorff (2006) also show that Chinese scientists have been very active, having become a major research group in the field of nanotechnology, which is widely believed to have huge economic potential.

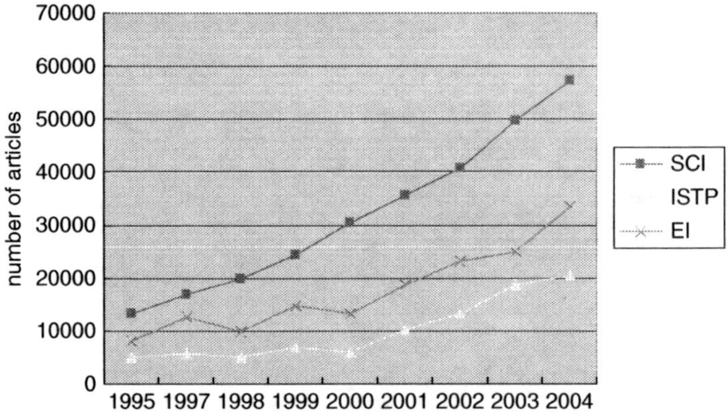

Figure 4.3 Increasing number of scientific publications by Chinese scholars.
Note: SCI: Science Citation Index; ISTP: Index to Science and Technical Proceeding; EI: Engineering Index.
Source: NBS & MOST (2006: 302).

Table 4.1 China's ranking in scientific publications

	1995	*1997*	*1998*	*1999*	*2000*	*2001*	*2002*	*2003*	*2004*
SCI	15	12	12	10	8	8	6	6	5
ISTP	10	9	10	8	8	6	5	6	5
EI	7	4	5	3	3	3	2	3	2

Note: SCI: Science Citation Index; ISTP: Index to Science and Technical Proceeding; EI: Engineering Index.
Source: NBS & MOST (2006: 302).

Table 4.2 Major research fields of Chinese scholars

Discipline	*Ranking*
Mathematics	7
Physics	2
Chemistry	1
Earth Science	9
Biology	6
Material Science	4
Power and Electrical Engineering	8
Electronics, Communication and Automation	3
Computer	5
Chemical Engineering	10

Note: Major research fields are identified based upon the number of academic publications (listed in SCI, ISTP, and EI).
Source: NBS & MOST (2006: 303).

Additionally, as shown in Tables 4.3 and 4.4, both the number of patent applications in China and the number of international patent applications by China-based entities has grown sharply in recent years. China has successively caught up to advanced countries, ranking eighth in terms of patent application through the Patent Cooperation Treaty (PCT) in 2006 (SIPO 2007.3.14).[1] Moreover, patent grants offered to China-based entities by the USPTO increased from 119 in 2000 to 404 in 2004, and to 661 in 2006 (SIPO 2007).

Another meaningful indicator of China's technological power is the number of university students. As shown in Figure 4.4, Chinese universities have expanded enrollment since the late 1990s and accordingly, the number of university graduates has begun to take off since 2002. The increase is most prominent in the field of engineering and business administration, which could be assumed as the majors most directly related to creating and exploiting technological knowledge for economic uses.

From the above discussions, one could see that China has ambitiously increased S&T input and has drawn more S&T output. In fact, R&D expenditure, scientific publication, patent application, and university graduates are widely accepted and frequently used factors to appraise the technological power of a country. Then, is everything clear about China's technological power? Perhaps not! Although many aggregate-level statistics show sharp rises in China's technological power, which

Table 4.3 China's patent grant for indigenous and foreign entities

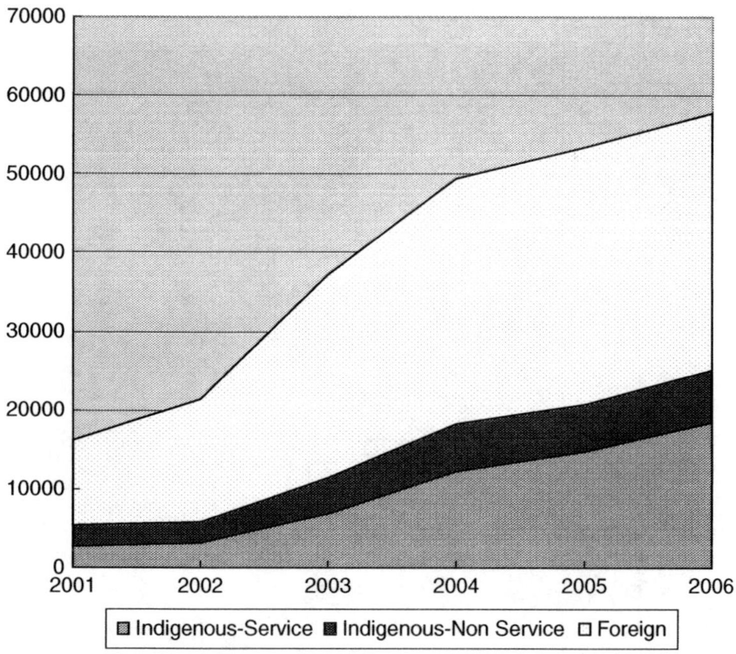

Source: SIPO, www.sipo.gov.cn.

Table 4.4 International patent applications (through PCT)

	2000	*2001*	*2002*	*2003*	*2004*	*2005 estimate*	*2005 percent*	*2005 growth*
EPC Member States	36,031	40,681	42,506	43,299	44,032	46,446	34.6%	5.5%
United States of America	38,007	43,055	41,292	41,023	43,464	45,111	33.6%	3.8%
Japan	9,567	11,904	14,063	17,393	20,223	25,145	18.8%	24.3%
Germany	12,582	14,031	14,326	14,682	15,255	15,870	11.8%	4.0%
France	4,138	4,707	5,089	5,172	5,181	5,522	4.1%	6.6%
United Kingdom	4,795	5,482	5,376	5,205	5,041	5,115	3.8%	1.5%
Republic of Korea	1,580	2,324	2,520	2,949	3,554	4,747	3.5%	33.6%
Netherlands	2,928	3,410	3,977	4,480	4,236	4,435	3.3%	4.7%
Switzerland	1,989	2,349	2,755	2,860	2,881	3,096	2.3%	7.5%
Sweden	3,091	3,421	2,990	2,612	2,844	2,784	2.1%	-2.1%
China	784	1,731	1,018	1,295	1,706	2,452	1.8%	43.7%
Canada	1,801	2,114	2,260	2,270	2,109	2,315	1.7%	9.8%
Italy	1,394	1,623	1,982	2,163	2,196	2,309	1.7%	5.1%
Australia	1,576	1,664	1,759	1,680	1,837	2,022	1.5%	10.1%
Finland	1,578	1,696	1,762	1,557	1,672	1,866	1.4%	11.6%
All Others	3,894	4,758	4,972	5,289	5,682	5,835	4.4%	2.7%
Total	**93,240**	**108,231**	**110,390**	**115,198**	**122,607**	**134,073**	**100.0%**	**9.4%**

Source: WIPO, www.wipo.int.

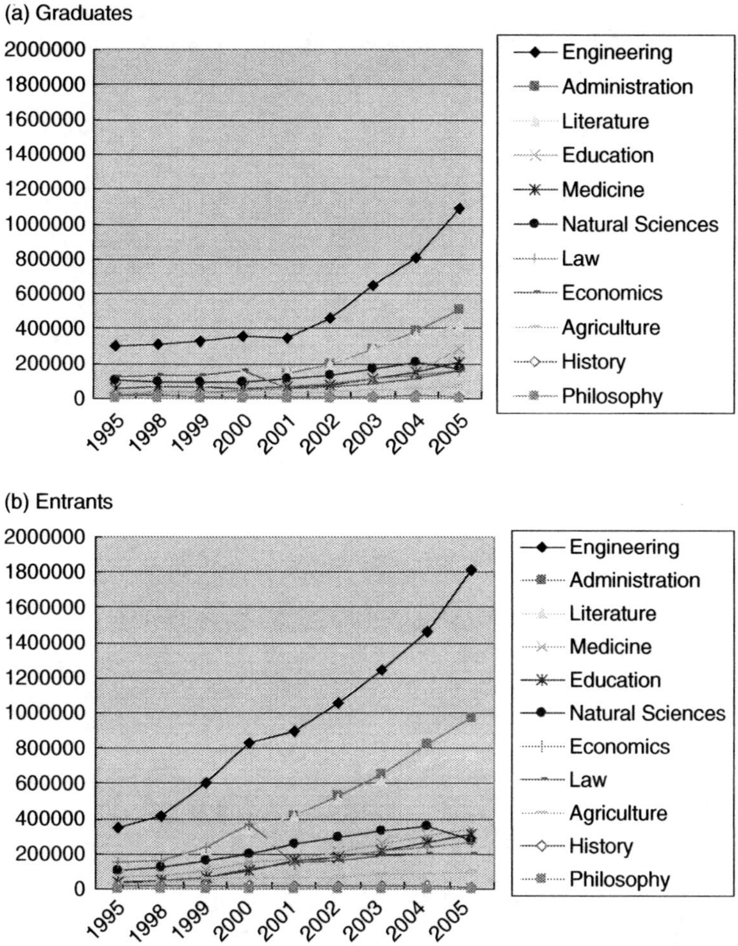

Figure 4.4 University graduates and entrants by field of study in China
Source: NBS & MOST (2006: 20–2).

as a result already has China placing itself as one of the major players in S&T activities, there remain, however, several critical issues that should be taken into consideration in assessing China's technological power.

When we are making international comparisons, we should first choose the level of comparison. For example, we should choose the level of aggregation. Actually, many national-level aggregate statistics show that China has already become a major player in S&T activities, but the per capita statistics (e.g. per capita R&D expenditure) still rank China far below the U.S., Japan, Germany and several quite smaller countries in many aspects. Here, I suggest a tentative rule of selection. Aggregate number might be more meaningful when the S&T resources (including money, manpower) are mobilized at the national level by a few entities, as in the aerospace industry, but it would have quite limited significance when it is typically split at the local or individual firm level and the resources used by many entities in a redundant manner. Thus, in the latter case, one had better disaggregate the national-level statistics from the international comparison of technological capability. However, the frequently cited statistics on China's S&T, which we have reviewed above, are mostly the ones aggregated at the national level. Therefore, we should be aware of the fact that the international comparison based upon those aggregated numbers would easily *overstate* the technological power of China with a population of over 1.3 billion.

Another technical issue that arises when we try to compare S&T activities measured by amount of money is the choice of an appropriate exchange rate. As we have seen in the above, the choice could shift China's position (or ranking) among other countries. Theoretically, PPP, which equalizes the price levels of the countries under comparison, is desirable when the goods and services used in S&T activities are different only in cost without a considerable quality gap. On the other hand, MER might be a better basis of comparison when the quality gap is significantly large and widespread, and the difference in the price of the baskets of goods and services used in S&T activities is mostly due to the quality gap.

One can hardly argue that any one of the two exchange rates perfectly describes the reality in China. However, I would like to point out that the ranking or the image of the Chinese technological power created upon the PPP easily exaggerates the real capability of China. First of all, China ranked only 124th in the average number of citations per paper – a measure of the quality of a paper (*Financial Times* 5.1.2007). It means that there could be a significant quality gap between China and more advanced countries in S&T activities, which makes PPP less reasonable. Second, a considerable portion of the facilities and equipment used in S&T activities in China is imported from abroad at almost the same cost that advanced countries allow. Thus, we should not simply multiply the digit that represents the gap in general price level and assume it to have genuine S&T input in China. In addition, the scientists and engineers returning from abroad, who play increasingly important roles in the Chinese S&T activities, are usually paid four or five times higher than the ones educated in China.[2] This indicates that the wage level of scientists and engineers in China gradually equals that in advanced countries. Still, even if the same quality scientists and engineers are paid less in China than in advanced countries, the gap might be smaller than the general price gap between China and advanced countries.

The above-mentioned issues of choosing a basis for comparison (aggregate vs. per capita, PPP vs. MER) needs more elaboration in order to assess more accurately the technological power of a country. If there is a detailed enough manual that could determine which basis is more adequate in certain cases (e.g. appropriate basis for comparison might be different across industrial fields), and based on a sound theoretical foundation, the assessment of a country's technological power and the international comparison could become more reliable because the authors' possible intents of exaggeration or understatement could be checked with the manual. However, preparing the detailed manual or guide of choosing a basis for comparison is beyond the scope of this study. Thus, I leave this task for future studies.

3. A new conceptual framework

In the previous section, I have discussed that choosing the right option as a basis for international comparison (e.g. aggregate vs. per capita, PPP vs. MER) is important in order to avoid a biased image of the technological power of a country. Besides the *technical* issue of choosing the correct standard, however, there are some *fundamental* issues that should be addressed. Unfortunately, in many existing discussions on the Chinese technological power, these issues have often been neglected. The fundamental issues are as follows.

First of all, the traditional approach has paid a lopsided attention to only a specific type of S&T knowledge that is well-documented in the form of, for instance, scientific papers or patent documents. Actually, it is quite a widespread tradition in mainstream economics to use the quantity of scientific papers and patents as representatives for scientific or technological power because they are easily available in official statistics. However, the increasing literature of technology economics and innovation studies has revealed that the well-documented knowledge, say, *codified* (or *explicit*) knowledge could not cover all the economically useful S&T knowledge. In other words, the traditional approach largely neglects another economically important type of knowledge – *tacit* knowledge. Although the university graduate statistics frequently referred to could capture something more than codified knowledge, it however also reflects the attention on the codified knowledge that is *embrained* (Lam and Lundvall 2004) in a human being.

Tacit knowledge is usually *embodied* in human beings through on-site experiences. Nobel Prize laureate, Kenneth Arrow (1962), identified the importance of 'learning by doing' or experience-based learning in the competency of individual firms. Lundvall and Johnson (1994) and OECD (2000) pointed out that the *know-how* type knowledge, which is tacit in nature, takes an important place in building and maintaining the competence of individuals or firms. They argue that tacit knowledge constitutes a core part of a firm's competency because tacit knowledge cannot be easily transferred to or copied by others. Extending their discussions (i.e. from firm level to national level), we might argue that tacit knowledge, in addition to codified knowledge, which is accumulated in a national border, to a considerable degree contributes to the technological power of the country.

The deficiency of the traditional approach, which is biased towards codified knowledge in assessing the technological potential of an economic entity (an individual, a firm or a country), could be reaffirmed by Pavitt's findings.[3] By analyzing 2000 important technical innovations in the United Kingdom, Pavitt (1984) showed that the codified knowledge injected from universities and research institutions is the major source of innovation only in *some* industries – what he categorized as 'science-based producers.' According to him, in many other industries, important innovations are propelled by something other than codified knowledge. In the same vein, I propose to take the creation of tacit knowledge, often occurring in industrial workplaces, into account in evaluating the technological power of China.

Second, the traditional approach did not pay much attention to *who* (especially, indigenous firms vs. foreign firms) produces, possesses, and handles the S&T

knowledge in assessing a country's technological power. This ignorance of the *structure* of the S&T knowledge distribution could lead to a wrong image of a country's technological power, especially when the country hosts many foreign countries, as in China. The reasons are as follows.

When firms produce S&T knowledge, one major outcome is innovation (e.g. new products) but another major outcome is 'competence' accumulated within the innovators (e.g. firms) (Lundvall 2004). Because competence is not automatically leaked out (or spilled over) to other organizations even within the same national border, it is important to determine who produces the knowledge and accumulates the competence. If foreign companies account for a lion's share of the knowledge production and competence accumulation within the country concerned, the technological power of the country could be weaker, as compared to the opposite case wherein indigenous firms play major roles in knowledge production.[4]

Moreover, whether foreign companies are mostly joint ventures with domestic firms or wholly owned foreign firms could make a difference. In the case of a joint venture, the spillover effect might be bigger than in the case of wholly owned foreign firms. This indicates that an accurate assessment of the technological power of a country requires a micro-level understanding of the structure of the country, which is lacking in the traditional approach.

The blind spots of the traditional approach could be illustrated in Figure 4.5. The vertical axis of Figure 4.5 differentiates different types of knowledge – codified (or science-based, disembodied) knowledge versus tacit (or experience-based, embodied) knowledge, and the horizontal axis differentiates different

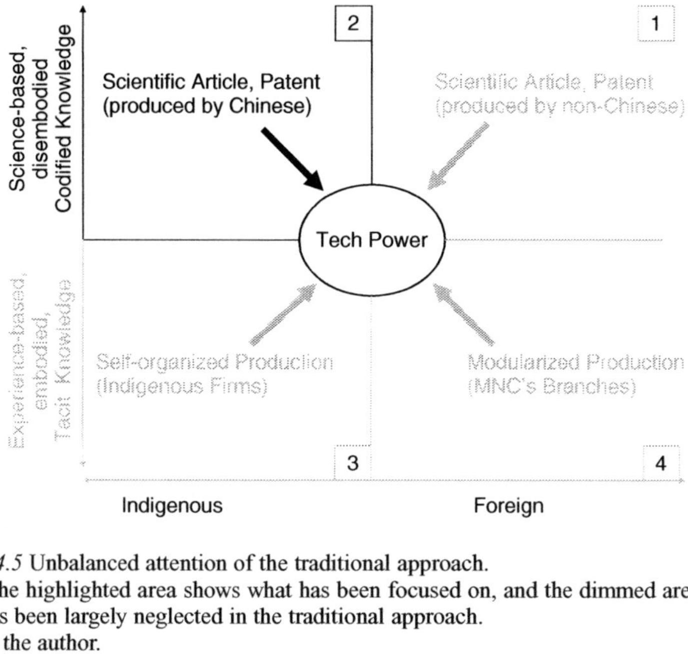

Figure 4.5 Unbalanced attention of the traditional approach.
Note: The highlighted area shows what has been focused on, and the dimmed area shows what has been largely neglected in the traditional approach.
Source: the author.

actors – that is, indigenous firms vs. foreign firms. With this, the new framework identifies four different sources of technological power building.

The traditional approach has put an excessive emphasis on *codified* knowledge and it often failed to differentiate the importance of S&T activities performed by different entities: *indigenous* vs. *foreign* companies. In other words, the traditional approach has been biased toward quadrant 2 in Figure 4.5, neglecting the other three quadrants. In point of fact, what we have seen above is mostly about the activities that fall into quadrant 2 in Figure 4.5. This means those frequently cited statistics presented above fall short of showing an unbiased, full picture of the Chinese technological potential.

In addition to the two deficiencies mentioned above (i.e. ignorance of the tacit knowledge and the structure of the knowledge distribution between indigenous and foreign entities), the traditional approach has another major drawback. It has mainly focused on the *stock* of knowledge *per se*, neglecting the *process* in which the pieces of knowledge transform themselves into the technological power. However, newly created S&T knowledge must be re-processed to constitute the technological power and ultimately contribute to the economy. The process also requires considerable effort. To use a metaphor, a *barrier* must be penetrated for S&T knowledge to be exploited in order to ultimately contribute to the economy. Acs *et al.* (2003) conceptualized the barrier as a 'knowledge filter' – a semi-permeable barrier limiting the efficient conversion of new knowledge into economic knowledge. Furthermore, Acs (2006) and Mueller (2006) hinted that the knowledge filter could be reduced by 'entrepreneurship' and 'absorptive capacity.' In order to penetrate or reduce the knowledge filter, there must be efforts, I believe, not only to enhance the absorptive capacity and entrepreneurship, but also efforts to improve the 'institutional environment' are necessary. The dynamic process of technological power building is not limited to penetrating or reducing the knowledge filter as well. The S&T activities in a specific field, as illustrated by each of the four quadrants in Figure 4.6, could either facilitate or constrain other S&T activities in other fields (i.e. other quadrants).

By incorporating the preceding discussions, I propose a new conceptual framework with which one could assess a country's technological power in a more balanced approach. The new framework explicitly takes into account *tacit knowledge* in addition to codified knowledge, as well as the *structure of S&T knowledge distribution* among indigenous and foreign firms in assessing the technological power of a country, with additional consideration of the dynamic process of technological power building (see Figure 4.6).

The dotted grey area around the 'technological power' in Figure 4.6 indicates the knowledge filter. The density of the knowledge filter indicates how hard it might be to penetrate it. Because of the knowledge filter, some pieces of S&T knowledge fail to contribute to the technological power, which is illustrated by the curbed arrows. The dotted arrows show these cross-field effects. For example, if a country succeeded in transforming the codified knowledge contained in scientific articles produced by indigenous scholars, the events could enhance the country's ability to absorb other scientific articles produced by foreign scholars and could

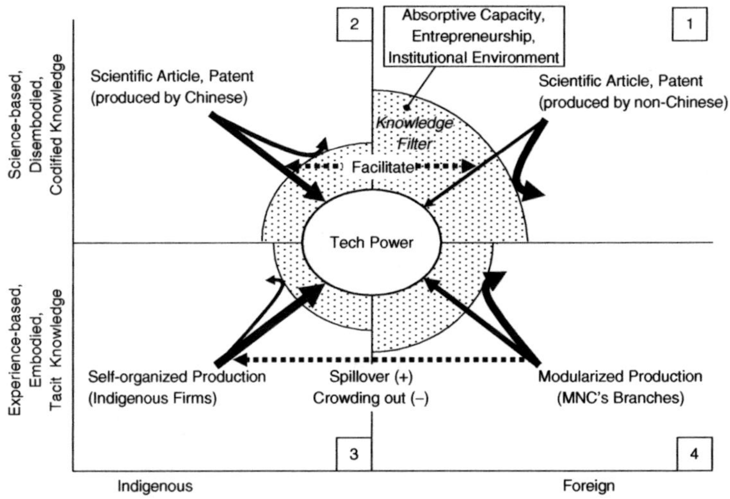

Figure 4.6 A broader perspective on the technological power building mechanism
Source: the author.

let them contribute to the country's technological power (see the dotted arrow drawn across quadrant 1 and 2). Also, the presence of foreign companies could bring both positive (i.e. *spillover* of technological and administrative skills) and negative (i.e. *crowding-out* of business opportunities and scarce resources) impacts to the indigenous firms (see the dotted arrow drawn from quadrant 4 to quadrant 3).

The new framework is, in principle, applicable to assessing the technological power of any country. However, in the following section, we will examine China's case within the framework developed above.

4. Re-evaluating China's technological power

In this section, I will examine the aspects that have been largely neglected in the traditional approach in order to assess the current technological power of China in a more balanced way. As mentioned above, the existing discussions are mainly focused on the aspect illustrated by quadrant 2 in Figure 4.6. Thus, in this section, I will pursue a more balanced perception of Chinese technological power by additionally taking into account what is happening in the rest of the three quadrants on top of the existing discussions on quadrant 2: Sub-section 1 matches quadrants 3 and 4; Sub-section 2 matches quadrant 1; Sub-section 3 matches the central area of Figure 4.6, which represents the dynamic process of technological capability building that has often been neglected in previous studies.

1) Foreign presence and tacit knowledge

Due to China's Open Door policy, initiated in 1978 and which continued for about 30 years without a major setback (the aftermath of the Tiananmen Square incident in 1989 is a remarkable exception), the *globalization* of the Chinese economy has significantly progressed. Particularly since the early 1990s, foreign companies have rushed into the Chinese market to take advantage of the market opportunities of the booming economy and the preferential policies (e.g. tax exemption) provided for foreign companies, bringing in capital and technology which China has long sought.

On the other hand, the foreign companies' recent scuttle to China was further facilitated by the *new technological regime* which could be characterized by codification, digitalization, and modularization of the (previously analogue and less dividable) production process (Lau and Yam 2005; Doran 2003; Takeishi and Fujimoto 2001). Thanks to the so-called IT revolution and what Nolan (2001) calls 'business revolution' in the late twentieth century, firms in many industries have become able to divide their production process into several chunks (or modules) and outsource the labor-intensive and low value-added ones to low-income countries. Under this new technological regime, the open China with cheap land and labor provided a huge opportunity for foreign companies to further optimize their global production system. In reality, many multinational corporations (MNCs) have responded to China's opening by further globalizing their production system.

Considering the highly globalized Chinese situation, one should be more cautious in interpreting the S&T-related statistics of China. As discussed in the previous section tacit knowledge, which is another important building block of a country's technological power, is usually produced and accumulated by on-site experiences and is not easily transferred to others.[5] Thus, who (i.e. foreign or indigenous entity) really does the job and accumulates experiences is key in tacit knowledge accumulation. In this respect, I propose to make a distinction between the industrial practices performed by foreign firms and the ones done by indigenous firms. This differentiation is also based on the idea that a *modularized* and thus *fragmented* production performed by foreign (or multinational) branches under a global division of labor (or global production system) has a relatively limited positive impact on the host developing country in terms of the employees' learning by doing (because knowledge-intensive chunks could be deliberately excluded from the production in the country at the outset), but has a chain-wise positive impact on upstream and downstream industries because the chunk of production in the country might not be closely linked to domestic upstream and downstream industries.

The Chinese industrial structure seems to have been improved quite a lot during the last decade. At least, it is true that the share of the so-called 'high-technology industries' has expanded in the Chinese industrial production (see Figure 4.7) and export (the share of the so-called high-technology products in total exports of China has increased from 17.5 per cent in 2001, to 25.1 per cent in 2003, and to 28.9 per cent in 2005). Although this is often referred to as evidence of China's enhanced technological power, we need to examine in more detail and check who (e.g. foreign or indigenous firm) plays the major role in those industries in order to properly evaluate China's technological power. From Figure 4.8, we could see

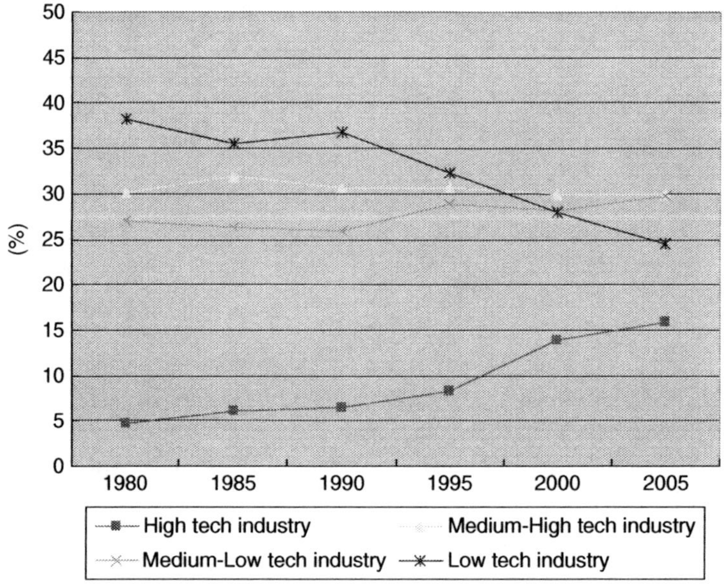

Figure 4.7 Industrial production in China.
Note: The classification of industries into four categories follows Hatzichronoglou (1997) based on the International Standard Industrial Classification (ISIC, Rev.3).
Source: Adjusted from Yang (2006: 116).

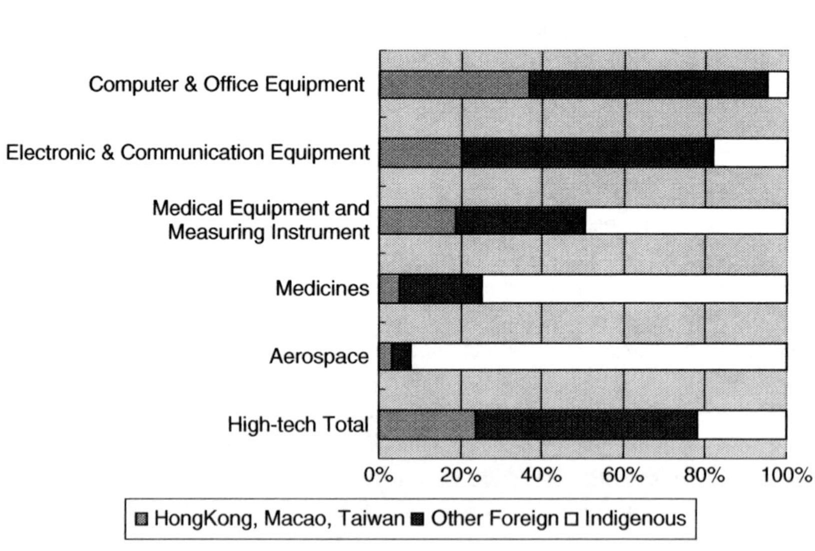

Figure 4.8 Share of foreign-invested firms in Chinese high-technology industries (by industrial production).
Source: NBS & MOST (2006: 184–9).

that foreign companies occupy the dominant position in many high-technology industries (except aerospace industry), ahead of large Chinese state-owned enterprises. Also, Figure 4.9 shows that foreign companies have played increasingly important roles in China's high-technology exports. By 2005, the foreign companies' share in the Chinese export of high-technology products will have continuously grown to about 88 per cent. Such heavy foreign presence in China is extremely apparent in high-technology sectors (especially in the ICT industry), but even in other industries, foreign companies also play important roles: Foreign companies account for 28.6 per cent of the total industrial production and 58.3 per cent of the total export from China. This indicates that a very large part of tacit knowledge produced from actual industrial production in China belongs to foreign companies rather than indigenous firms, requiring us to depreciate the Chinese technological power originally estimated from the simple aggregate industrial statistics.

Furthermore, the chunks of high-technology industries outsourced to China by MNCs are, in many cases, practiced in highly automated, digitalized factories, giving only limited chances for Chinese laborers to learn by doing something technologically important. In this sense, one might argue that the MNC-driven

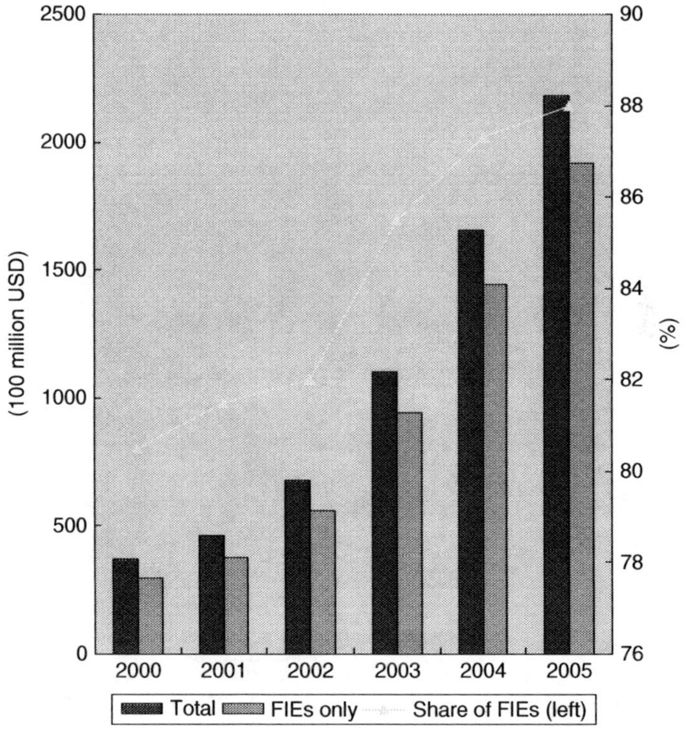

Figure 4.9 Share of foreign-invested firms in Chinese high-technology exports.
Source: China Customs, www.customs.gov.cn.

international division of labor based on codification, digitalization, and modularization of production process has facilitated the nominal improvement of the Chinese industrial structure on the one hand, but limited the chance for Chinese people to produce and accumulate tacit knowledge on the other hand. Consequently, against common sense, many high-technology industries in China are actually 'labor-intensive' rather than 'knowledge-intensive.'[6] Additionally, a recent trend in which Sino-foreign joint ventures (JVs) restructure themselves to become wholly owned foreign companies (Eun 2006) seems to further limit learning by doing on the Chinese side[7] (see Figure 4.10).

2) Foreign presence and codified knowledge

We have seen that China's increasing academic papers and patents (i.e. codified knowledge stock) are often understood as evidence of growing Chinese technological power. However, one should be cautious in interpreting the related statistics because many of them are produced by foreign entities in China. According to Fuller (2006), out of the total 939 corporate IT US utility patents originating from China, 689 (73.4 per cent) are from Taiwanese firms (Fuller 2006: 20–1). Furthermore, Fuller found that the Taiwanese assemblers of electronics and other products have not contributed much to China's development because of their closed manufacturing networks.

Fuller's argument lets us conceive that 'foreign enclaves' are located in but are largely disconnected from China. Another sign of major roles of foreign entities in China is that foreign-invested enterprises hold more than a quarter of all corporate R&D spending in China. Especially in high-technology industries, the share of R&D performed by foreign firms is as high as 42.1 per cent (see Table 4.5).

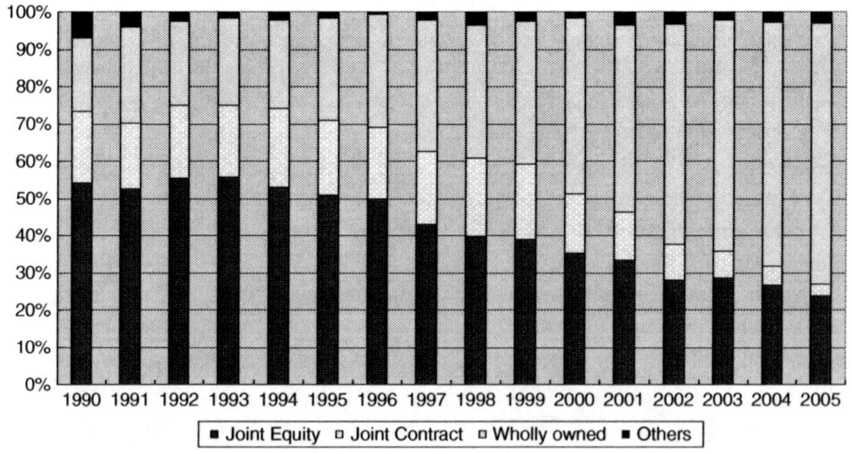

Figure 4.10 Increasing share of wholly owned foreign companies.
Source: CEIC.

Table 4.5 Corporate R&D: Indigenous vs. foreign firms

	Indigenous Firms	*Foreign Firms*	
All industries	74.0%	26.0%	
		Wholly Owned Foreign	Joint Venture
		8.6% (33.0%)	17.4% (67%)
High Technology Only	57.9%	42.1%	

Source: NBS & NDRC (2006: 287).

The leading role of foreign companies in the Chinese knowledge intensive sector could also be captured by China's domestic patent statistics: Out of 139,566 patents filed in China in 2005, 77,575 patents (55.6 per cent) were applied by foreign companies. Among the big 30 corporate patent applicants, 21 applicants were foreign companies in 2005, and those foreign companies accounted for 68.9 per cent of all the patents filed by the big 30 (SIPO 2006).

The earlier discussions show that in assessing the technological power of a highly globalized country such as China, we should be more careful in interpreting the aggregate statistics. It is also necessary to examine whether the S&T activities under concern are performed by indigenous entities or foreign ones. Once the differentiation is applied, the amazing features of China's national-level statistics on S&T activities presented in Section 2 are largely diluted. In other words, the heavy influx of foreign firms into China (I would call this 'inbound globalization') and their significant role in China requires us to *depreciate* the nominal figures in China's S&T statistics.

However, we also have to take into account the overseas Chinese peoples' active roles in other countries' universities, research institutes, and high-technology firms in assessing China's technological power, the reason being, the overseas Chinese's S&T capabilities could be mobilized in enhancing China's technological power. This 'outbound globalization' of China might provide external inputs, which are not usually captured by traditional indicators. Therefore, we have to *appreciate* China's technological power beyond the figures in the Chinese domestic S&T statistics.

As such, the two aspects of the globalization (i.e. inbound globalization and outbound globalization) of China complicate the task of assessing the technological power of China. There co-exists the need of *depreciation* and the need of *appreciation* on China's domestic S&T statistics in assessing the real technological power of China. However, most of the depreciation should be done immediately while the larger part of the appreciation could only be considered in the (near or distant) future because the S&T competence acquired by overseas Chinese could be realized and contributed to China's technological power only when overseas scientists and engineers choose to return to China, or when Chinese indigenous entities successfully utilize overseas Chinese's S&T capabilities by forming international links with them. Moreover, the scale and quality of returnees and the significance of the international linkages would depend upon not only the *economic* but also the *socio-political* conditions in China, for which, allegedly, many overseas Chinese still wait for improvements, although a number of returnees have recently picked up.[8] Therefore, there seems to be a *time lag* between the depreciation and appreciation. This time lag leads us, for now, to depreciate China's technological power below the image created by the frequently mentioned China's S&T statistics referred to in Section 2.

3) Technological power building process: knowledge filter, spillover, and crowding-out

In the previous section, we pursued a more balanced picture of the Chinese technological power by breaking the aggregate statistics and differentiating the S&T activities performed by indigenous and foreign entities. This task is necessary because different players (i.e. indigenous vs. foreign) are assumed to be different in degrees of the contribution to the technological power of the country under concern. Yet, the discussions are mostly about the *static distribution* of S&T knowledge rather than *dynamic process* of knowledge exploitation/utilization. However, as mentioned in Section 3.3, we need to further examine the 'knowledge filter' that prevents or constrains the transformation of new S&T knowledge into economically relevant knowledge, and the Chinese efforts to penetrate it in order to assess the real technological power of China.

I would now like to focus on the *dynamic process* of technological power building, which includes spillover and crowding-out effects between indigenous and foreign entities.[9] Although mainly utilized as a depreciator in the static analysis, the heavy presence of foreign firms in China, in itself, could also provide new opportunities for indigenous firms to take advantage of. One important thing indigenous firms could acquire from bigger exposure to foreign companies is the increased chance of 'parallel learning' (Eun *et al.* 2006) from foreign companies through intended technology transfer by friendly foreign companies, by unintended spillover from foreign companies, or even by (sometimes illegal) technological intelligence performed by indigenous firms in spite of foreign companies' security efforts. Some Chinese firms have successfully learned or copied key technologies from foreign firms of a particular industry or from the foreign partners in Sino-foreign joint ventures. However, as more and more Sino-foreign joint ventures have recently (especially since China's accession to the WTO) re-structured themselves to become wholly owned foreign companies (see Figure 4.10), the Chinese local firms might have a harder time gaining access to key technologies in foreign companies' hands.

In addition to the 'spillover effect' from the foreign companies, 'crowding-out effects' could also occur. Indigenous firms could lose opportunities (i.e. be crowded out) by the influx of foreign companies. For instance, recently increasing foreign R&D centers in China might take up the best scientists and engineers, limiting the development of indigenous R&D centers or indigenous high-technology firms. There are allegedly approximately 800 foreign R&D centers in China whose growth rate (in number) is much faster than the Chinese GDP growth rate.

In fact, in the UNCTAD's recent survey (2005), China was ranked first as the most attractive prospective R&D location for multinational corporations.[10] From these R&D centers, China could expect technology spillover effects. On the other hand, crowding-out effects are also very probable: If talented Chinese engineers (from China and abroad) are attracted to foreign R&D centers established in China, indigenous Chinese firms might find it harder to recruit first-grade engineers. The influx of foreign capital could also crowd out the indigenous industry by international M&As in China, which have increased rapidly since China's accession to the WTO in 2001. In China, there are concerns about the 'foreignization' of domestic assets, especially indigenous firms in early stages but with huge growth potentials (Eun 2006). This shows that foreign existence could mean something quite different according to the host country's learning capability and the actual pattern of interaction between indigenous and foreign firms.

In discussing international spillover or crowding-out effects, existing studies have mainly focused on the *foreign actors* who are assumed to play *active* and *major* roles in either case. Conversely, *indigenous actors* have been put into the spotlight less, largely ignored, and considered as *passive* beneficiaries (in case of spillover) or victims (in case of crowding-out). Nevertheless, in the dynamic process of technological power building, indigenous actors also play a major role. In all likelihood, whether the foreign influence, which has both positive and negative potentials, is actually realized as spillover or as crowding-out largely depends on the indigenous actors' characteristics. The 'absorptive capacity' of indigenous actors, in particular, plays an important role. Even the codified knowledge produced by foreign entities (illustrated by quadrant 1 in Figure 4.6) could be utilized in China's technological power building if China has enough absorptive capacity. As Cohen and Levinthal (1990) arguably pointed out, only when the knowledge users have invested in building 'absorptive capacity' in advance, can they utilize the knowledge, which is seemingly limitlessly accessible to anyone.[11] Therefore, if a country has a huge absorptive capacity, scientific knowledge in the public domain could be effectively used in the country's technological power building, even though the scientific knowledge was not produced by its own people. In the opposite case of a country with very weak absorptive capacity, not only the scientific knowledge produced by foreign entities but also the one by its own people, cannot be effectively utilized in enhancing the country's technological capability, although the scientific knowledge is open for everybody without charging any fees.

The previous discussion indicates the need to measure the absorptive capacity of China in order to assess its technological power. However, we should first acknowledge that absorptive capacity cannot easily be measured or calculated from the existing statistics[12] because the ability to absorb external knowledge depends on many things, including the degree of mastery of the pre-requisite knowledge that is helpful in absorbing new knowledge, the recipient's will and incentive to absorb external knowledge, and various environmental factors.

Yet, the rapidly increasing tertiary education admissions (Figure 4.4) indicate that China is enhancing its absorptive capacity as a whole. Also, we could check the Chinese firms' investment in absorbing or assimilating imported technologies.

Table 4.6 Indigenous firms' technology import and assimilation (unit: 10,000 RMB)

	2000	*2001*	*2002*	*2003*	*2004*	*2005*
Technology Import	245,422,0	285,865,9	372,503,3	405,407,5	367,949,6	296,765,0
Assimilation	181,809	196,273	257,438	270,957	539,700	693,824
Domestic Technology Purchase	264,444	363,335	428,933	543,258	699,192	833,876

Source: NBS & NDRC (2006: 4).

Chinese firms have been criticized for their lukewarm investment in assimilation of imported technology (MOST 2005). However, as shown in Table 4.6, Chinese firms have recently leveled-up their investment in assimilation, especially since 2003. The trend likewise has coincided with the decreasing dependence upon the imported technologies.

By breaking the investment on assimilation of imported technology by different types of firms, one could see that the Chinese *private* firms are most active in assimilating imported technology and, on the other hand, state-owned enterprises invest less in absorbing imported technology, indicating a problematic incentive structure for state-owned enterprises (see Table 4.7). Foreign enterprises' reduced interest in assimilation might be due to the fact that they do not need to newly invest in absorbing technologies imported from their headquarters, which have already been mastered by expatriate engineers dispatched from the headquarters to branches in China. This also indicates that foreign enterprises' (especially the wholly owned foreign enterprises) contribution to enhancing the absorptive capacity of China is relatively limited.

As discussed in Section 3, entrepreneurship and institutional environment as well as the absorptive capacity could facilitate the conversion of new S&T knowledge into economically useful S&T data. Therefore, one should consider these factors in order to assess China's technological potentials. I will overlook this and leave it for future study, briefly acknowledging that the Chinese government has recently initiated a series of measures to enhance entrepreneurship and improve the institutional environment for the so-called knowledge industrialization, although the outcome still needs to be seen (Eun 2005).

5. Summary and conclusions

A series of statistics on the S&T activities in China, for instance, R&D expenses, scientific publication, patent application, and university graduates, and the like, has recently showed rapid and simultaneous increases, creating a new image of China, that is, a scientific and technological powerhouse. However, assessments of the technological power of China based on those traditional indicators have

Table 4.7 Technology import and assimilation by different types of firms (2005)

			Technology import (a)	*Assimilation (b)*	*Domestic technology purchase (c)*	*b / a (%)*	*a / c (%)*
Indigenous Firms Total			164,254,7	390,394	716,819	23.8%	229.1%
		State-Owned	378,686	55,253	140,108	14.6%	270.3%
		Private	68,933	28,570	51,178	41.4%	134.7%
Foreign Firms Total			132,510,3	303,430	117,057	22.9%	1132.0%
	HTM	Total	221,409	64,709	31,793	29.2%	696.4%
		Wholly Owned	64,007	7,640	3,111	11.9%	2057.4%
	Other Foreign	Total	110,369,4	238,721	85,264	21.6%	1294.4%
		Wholly Owned	222,921	10,203	4,335	4.6%	5142.4%

Note: HTM: Hong Kong, Macao, and Taiwan.
Source: NBS & NDRC (2006: 387).

often been biased (typically, exaggerated) not only because they arbitrarily chose the method of calculation (or basis for comparison) among alternatives (e.g. PPP vs. MER, aggregate vs. disaggregate) which could possibly be contaminated by the author's hidden intention, but also because they failed to consider the characteristics of the newly emerging global production systems based on intra-industry division of labor and modularization between opened China and the rest of the world (especially advanced countries).

We have seen that a considerable part of corporate R&D expenses and patent applications is actually led by foreign companies (especially MNCs) that infiltrated into China to exploit the cheap labor and land, and increasingly the inexpensive but talented engineers. Although the transnational agents could be regarded as a part of the hosting country (i.e. China), however, it is clear that the rapid increases in statistics on S&T activities performed in the national boundary of China propelled by MNCs' changed pattern of behaviors do not accurately represent the actual technological power of China.

In order to remedy the bias and treat the discordance between the newly emerged global production system and the traditional way of assessing a country's technological power, this study proposed a new conceptual framework reflecting rich discussions in technology economics and innovation studies. The new conceptual framework helps one to broaden the perspective in assessing a country's technological power from excessively focusing on the 'codified knowledge stock' taking into additional account the 'tacit knowledge creation,' the 'structural power of the knowledge distribution between indigenous and foreign entities in the national boundary,' and the 'dynamic process of knowledge production.' Although the broadened perspective could not immediately provide the accurate ranking of China in terms of technological power, it could show several additional points that deserve careful observation, which are also relevant to the technological power of a country but largely neglected so far in the traditional approach.

Within the newly constructed framework, this study tried to reassess the *current* technological power of China by checking the *structural* and *dynamic* aspects of the Chinese technological potential. We found that the supposed technological power of China at the present stage needs to be depreciated to a certain degree due to the heavy dependency upon the foreign entities and the modularized, black-boxed, fragmented nature of the technologies scattered in China which are actually, in many cases, in the hands of MNCs. Recent achievements in attracting R&D centers of MNCs, which many Chinese call over, could also create another source of concern because it could involve losses of technical talents – many of the best and brightest both among those reared in the Chinese educational system and returnees from abroad – to foreign companies (i.e. crowding-out).

In the long run, however, if the Chinese firms' increasing investments in assimilation and absorption of external knowledge and the Chinese government policy efforts to enhance the higher education and indigenous innovation would bear fruits, China could improve the *structural* deficiency and further catalyze the *dynamic* process of the transformation of the fragmented set of S&T knowledge into organically combined and economically useful knowledge.

Notes

1 Patent Cooperation Treaty (PCT) is a patent filing system which allows for a single international patent application to have effect in multiple designated states.

2 The author's interview with three professors in Beijing took place on 24.4.2007.

3 Pavitt (1984) defined four categories of knowledge production based upon sectoral differences: (1) 'supply-dominated sectors,' in which firms develop few important innovations on their own but obtain some from other firms (e.g. clothing, furniture), (2) 'scale-intensive sectors,' which focus their innovation activities on developing more efficient process technology (e.g. food, cement), (3) 'specialized suppliers,' who carry out frequent product innovations, often in collaboration with customers (e.g. engineering, software, instruments), (4) 'science-based producers,' who develop new products as well as processes in close collaboration with universities (e.g. chemical industry, biotechnology, electronics).

4 In assessing the S&T power of a country, the 'GNP-type' perspective (i.e. S&T behavior performed by its own people would contribute to the S&T power of the country) could be more appropriate when (1) the spillover in a geographical region is highly restricted and (2) the global ethnic network works fairly well, while the 'GDP-type' perspective (i.e. S&T behavior performed in the national border would contribute to the S&T power of the country) might be more appropriate in the opposite case. However, when neither the geographical spillover nor the global ethnic network works very well, we might adopt 'GNP Minus-type' perspective, which regards the S&T behavior performed by its own people in the national border as the sole contributor to the country's S&T power. On the other hand, when both the geographical spillover and the global ethnic network works very well, we might adopt 'GDP (or GNP) Plus-type' perspective, which states that the following would contribute to the country's S&T power: S&T behaviors performed by its own people across the World and the ones performed by foreign entities in the national border.

5 It is very difficult to directly capture know-how type tacit knowledge production in a country simply because the outcome (i.e. tacit knowledge) is neither officially documented nor summed up as a statistic at a national level. However, we could figure out how actively tacit knowledge is being produced by examining industrial activities, because tacit knowledge is mainly produced through learning by doing in the workplaces.

6 The most popular definition of the 'high-technology industry' is provided by the OECD. The OECD classifies some industries as high-technology when the R&D expenditure/output ratio exceeds a certain point. However, the OECD's classification is based upon a survey on the practices of twelve OECD countries, all of which are advanced countries. Considering the new trend of MNCs (i.e. global division of labor within an industry), however, we should be careful in applying the industry classification (e.g. high-technology vs. low-technology) to developing countries, such as China. It is highly possible that Chinese workers simply assemble parts imported from advanced countries in an industry which is classified as a high-technology industry according to the OECD. See Kuwahara (2006) for further discussion.

7 The trend is further accelerated after China's accession into the WTO in 2001.

8 About a quarter of foreign Ph.D. candidates in the US are Chinese. Beijing says that 170,000 Chinese who study abroad have returned, 30,000 of them in 2006 (*Financial Times*, 5.1.2007).

9 For the discussion on the interactions between codified and tacit knowledge, see Nonaka and Takeuchi (1995).

10 Sixty-one per cent of surveyed MNCs selected China as their most preferred R&D location during 2005–2009, and second-ranked United States and third-ranked India were preferred by 41 per cent and 29 per cent of the surveyed MNCs, respectively.

11 This is why many manufacturing firms also undertake basic research which is traditionally regarded as the main function of universities and public research institutes.

12 Existing empirical studies have used R&D spending, patents, new products, and some human capital measures as proxies for absorptive capacity (Cohen and Levinthal 1990; Borenzstein *et al.* 1998; Narula 2003; Eun 2005).

References

Acs, Z. *et al.* (2003) 'The Missing Link: The knowledge Filter and Endogenous Growth,' presented at Center for Business and Policy Studies. Stockholm Sweden.

Acs, Z. (2006) 'Penetrating the 'Knowledge Filter' in Regional Economics,' Mimeo.

Arrow, K.J. (1962) 'The Economic Implications of Learning by Doing,' *Review of Economic Studies*, Vol. 29, No. 3, pp. 155–73.

Borensztein, E. *et al.* (1998) 'How does foreign direct investment affect economic growth?,' *Journal of International Economics*, 45, pp. 115–35.

Chen, C.H. and Shih, H.T. (2005) *High-Tech Industries in China.* Cheltenham: Edward Elgar.

Cohen, W.M. and Levinthal, D.A. (1990) 'Absorptive capacity: A new perspective on learning and innovation,' *Administrative Science Quarterly 35*, pp. 128–52.

Dahlman, C. and Aubert, J.E. (2001) *China and the Knowledge Economy: Seizing the 21st Century*. Washington D.C.: World Bank Publications.

Doran, D. (2003) 'Supply chain implications of modularization,' *International Journal of Operations & Product Management*, Vol. 23, No. 3, pp. 316–26.

Eun, Jong-Hak, Lee, K. and Wu, G. (2006) 'Explaining the 'University-run enterprises' in China: A theoretical framework for university-industry relationship in developing countries and its application to China,' *Research Policy*, Vol. 35, No. 9, pp. 1329–46.

Eun, Jong-Hak (2006) 'Changes in China's Business Environment and the Strategies of Foreign-Invested Enterprises: Optimalization of Corporate Organization,' In: Park, W. *et al.*, *Changes in China's Business Environment and the Strategies of Foreign-Invested Enterprises*. Seoul: Korea Institute for International Economic Policy, pp. 93–128.

Eun, Jong-Hak (2005) *The Academy-run Enterprise in China: A Governance Form of Knowledge Industrialization*, unpublished PhD dissertation. Beijing: Tsinghua University.

Fuller, D. (2006) 'Adversaries and Partners: The Impact of the Cross-Strait Economic Relationship on the Development of the Taiwanese and Chinese Economies,' presented at Shorenstein APARC Research Seminar, Stanford University. Available at: http://iisdb.stanford.edu/evnts/4426/Adversaries_and_Partners.pdf.

Hatzichronoglou, T. (1997) 'Revision of High-Technology Sector and Product Classification,' *OECD Science, Technology and Industry Working Papers 1997/2*. Paris: OECD.

Huang, Y. (2005) *Selling China: Foreign Direct Investment during the Reform Era*. Cambridge University Press.

Iammarino, S. and McCann, P. 'The structure and evolution of industrial clusters: Transactions, technology and knowledge spillovers,' *Research Policy 35*, pp. 1018–36.

Kuwahara, S. (2006) 'Empirical Analysis of the Trade Structure Changes in East Asia under Modularization of Product Architecture,' *RIETI 2006/11 Research & Review*. Available at: http://www.rieti.go.jp.

Lau, A. and Yam, R. (2005) 'A case study of product modularization on supply chain design and coordination in Hong Kong and China,' *Journal of Manufacturing Technology Management*, Vol. 16, No. 4, pp. 432–46.

Lam, A. and Lundvall, B.A. (2004) 'The learning organization and national systems of competence building and innovation,' presented at Loc Nis Workshop on How Europe's Economies Learn, European Commission, Brussels.

Lee, Keun, Jee, M., and Eun, J.H. (2006) 'China's Economic Catch-up in a Comparative Perspective: Washington Consensus, East Asian Consensus or Beijing Model,' Mimeo.

Lundvall, B.A. (2004) 'The Economics of Knowledge and Learning,' Mimeo.

Lundvall, B.A. and Johnson, B. (1994) 'The Learning Economy,' *Journal of Industry Studies*, Vol. 1, No. 2, pp. 23–42.

Minstry of Science and Technology (MOST) (2005). *China Science and Technology Indicators 2004* (in Chinese). Beijing: Kexue jishu wenxian chubanshe.

Mueller, P. (2006) 'Exploring the knowledge filter: How entrepreneurship and university-industry relationships drive economic growth,' *Research Policy 35*, pp. 1499–508.

National Bureau of Statistics (NBS) and Ministry of Science and Technology (MOST) (Eds) (2006) *2006 China Statistical Yearbook on Science and Technology* (in Chinese). Beijing: China Statistics Press.

National Bureau of Statistics (NBS) and National Development and Reform Commission (NDRC) (Eds) (2006) *2006 Statistics on Science and Technology Activities of Industrial Enterprises* (in Chinese). Beijing: China Statistics Press.

Narula, R. (2003) 'Understanding Absorptive Capacities in an Innovation Systems Context: Consequences for Economic and Employment Growth,' *DRUID Working Paper*, No. 04–02.

Nolan, P. (2002) 'China and the global business revolution,' *Cambridge Journal of Economics 26*, pp. 119–37.

Nonaka and Takeuchi, (1995) *The Knowledge-Creating Company: How Japanese Companies Create the Dynamics of Innovation*. New York: Oxford University Press.

OECD (1996) *The Knowledge-based Economy*. Paris: OECD.

OECD (2000) *Knowledge Management in the Learning Economy*. Paris: OECD.

OECD (2005) *OECD Science, Technology and Industry Scoreboard 2005*. Paris: OECD.

OECD (2006) *OECD Science, Technology and Industry Outlook 2006*. Paris: OECD.

Pavitt, K. (1984) 'Sectoral patterns of technical change: Towards a taxonomy and a theory,' *Research Policy*, Vol. 13, No. 6, pp. 311–79.

Polanyi, M. (1966) *The Tacit Dimension*. New York: Doubleday and Co.

Rooney, D., Hearn, G., and Ninan A. (2005) Handbook on the Knowledge Economy. Cheltenham: Edward Elgar.

Senge, P. (1990) *The fifth discipline: The art and practice of learning*. New York: Doubleday and Co.

SIPO (2006) *Patent Statistics Brief* (in Chinese), 1.11.2006.

SIPO (2007) *Patent Statistics Brief* (in Chinese), 5.4.2007.

Takeishi, A. and Fujimoto, T. (2001) 'Modularization in the auto industry: interlinked multiple hierarchies of product, production, and supplier systems,' *IIR Working Paper WP#01–02*. Tokyo: Hitotsubashi University.

UNCTAD (2005) *World Investment Report 2005: Transnational Corporations and the Internationalization of R&D*. New York and Geneva: United Nations.

Yang, P. (2006) *A Study on the Determinants of China's Imports from the Republic of Korea*, unpublished PhD dissertation. Seoul: Hankuk University of Foreign Studies.

Yang, Y.R. and Hsia, C.J. (2005) 'Local Clustering and Organizational Governance of Trans-border Production Network: A Case Study of Taiwanese IT Companies in the Greater Suzhou Area, China,' presented at the Association of Asian Studies Annual Meeting, Chicago, IL.

Zhou, P. and Leydesdorff, L. (2006) 'The Emergence of China as a leading nation in science,' *Research Policy*, Vol. 35, No. 1, pp. 83–104.
Chosun Ilbo, 5.12.2006.
Financial Times, 4.12.2006., 5.1.2007.
Joongang Ilbo, 25.1.2007.
Korea Economic Daily, 5.12.2006.
China Customs, www.customs.gov.cn
State Intellectual Property Office of P.R.C (SIPO), www.sipo.gov.cn
World Intellectual Property Organization (WIPO), www.wipo.int
CEIC
UN World Development Indicators (WDI) 2006.
Penn World Table (PWT) 6.2.

Part 2

Assessing the capabilities of the Chinese state

5 Assessing China's capability to manage the high-probability risks to economic growth: fiscal, governance and ecological problems[1]

Wing Thye Woo

The road to prosperity might not be a smooth one

China's economy has been like a speeding car for almost 30 years. Not surprisingly, it is becoming more common to hear glowingly optimistic assessments of China's future than dismissively pessimistic ones. For example, Jim O'Neill *et al.* (2005) of Goldman Sachs have predicted that China's GDP would surpass that of the United States in 2040 even after assuming that China's GDP growth rate would slow down steadily from its average annual of 10 per cent in the 1979–2005 period to 3.8 per cent in the 2030–2040 period.[2]

The past, however, is not a good predictor of the future. Otherwise, there would not be any turning points in history like the fast disintegration of the Soviet Union and the rapid, radical transformation of Japan upon the Meiji restoration. So there is not a modicum of innocence or of malevolence in asking whether the speeding car that is China could slow down drastically or even crash, and what factors could bring about this negative development.

I think that a good clue as to what the most likely precipitating factors are is found in the discussions of the 6th Plenum of the 16th Central Committee of the Communist Party of China (CPC) that concluded on October 11 2006. The 6th Plenum passed a resolution to commit the CPC to establish a harmonious society by 2020. The obvious implication from this commitment is that the present major social, economic and political trends within China might not lead to a harmonious society or, at least, not lead to a harmonious society fast enough.

Among the disharmonious features mentioned in the fifth paragraph of the 'resolutions of the CPC Central Committee on major issues regarding the building of a harmonious socialist society' were:

1. there is serious imbalance in the social and economic development between the urban and rural areas, and across China's 31 provinces;
2. the population and environmental problems are worsening;
3. a large proportion of the population find the national situation in employment, social safety nets, income distribution, education, medical care, housing, occupational safety and public order to be seriously deficient;

4. the system of public management needs improvement;
5. democracy and the rule of law are still not adequately institutionalised;
6. the capability and work style of some leaders do not meet the requirements of the new situation and the new tasks; and
7. corruption in some areas is still very serious.

The harmonious socialist society proposed by the 6th Plenum would encompass:

- a democratic society under the rule of law;
- a society based on equality and justice;
- an honest and caring society;
- a stable, vigorous and orderly society; and
- a society in which humans live in harmony with nature.

What is revealing is not the existence of these disharmonious features in Chinese society, polity and economy in 2006, but that most of the official descriptions of the envisaged harmonious society downplay the prominence of achieving a prosperous society.[3] Of the nine objectives listed in the Communique of the 6th Plenum, 'the objective of building a moderately prosperous society' was not only listed last, it was also qualified with the condition that the prosperity should be shared 'all-around.' And this qualifier is actually a repetition because the narrowing of income gaps had already been listed as the second objective.

This new emphasis on democratic practice, the rule of law, and income equality represents a turning point that is just as significant as the turning point in 1992 when Deng Xiaoping omitted the word 'plan' (which had been ubiquitous since 1949) from the CPC's description of its proposed 'socialist market economy with Chinese characteristics.' Even the 2005 Plenum had reiterated the Dengist mantra that 'economic development is the top priority for the CPC, all efforts should be focused on economic development ...'[4] This departure in 2006 from past practice can also be seen in that the 2005 Plenum stressed the centrality of scientific guidance in economic construction, while the 2006 Plenum stressed the centrality of 'putting people first' in social harmonisation.

What is the origin of the CPC's decision to change its primary focus from 'economic construction' to 'social harmony'? And why include a target date of 2020? I do not believe that this change is merely the consequence of two leaders coming to their final term in office trying to establish their historical legacy by moving out of the shadow of their predecessors. I also do not believe that this change is the response to developments that had occurred since the promotion of Hu Jintao to General Secretary of CPC and the designation of Wen Jiabao as the next Prime Minister in late 2002. Instead I believe that this switch in emphasis from 'economic construction' to 'social harmony' occurs because the Hu-Wen leadership is well aware that the political legitimacy of CPC rule rests largely on maintaining, one, an economic growth rate that is high enough to keep unemployment low, and, two, a growth pattern that diffuses the additional income widely enough.

Specifically, I believe that the policy change has come about because the younger and better educated CPC leadership led by Hu Jintao and Wen Jiabao recognises that:

1. material conditions and public expectations in China have changed so much since 1978 that without accelerated institutional reforms and new major policy initiatives on a broad front, economic construction that continues using the 1978–2005 policy framework, which had produced an average annual GDP growth rate of almost 10 per cent, is unsustainable; and
2. unless their new policies could produce significant improvements in social harmony by 2020, social instability would reduce China's economic growth, hence, making the leadership of CPC in Chinese politics unsustainable.

The realisation of the above two points is, in my opinion, the most important reason why China has changed its development policy from single-minded pursuit of high GDP growth to building a harmonious society. In other words, to return to the analogy of China's economy being like a speeding car, the Hu-Wen leadership saw that the car could crash in the near future because there were several high-probability failures that might occur and cause an economic collapse.

To be specific, there are three classes of failures that could occur:

1. hardware failure,
2. software failure, and
3. power supply failure.

A *hardware failure* refers to the breakdown of an *economic mechanism*, a development that is analogous to the collapse of the chassis of the car. Probable hardware failures are:

1. a banking crisis that causes a credit crunch that, in turn, dislocates production economy-wide, and
2. a budget crisis that necessitates reductions in important infrastructure and social expenditure (and also possibly generates high inflation, and balance of payments difficulties as well).

A *software failure* refers to a flaw in *governance* that creates frequent widespread social disorders that disrupt production economy-wide and discourage private investment. This situation is similar to a car crash that resulted from a fight among the people inside the speeding car. Software failures could come from:

1. the present high-growth strategy creating so much inequality, and corruption that, in turn, generates severe social unrest which dislocates economic activities; and
2. the state not being responsive enough to rising social expectations, hence causing social disorder.

A *power supply failure* refers to the economy being unable to move forward because it hits either *a natural limit or an externally imposed limit,* a situation that is akin to the car running out of gas or having its engine switched off because an outsider reached in and pulled out the ignition key. Examples of power supply failures are:

1. an environmental collapse, e.g. climate change, a type of disaster that has happened quite often in history, e.g. Diamond (2005); and
2. a collapse in China's exports because of a trade war.

My perception is that the Chinese leadership is quite confident that it could prevent most hardware failures and that it could respond appropriately to them if they were to occur. The leadership is less confident however about its ability to prevent, and react optimally to, software failures and power supply failures. Even more, the leadership knows that the negative trends since the mid-1990s of widening income disparity, worsening corruption, rising social expectations, growing trade imbalances, and deteriorating natural environment have increased the probability of software failures and power supply failures. The thesis here is that this increased attention by the Hu-Wen leadership on possible software failures and power supply failures is the origin of China's quest for a harmonious society.

The discussion of most of the high-probability events that could make China's high growth unsustainable is beyond the scope of this paper. I will limit my discussion to the event in each class of failure that has the highest probability of occurring under the present economic policy regime. My assessment is that the highest probability event in hardware failure is the weakening of China's fiscal position; the highest probability event in software failure is social disorder, and the highest probability event in power supply failure is water shortage. And my ranking of the probability of these three specific negative events in descending order is social disorder caused by outmoded governance, water shortage as a result of inept environmental management, and fiscal crisis generated by the repeated recapitalisation of the state banks and the rapid aging of the population.

I must emphasise that these three events have the highest probability of happening only as long as the present socio-economic policy regime continues. These events need not happen. With the root-and-branch reform of China's society as specified in the Harmonious Society program, and with drastic reform of the economic system and of the economic management system, China can move to a sustainable mode of economic development. This fundamental change in the overall policy regime will not only reduce poverty, income inequality, and financial shenanigans, but also enhance macroeconomic stability, strengthen the fiscal basis of the state, raise the efficiency of the financial sector, and lower the tensions in international economic relations.[5]

The need for improved governance to sustain economic growth

The present economic development strategy does not only generate high growth, it also generates high social tensions. At the present stage of economic development, this development strategy has great difficulties in reducing extreme poverty further and in improving income distribution significantly; see Woo *et al.* (2004), and Dèmurger *et al.* (2002). Furthermore, this mode of economic development also generates immense opportunities for embezzlement of state assets, and corruption (see Woo, 2001). These features certainly make social harmony hard to sustain.

The prevention of the above negative events would be helped if China had better governance. Specifically, there would be more pre-emptive efforts at conflict mediation by the government and less abuse of power by government officials if the government's actions were monitored more closely by an independent mechanism, and the government were also held more accountable for its performance. I therefore do not think that it is naive to see the Harmonious Society program as a serious attempt at fundamental reform of China's institutions of governance, going well beyond the reform of economic institutions. This assessment is substantiated by the identification of the first component of a harmonious society as 'a democratic society under the rule of law.' This point was confirmed in a meeting between Premier Wen and the Brookings Board of Trustees in October 2007, where Premier Wen dwelt at length on how China intends to make greater use of democratic mechanisms (e.g. extending free elections to above the village level) to mediate social conflicts and to improve public administration.

The desire by the Hu-Wen leadership to improve the institutions of governance is also borne out by the following report from the *South China Morning Post* about what Premier Wen said when he met a group of Chinese citizens in Japan in April 2007:[6]

> During 30 minutes of impromptu remarks, he said the key to pursuing social justice, the mainland's most important task, was to 'let people be masters of their houses and make every cadre understand that power is invested in them by the people.'
>
> . . . Although he did not deviate from the official line and spoke informally on both occasions, Mr Wen is known for being careful about what he says, whether in prepared remarks or speaking off the cuff. The fact that he highlighted, in the presence of Hong Kong and overseas journalists, the need for political reform is uncharacteristic and interesting, particularly in the context of the leadership reshuffle looming at the Communist Party's 17th congress later this year.
>
> There have been signs that the leadership under President Hu Jintao is under increasing pressure to undertake drastic political reforms to consolidate the party's grip on power and stamp out widespread corruption.

While a cynical observer might doubt the sincerity of Premier Wen's words, he cannot doubt that Premier Wen is at least aware that democracy is one way to solve many of China's problems of governance. More importantly, the cynic cannot doubt that Premier Wen, like many of his countrymen, must be well acquainted with the history of democratic development in Eastern Europe and in East Asia, particularly in Taiwan and Hong Kong.

To understand the reasons behind Hu-Wen's switch to democracy as the new important instrument to introduce external supervision and accountability into governance, it is worth quoting at length from two recent insightful analyses on social unrest in China.

In Albert Keidel's (2006) assessment:

> Large-scale public disturbances have been on the rise in China for more than a decade. Media reports describe violence, injuries, and even deaths. ... Issues include labor grievances, taxation, land confiscation, and pollution. Corruption worsens common injustices and further inflames citizen anger. ...
>
> ... It is important to emphasize that China's social unrest is not made up of street demonstrations demanding a new government or western-style democracy ... China's social unrest should be understood as the unavoidable side effects – worsened by local corruption – of successful market reforms and expanded economic and social choice... Managing this unrest humanely requires accelerated reform of legal and social institutions with special attention to corruption.

Murray Scot Tanner (2004) reports from his examination of documents prepared by China's police that:

> Most available police analyses now blame unrest primarily on approximately the same list of social, economic, and political forces..., implicitly relegating enemy instigation [i.e. conspiracy theories] to the role of a secondary catalyst... In terms of internal security strategy, this characterization typically, though not always, reduces reliance on coercion...
>
> [Many] police see a new social logic taking hold, with disgruntled citizens increasingly convinced that peaceful protest is significantly less dangerous and not only effective but often unavoidable as a means to win concessions. Police sources now routinely quote a popular expression: 'Making a great disturbance produces a great solution. Small disturbances produce small solutions. Without a disturbance, there will be no solution.'
>
> ... Socioeconomic change may generate these underlying demands and clashes of social interest, but it is usually government failures that cause these contradictions to turn antagonistic and dangerous.

Clearly, the large economic dislocations caused by the reform of the planned economy, and the institutional failures in governance[7] are important factors behind the higher frequency of large social disturbances.[8] However, like Tanner, I am of the opinion that there is a third important factor behind the increasing readiness to resort to civil disorder, which is that the richer and more knowledgeable Chinese population now has higher expectations about the performance of the government.[9] The implication of the third factor is that 'Beijing may be kidding itself if it believes economic growth alone will bring unrest under control.'[10]

The CPC is too astute to kid itself. In its search for new mechanisms to improve its performance on governance, it naturally had to consider democratic institutions as an option because democracy is the well-tested means of governance in the developed world. The two basic considerations for the CPC in deciding upon whether democracy should become the new centerpiece in its governance structure are:

1. whether democracy, the rule of law, and a stable income distribution comprise an indivisible combination that is necessary to ensure the social stability that will keep the economy on the high growth path to catch up with the United States (a vision which acts as the bedrock of CPC's legitimacy to rule)?
2. whether the CPC will be skilful and lucky enough to lead the democratic transition and emerge afterward as the most important political force?

By proposing the Harmonious Society program, the Hu-Wen leadership has replied affirmatively to both questions.

Objectively, this attempt by the CPC to reinvent itself is a difficult and risky undertaking. A functioning democracy requires not just free elections but also a free press that is responsible and a competent judiciary that is independent. So, how would the rank and file of CPC (who are used to exercising unchallenged power for 50 years) react to these institutional changes which produce a power-sharing arrangement that is alien and chaotic? Furthermore, a plan of gradual democratisation might be initially lauded and endorsed by most segments of society but subsequent changes in social expectations about governmental responsiveness and personal freedom could easily outpace the actual developments as implemented according to the plan.[11] So, would the CPC then be sufficiently pragmatic to accelerate the plan to avoid being run over by events?[12]

One possible answer to both these questions is that the CPC would rise to the demands of the occasions and transform itself into a social democratic party. An alternative answer based on the experiences from the Soviet bloc is that CPC would split and social instability would follow. While any answer to the two previous questions is necessarily speculative, what is much more definitive is the genesis of the program to achieve a harmonious society by 2020. The fact that the Hu-Wen leadership, which is well-known for its political caution, has embarked on this technically difficult and politically risky project suggests that it has concluded that new far-reaching reforms are less dangerous than partial reforms, and that, given the deep entrenchment of the disharmonious elements, time might not be on its side.[13]

The need for environmental protection to sustain economic growth

The present mode of economic development has given China the dirtiest air in the world, is polluting more and more of the water resources, and is, possibly, changing the climate pattern within China. The reality is that CPC's new objective of living in harmony with nature is not a choice because the Maoist adage of 'man conquering nature' is just as unrealistic as creating prosperity through central planning. China's fast growth in the last two decades has done substantial damage to the environment. Elizabeth Economy (2004, pp. 18–19) summarised the economic toll as follows:

> China has become home to six of the ten most polluted cities in the world.[14] Acid rain now affects about one-third of China's territory, including approximately one-third of its farmland. More than 75 per cent of the water in rivers flowing through China's urban areas is [unsuitable for human contact][15] ... deforestation and grassland degradation continue largely unabated[16]... The [annual] economic cost of environmental degradation and pollution ... are the equivalent of 8–12 per cent of China's annual gross domestic product.

Water shortage appears to pose the most immediate environmental threat to China's continued high growth.[17] Presently, China uses 67 to 75 per cent of the 800 to 900 billion cubic meters of water available annually, and present trends in water consumption would project the usage rate in 2030 to be 78 to 100 per cent.[18] The present water situation is actually already fairly critical because of the uneven distribution of water and the lower than normal rainfall in the past 15 years. Right now, '[about] 400 of China's 660 cities face water shortages, with 110 of them severely short.'[19]

The extended period of semi-drought in northern China combined with the economic and population growth have caused more and more water to be pumped from the aquifers, leading the water table to drop from three to six meters a year.[20] And a study using measurements from satellites (the Global Positioning System) has established that the part of China north of the 36th parallel latitude has been 'sinking at the rate of 2 mm a year.'[21] Specifically, 'Shanghai, Tianjin, and Taiyuan are the worst hit in China, with each sinking more than two meters (6.6 feet) since the early 1990s.'[22]

The overall water situation in northern China is reflected in the fate of the Yellow River,

> which started drying up every few years from 1972, did so for increasing periods of time over longer distances in the 1990s until 1997, when it dried up for almost the entire year over a stretch of several hundred kilometres.[23]

The utilisation rate of Yellow River's water is 60 per cent, far exceeding the internationally recommended utilisation limit of 40 per cent. All the mentioned factors have contributed to lowering the 'amount of Yellow River water feeding into the Bohai Sea' from an annual 49.6 billion cubic meters in the 1960s to 14.2 billion cubic meters in the 1990s to the present 4.65 billion cubic meters.[24]

Water shortage and the increasing pollution of what water there is[25] are not the only serious environmental threats to the economy of northern China. The desert is expanding (possibly, at an accelerating pace), and man appears to be the chief culprit. The State Forestry Administration reported that 28 per cent of the country's land mass was affected by desertification in 1999, and 37 per cent was affected by soil erosion. The report identified about 65 per cent of the desert as having been created by 'over-cultivation, overgrazing, deforestation and poor irrigation practices.'[26] The rate of desertification is 3,900 square miles a year,[27] an annual loss of a land area twice the size of Delaware. One direct upshot is a great increase in the frequency of major sandstorms[28] that play 'havoc with aviation in northern China for weeks, cripples high-tech manufacturing and worsens respiratory problems as far downstream as Japan, the Korean peninsula and even the western United States.'[29] In the assessment of Chen Lai, Vice-Minister of water resources: 'It will take nearly half a century for China to control the eroded land and rehabilitate their damaged ecosystems in accordance with China's present erosion-control capabilities.'[30]

While northern China has been getting drier and experiencing desertification, nature as if in compensation (or in mockery) has been blasting southern China with heavier rains, causing heavy floods which have brought considerable deaths and property damage almost every summer since 1998. The sad possibility is that the northern droughts and southern floods may not be independent events but a combination caused by pollution that originates in China. I will have more to say about this possibility later.

Clearly, without water, growth cannot endure. And in response, the government begun implementation in 2002 of Mao Zedong's 1952 proposal that three canals be built to bring water from the south to the north: an eastern coastal canal from Jiangsu to Shandong and Tianjin, a central canal from Hubei to Beijing and Tianjin, and a western route from Tibet to the northwestern provinces, and each canal will be over a thousand miles long.[31] Construction of the eastern canal (which would be built upon a part of the existing Grand Canal) started in 2002, and the central canal in 2003. Work on the western canal is scheduled to begin in 2010 upon completion of the first stage of the central canal.

The scale of this water transfer project is simply unprecedented anywhere:

> Together, the three channels would pump about 48 billion litres of water a year – enough to fill New York's taps for a quarter century. Only a tenth as much water flows through the next-largest water diversion project, in California.[32]

This massive construction project will not only be technically challenging but also extremely sensitive politically and fraught with environmental risks. The central canal will have to tunnel through the foot of the huge dyke that contains the elevated Yellow River, and the western canal will have to transport water through regions susceptible to freezing. The number of people displaced by the Three Gorges Dam was 1.1 million, and this water transfer scheme is a bigger project. The enlargement of the Danjiangkou Dam (in Hubei) alone to enable it to be the source of the central canal will already displace 330,000 people.[33] Moving people involuntarily is certainly potentially explosive politically. The project could also be politically explosive on the international front as well. One plan for the western canal calls for 'damming the Brahmaputra river and diverting 200 billion cubic metres of water annually to feed the ageing Yellow river,' a scenario that is reportedly 'giving sleepless nights to the Indian government ... [which is concerned that this 'Great Western Water Diverson Project] could have immense impact on lower riparian states like India and Bangladesh.'[34]

The environmental damages caused by this project are the most serious for the central and western canals. In the case of the central canal,

> environmental experts [in Wuhan where the Hanjiang River flows into the Yangtze] are worried about ... [whether the annual extraction of eight billion cubic metres of water could affect] the river's ability to flush out the massive pollution flows released by the thousands of factories and industries along the tributaries ... The reduced flows could increase the frequency of toxic red algae blooms on the Yangtze near the confluence with the Hanjiang River. There have already been three blooms ... [by May of that year, 2003].[35]

The western canal has generated a lively controversy. Some scientists are contending that it 'would cause more ecological damage than good'[36] because it 'could cause dramatic climate changes ... [and] the changed flow and water temperature would lead to a rapid decline in fish and other aquatic species.'[37]

Many opponents of the water transfer project have argued that water conservation could go a long way toward addressing this problem because currently a tremendous amount of the water is just wasted, e.g. only 50 per cent of China's industrial water is recycled compared to 80 per cent in the industrialised countries,[38] and China consumes 3,860 cubic meters of water to produce $10,000 of GDP compared to the world average of 965 cubic meters.[39] The most important reason for this inefficient use of water lies in the fact that 'China's farmers, factories and householders enjoy some of the cheapest water in the world'[40] even though China's per capita endowment of water is a quarter of the world average.[41]

I now want to raise the unhappy possibility that neither the price mechanism nor the three canals can solve China's water problem and make its growth sustainable unless the present mode of economic development is drastically amended. There is now persuasive evidence that China's voluminous emission of black carbon (particles of incompletely combusted carbon) has contributed significantly to the shift to a climate pattern that produces northern droughts and southern floods of increasing intensity.[42] The biggest source of what has been called the 'Asian brown cloud' in the popular media is burning of coal and bio-fuels in China. If the pollution-induced climate change analysis is valid, it means that:

1. China's massive reforestation program will not succeed in reducing sandstorms in the north because trees cannot survive if the amount of rainfall is declining over time; and
2. the number of south-north canals will have to be increased over time in order to meet the demand for water in northern China;

until China reduces its emission of black carbon significantly (presuming no new large emissions from neighboring countries, like Indian).

The general point is that effective policy-making on the environmental front is a very difficult task because much of the science about the problem is not known. For example, China must no longer select its water strategy and its energy strategy separately. A systems approach in policymaking is necessary because the interaction among the outcomes from the different sectoral policies can generate serious unintended environmental damage. If part of the shift in China's climate is integral to global climate change, then a sustainable development policy would require a complete rethinking about the location of population centers, and types of enhanced international cooperation on global environmental management.

The uncomfortable reality for China is that unless ecological balance is restored within the medium-term, environmental limits could choke off further economic growth. And the uncomfortable reality for the rest of the world is that the negative consequences of large-scale environmental damage within a geographically large country are seldom confined within that country's borders. The continued march of China's desertification first brought more frequent sand storms to Beijing and then, beginning in April 2001, sent yellow dust clouds not only across the sea to Japan and Korea but also across the ocean to the United States. China's environmental management is a concern not only for China's welfare but for global welfare as well.

In discussing the environmental aspects of the water transfer plan, it is important to note that there is now an open controversy in China involving a key government infrastructure project, and that this controversy is not limited to members of the technocracy. The very public nature of the controversy and the involvement of more than just scientists, engineers and economists in it reveal how very far social attitudes have progressed. The important point is that this change in social expectations will require any government in China to live in harmony with nature. However, any government will have great difficulties in doing so even if it wants to because a green growth policy involves a systems approach, and scientific understanding of many ecological sub-systems and the nature of their interactions is still rather incomplete.

The challenge of fiscal sustainability

Among doomsayers, one favorite mechanism for the forthcoming collapse of an economy is the inevitable fiscal crisis of the state. What is noteworthy is that this fiscal mechanism is used by doomsayers of all stripes. The Marxist economist, James O'Connor (1973), predicted that the dynamics of capitalist America would precipitate a fiscal crisis that would destabilise the economy completely. In turn, the capitalist lawyer, Gordon Chang (2001), predicted that a fiscal crisis could be the triggering event in the unavoidable disintegration of socialist China.

This fixation of the doomsayers upon a large negative fiscal shock as a totally destructive systemic shock is understandable because fiscal imbalance is the proximate cause in most crises. The reason is that the state budget is often faced with the task of defusing the cumulative tensions unleashed by deeper, more fundamental social processes. To a first approximation, fiscal capacity is a fundamental determinant of system stability because economic sustainability depends on the ability to cover production costs, and political viability depends on the ability to reward one's supporters and to pay off one's enemies.

The reality in many cases is that fiscal sustainability is the prerequisite for both economic sustainability and political viability, and that economic sustainability and political viability are intricately linked and mutually reinforcing. To see the mutual interdependence of the two, one has only to recall the many times that near-bankrupt governments have been driven out of power after raising the prices of a subsidised item like food, petrol, or foreign exchange.[43] One could indeed go so far as to say that the degree of economic and political resilience of a state can be measured by the state's ability to cover an unexpected, prolonged increase in expenditure or an unanticipated, protracted shortfall in revenue.[44]

A recent OECD (2006) report has raised grave concerns about China's fiscal management. Specifically:

> China's officially reported spending figures reflect only about three-quarters of total government spending. Extra-budgetary spending, social security outlays and central government bond financing of local projects are not part of the official budget. Notwithstanding recent reforms, the government remains overly exposed to extra-budget and off-budget activities, which make public expenditures difficult to plan and control and which impair their accountability and transparency. Contingent liabilities have been a major source of unplanned spending and pose perhaps the greatest risk to the controllability of future expenditure. (p. 10)

I share the concerns expressed in this OECD report. I want to add that there are other equally important concerns about China's fiscal situation (e.g. there are fundamental improvements that should be made to the public revenue side), and there is also the even more important issue of fiscal sustainability. In my opinion, fiscal sustainability is more important than fiscal efficiency because the former determines the survival of the system, while the latter only influences the output growth rate.

The fact that fiscal sustainability is central to economic management can be seen in the two fiscal targets that the original Growth and Stability Pact of the countries in the Euro-Zone specified for its members to meet:

- the consolidated government budget deficit should not exceed 3 per cent of GDP except in the case of an unusually severe downturn; and
- the debt-GDP ratio should be brought down to 60 per cent or lower.

Table 5.1 gives an international perspective on the fiscal situation in China by comparing it with those in the OECD countries. I chose the year 2001 for China because I want to postpone until later the discussion on the fiscal consequences of the now ongoing recapitalisation of the state-owned banks (SOBs). I use the year 2003 for OECD because the cross-country data were conveniently available for this year.[45] Table 5.1 reports that China's official debt-GDP ratio was 16.4 per cent, which compared very favorably with the OECD average of 75.3 per cent. If the tiny state of Luxembourg is treated as an exception and excluded from the comparison, then the lower half of the OECD distribution of debt-GDP ratios ranges from 18.6 per cent (South Korea) to 55.5 per cent (Denmark); and the upper half of the distribution ranges from 58.1 per cent (Hungary) to 154 per cent (Japan).

As China's debt-GDP ratio of 16.4 per cent is below the 18.6 per cent of South Korea, and as China's annual budget deficit has nearly always been below 3 per cent of GDP, it would seem that China has a sounder fiscal situation than all the other OECD countries.[46] Such an impression needs to be qualified however. Many analysts have noted that China's official debt-GDP ratio understates the extent of China's fiscal burden because it does not include the nonperforming loans in the SOBs that the state would have to take over during recapitalisation, and it does not include many contingent liabilities (e.g. pension schemes of state enterprises) that the state would have to assume responsibility for in order to preserve economic and social stability. Citigroup (2002), for example, has estimated that the cost for SOB recapitalisation was 46.9 per cent of GDP, social security obligation was 26.1 per cent, and external debt was 15.6 per cent.

Part II of Table 5.1 uses estimates from Citigroup (2002) and Fan (2003) to revise China's official debt-GDP ratio. The outcomes are that China's debt-GDP ratio is:

- 57.4 to 65.9 per cent when only SOB recapitalisation is undertaken; and
- 74.7 to 114.9 per cent when all contingent liabilities are recognised.

This change in China's debt-GDP ratio:

- moves China from the bottom of the OECD distribution to the top half of the distribution; and
- in the worst case scenario, puts China in the group of the five OECD countries with the highest ratios; 74.7 to 114.9 per cent for China versus 75.7 per cent for Canada, 103.2 per cent for Belgium, 108.8 per cent for Greece, 121.4 per cent for Italy, and 154 per cent for Japan.

Should the much higher revised debt-GDP ratio raise concern about China's fiscal sustainability? Our cautious reading of the evidence is that a fiscal crisis is not imminent in China. China's ratio not only falls within the OECD experience, its worst-case ratio of 114.9 per cent is still lower than Italy, which has been performing satisfactorily in overall economic performance. Most importantly, China's ratio is still substantially lower than the highest OECD ratio of 154 per cent (Japan).

While I believe China's fiscal regime to be sustainable, there are two fiscal features that have rendered the fiscal system vulnerable to a crisis. The first fiscal feature is that China has a lower capacity to service its public debt than all the

OECD countries. While China's revenue-GDP ratio has been increasing rapidly from 10.7 per cent in 1995 to 16.8 per cent in 2001, and to an expected 21.6 per cent in 2007, the 2007 level of 21.6 per cent is still too low by OECD standards. The average revenue-GDP ratio in the OECD in 2003 was 36.3 per cent, with the three lowest ratios (25.3 per cent for Japan and South Korea, and 25.6 per cent for the United States) higher than China's. While China's best-case debt-GDP ratio of 57.4 to 65.9 per cent puts China in the same group as Denmark (55.5 per cent), Hungary (58.1 per cent), Sweden (59.8 per cent), and the Netherlands (61.9 per cent), China's revenue-GDP ratio is only 21.6 per cent compared with Denmark's 48.3 per cent, Hungary's 38.5 per cent, Sweden's 50.6 per cent, and the Netherland's 38.8 per cent. For the OECD countries with debt-GDP ratios that are similar to China's worst-case debt-GDP ratio of 74.7 to 114.9 per cent, all of them also have higher revenue-GDP ratios: 21.6 per cent for China versus 33.8 per cent for Canada, 45.4 per cent for Belgium, 35.7 per cent for Greece, and 43.1 per cent for Italy.

The important point about this first fiscal feature is that as China's public debt rises from 16.4 per cent of GDP to 74.7 per cent with the incremental assumption of the contingent liabilities, the state will have to reduce expenditure steadily to accommodate the additional debt service unless there is an increase in state revenue.

The second fiscal feature that renders China vulnerable to a fiscal crisis is the constant need to recapitalise the SOBs. In 1998–1999, the government injected new capital into China's banks and transferred a large proportion of the NPLs to the state-owned asset management corporations (AMCs) in order to raise the capital adequacy ratio (CAR) of the four largest SOBs, commonly referred to as the Big Four,[47] from 4.4 per cent at the end of 1996 to over 8 per cent at the end of 1998. However, the rapid appearance of new NPLs after 1998 has lowered the average CAR of the Big Four to 5.0 per cent by the beginning of 2002.

The outcome is that China has been engaging in a second round of recapitalisation of the SOBs since 2003. Some unorthodox methods have also been used, e.g. in late 2003, Bank of China and China Construction Bank received a capital injection of US $22.5 billion each from the foreign reserves of the People's Bank of China.[48] The results of this still-ongoing second recapitalisation, and the rapid expansion of loans in the last two years is that the NPL ratio has improved, and the CAR of the Big Four was about 8 per cent respectively at the end of 2004.

The important question is how many more rounds of bank recapitalisation can China afford without generating a fiscal crisis? The simple fact is that fiscal sustainability lies at the heart of whether a banking crisis would actually occur. As long as the state is perceived to be able and willing to bail out the SOBs, depositors would retain their confidence in the SOBs regardless of the actual state of their balance sheets. Since the stock of publicly-acknowledged government debt in 2004 is only about 33 per cent of GDP, it is usual to hear official assurances that the current fiscal deficits of less than 2 per cent of GDP do not pose a problem for debt servicing by the state.[49] However, the current value of the debt-GDP ratio is not a good indicator of the sustainability of the existing fiscal policy regime, a better indicator would involve working out the evolution of the debt-GDP ratio over time.

Briefly, a fiscal regime that causes the debt-GDP ratio to:

- grow explosively is unsustainable,
- decline secularly to zero is sustainable,
- attain an equilibrium steady-state value that is 'low' is unlikely to destabilise the economy; and vice-versa.

To put the issue formally, the evolution of the debt-GDP ratio is given by:

$$d\,(\ln[\text{Debt/GDP}])\,/\,d\,t = r + [\text{GDP/Debt}]\cdot[f + b] - y$$

where

r = real interest rate on government debt

f = primary fiscal deficit rate

= [state expenditure excluding debt service – state revenue] / GDP

b = NPL creation rate

= [change in NPL in SOBs] / GDP

y = trend growth rate of real GDP

As long as $y > r$, then the Debt/GDP ratio will have a steady-state value that is nonzero when sum of $(f + b) > 0$. Specifically,

$$(\text{Debt/GDP})_{\text{steady-state}} = (f + b) / (y - r) \text{ when } y > r$$

China appears to belong to this case because its post-1978 annual growth rate has averaged 9.4 per cent, its growth rate in the next ten years is likely to be above 8 per cent; and the real interest rate has been about 4 per cent. For the generation of likely future scenarios, I will make the conservative assumptions that y is 8 per cent, f is 1 per cent, and r is 6 per cent.[50] It is difficult to predict b, the rate that banks would generate NPLs, because it depends on the type of banking reform undertaken. If no meaningful reforms are undertaken, then b is likely to remain at the historic value of 6 per cent.

So conditional on the effectiveness of reforming the SOBs, the steady-state ratio is:

$$(\text{Debt/GDP})_{\text{steady-state}} = 350 \text{ per cent when } b = 6 \text{ per cent}$$

$$(\text{Debt/GDP})_{\text{steady-state}} = 200 \text{ per cent when } b = 3 \text{ per cent}$$

$$(\text{Debt/GDP})_{\text{steady-state}} = 100 \text{ per cent when } b = 1 \text{ per cent}$$

The noteworthy finding from the above scenarios is that China will produce a level of $(Debt/GDP)_{steady\text{-}state}$ that is high by international experience despite the optimistic assumptions that long-run growth rate is 8 per cent, that *b* will be lowered from 6 per cent of GDP to 1 per cent. The most optimistic outcome is still two-thirds larger than what the European Union has set to be the 'safe' debt-GDP target (60 per cent) for its members. The banking system has made China vulnerable to a fiscal crisis even though there is a theoretical steady-state level for the debt-GDP ratio. Of course, the creation of NPLs cannot be attributed entirely to the SOBs, their chief customers, the embezzlement-ridden and inefficiency-ridden SOEs,[51] deserve an equal share of the blame.

The important point from this second fiscal feature is that the present ongoing recapitalisation of the SOBs is the last time that the government can afford to recapitalise the SOBs, and possibly the last time that the government can do so without upsetting confidence in the financial markets about the soundness of China's fiscal regime.

Now, how difficult is it to raise China's revenue-GDP ratio and to stop losses in the SOBs in order to ensure fiscal sustainability? On the subject of raising state revenue, I make two inter-related observations.

The first observation is that since the state has the right to raise taxes, it is a mystery that fiscal crises have happened so often and in many parts of the world. In theory, a government faced with a repayment of principal could impose a new tax on bondholders and then use this new revenue to redeem the bonds from the same people. In practice, however, such an act would be perceived correctly as a confiscation of wealth by a profligate (possibly, also incompetent) government, and could lead to political unrest that topples the government. In short, even though governments can introduce new taxes any time, this is an option many governments are very cautious in exercising because of political reasons. The worry is that raising taxes might be interpreted by the populace in the same way that a currency devaluation is usually interpreted, the outcome of governance failure.

The second observation about tax-raising ability is that the G-7 countries with the highest revenue-GDP ratios are western European countries, e.g. France (43.4 per cent), Germany (35.5 per cent), Italy (43.1 per cent), and the United Kingdom (35.6 per cent) versus the United States (25.6 per cent) and Japan (25.3 per cent). In these western European countries, the citizens voted in politicians who then raised taxes to finance social democratic programs (e.g. subsidised universal healthcare, subsidised higher education, and public pension schemes).

The reasons why the United States has low taxes and fewer social programs than the western Europe countries are many and complex. Two of the reasons are that the United States was founded on the basis of a tax revolt against England, and that it has a stronger cultural emphasis on individualism. In short, a government could raise more taxes and survive politically only if the citizens like these state-provided services and are willing to pay for them. This explains why the highest tax burdens are found in democracies and not in authoritarian societies, the taxes could be collected in the former only because the people had agreed to their imposition and to their intended use.

On the issue of how to raise China's revenue-GDP ratio to make the fiscal regime sustainable, it is unlikely that the ratio will continue growing at the speed of the 1995–2001 period because the VAT and the company income tax are becoming the main sources of state revenue, and these are flat taxes and not progressive taxes. Therefore China's revenue-GDP ratio is unlikely to increase much more unless new taxes or higher tax rates are introduced. Because it would be highly unpopular for the Chinese government to raise taxes in the name of covering the losses of the banks and of taking over the pension schemes of the state enterprises, it might be politically more astute to generate the needed revenue by selling state assets instead.

On the issue of how to stop the losses in the SOB sector (the second requirement for fiscal sustainability), the solution lies in imposing a hard budget constraint on the SOBs. SOB managers have to be convinced that the present recapitalisation is indeed the last free supper (which the 1998 recapitalisation was announced to be), and that their compensation and promotion will depend only on the profitability of the SOBs relative to the profitability of private banks.

At the same time, the prudential supervision and monitoring of bank operations will have to be strengthened to prevent asset stripping and discourage reckless investments fostered by the asymmetrical reward system under the soft budget constraint.[52] The operations of SOBs could be further improved by bringing in foreign strategic investors who would be part of the management team, and by removing the influence of the local governments on bank operations.

One additional way to harden the budget constraint faced by the SOBs is to privatise some of their branches, and use the performance of the new private banks to gauge the performance of the remaining SOBs. The privatisation of some branches will also help convince the SOB managers that the government is indeed serious about the present SOB recapitalisation being indeed the last free supper.

In my discussion of the fiscal challenge, I have not addressed the adverse fiscal implications of China's demographic time bomb of a rapidly aging population. The state expenditure on social programs will expand with the growing ranks of the elderly, and this will be increasingly hard to cover with the tax revenue from the shrinking labor force – unless unanticipated massive productivity improvements were to appear.

Final remarks

It might seem surprising to hear that China needs fundamental and comprehensive reform of its social, political, and economic institutions when it has experienced high growth for almost 30 years. Why meddle with success? Why fix it if it is not broken?

There are two parts to the answer. The first part is that 'it is broken.' The reason why growth has stayed so high for so long is because the government has continually changed policies to keep marketising the economy, deepening integration into the international economy, and, since the mid-1990s, reducing the discrimination against the private sector. In short, policy changes were the reason for keeping past growth high, and they will have to continue if future growth is to remain high.

The second part of the answer is that satisfaction with the status quo depends inversely on the level of expectations, and the expectations of the Chinese people towards their government have risen along with income, and, more importantly, risen along with their growing knowledge of the outside world. A Chinese government that consistently fails to produce results in line with the rise in social expectations runs the increasing risk of being challenged by another faction within the CPC. However, there has not been just rising expectations but also diversification of expectations. In this new situation, the greater use of democratic procedures is a natural way to accommodate the rising social expectations and mediate the emerging differences in social expectations.

In today's China, more of the same economic policies will not produce the same salubrious results on every front because the development problems have changed. For example, in the first phase of economic development, the provision of more jobs (through economic deregulation) was enough to lower poverty significantly. At present, many of the people who are still poor require more than just job opportunities, they need an infusion of assistance (e.g. empower them with human capital through education and health interventions) first in order to be able to take up these job opportunities. This is why the poverty rate (defined by a poverty line of a daily income of US$1) in China has stayed at about 11 per cent since 1998.

Worse yet, it appears that after 1998, the post-1978 development strategy has not been able to prevent the poor from getting poorer. Woo *et al.* (2004) found that the average income of the rural poor fell from 72 cents in 1999 to 63 cents in 2002; and a recent World Bank[53] study found that the average income of the poorest 10 per cent of China's population fell 2.4 per cent in the 2001–2003 period. As the national average income went up in the 1998–2003 period, the implication is that the traditional trickling-down mechanism has morphed into a trickling-up mechanism. Development policymaking has now become even more challenging.

On the sustainable growth front, proper management of the environment has now become critical if China is to continue its industrialisation process. Pan Yue, deputy head of the State Environmental Protection Agency, summed up the present situation in China very well when he said:

> If we continue on this path of traditional industrial civilisation, there is no chance that we will have sustainable development. China's population, resources, environment have already reached the limits of their capacity to cope. Sustainable development and new sources of energy are the only road that we can take.[54]

On the fiscal management front, the state budget is often called upon to change the spending flows to stabilise the price level, to apply the grease of infrastructure investments to crash through the production bottlenecks that are hindering economic growth, and to supply the financial glue to hold the polity together. It is therefore hard to over-emphasise the importance of fiscal soundness in economic management. The strong conclusion to our analysis is that frequent bank recapitalisation is the biggest threat to China's fiscal solvency, and that the present ongoing second recapitalisation of SOBs since 1996 is the last one that China can afford. Because fiscal solvency is ensured when the state keeps interest rates low through regulation to contain the cost of debt service, China faces a difficult tradeoff between easy debt management and the promotion of financial market development via bank recapitalisation and interest rate deregulation.

The analysis suggests two main policy suggestions to reduce the vulnerability of China to possible future fiscal difficulties:

1. increase the extractive capacity of the state so that the revenue-GDP ratio would increase to 25 per cent in the medium term. This extra revenue will be the fiscal cushion that allows the state to accommodate unexpected expenditure demands or revenue shortfalls. As noted in the paper, the collection of revenue might probably first require overcoming the challenge of forging the political consensus for a tax increase.
2. Reform the management of state assets and the regulation of the financial sector to eliminate the phenomenon of repeated recapitalisation of the SOBs. The privatisation of some units of the SOBs, and the emergence of large domestic private banks will help in strengthening the budget constraints perceived by the managers of SOBs.

The fact that the probability of a software failure and the probability of a power supply failure are both higher than the probability of a hardware failure means that development policymaking in China has become more challenging. So, will China succeed in establishing a harmonious society and completing the overhaul of its economic system? My answer is a very cautious 'yes.' I am optimistic because both Chinese society and government want the economy to continue its convergence to a modern private market economy, exemplified by the developed world. My considerable caution comes from

1. the new major reforms being technically difficult to implement (e.g. setting up social safety nets), and having few, if any, successful precedents in the world to draw upon (e.g. designing market-compatible environmental regulation); and
2. the possibility that the many potential losers from these major reforms could successfully organise to resist meaningful implementation of the reforms.

The present social, economic and political ills of China have been perceptively analysed by Minxin Pei (2006) as coming from being in a *trapped transition*, 'a transformative phase in which half-finished reforms have transferred power to new, affluent elites'[55] who are using crony capitalism to generate high economic growth that is not sustainable. The Harmonious Society program (with its emphasis on democracy, rule of law, justice, equality, and harmony with nature), should therefore be recognised as the attempt by the Hu-Wen leadership to take China away from it's present state of *trapped transition* to a sustainable high growth path. However, in Minxin Pei's assessment,[56] the Hu-Wen leadership is unlikely to succeed:

> In a 'trapped transition', the ruling elites have little interest in real reforms. They may pledge reforms, but most such pledges are lip service or tactical adjustments aimed at maintaining the status quo.

While the sophisticated theoretical framework of Minxin Pei allows us to think through the problem of Chinese policymaking in a consistent manner, it is still not a fail-safe guide to the future for quite a number of reasons. Most fundamentally, because any model is a distillation of the average behavior of each identified group, and a summary of the most important shocks to the class of countries that China belongs to, an error term has to be included into each equation[57] of the model because unanticipated shocks (i.e. the excluded low-probability events) do happen. And these error terms are not necessarily white noise (i.e. self-offsetting), they could, for example, be random walks instead. In contrast to error terms that are white noise, error terms that are random walks have the mathematical property of actually shaping the long-term outcomes.

One real-world manifestation of this random-walk error term is the emergence of atypical leaders who are public-spirited rather than self-interested.[58] World history provides just too rich a menu of outcomes to allow us to indulge in the notion of inevitability. The French monarchy and the British monarchy reacted differently to the popular requests for reform, and the outcomes were very different. The lesson is that enlightened self-interest does sometimes prevail and allows a non-disruptive process of change to occur.

The research focus of this Seoul conference (for which this chapter is written) is to assess the power of China. My answer is that the most important measure of China's power today is the degree to which enlightened self-interest determines public policymaking within the Chinese Communist Party.

Table 5.1 Comparative perspective on the size of the national debt (as a percentage of GDP)

(i) OECD'S Fiscal situation

	General government gross financial liabilities		*Total tax revenue*	
	1995	*2003*	*1995*	*2003*
Luxembourg	6.7	6.7	42.3	41.3
Korea	5.5	18.6	19.4	25.3
Australia	43.4	18.9	29.8	31.6
Ireland	81.2	31.1	32.8	29.7
New Zealand	51.7	32.0	36.9	34.9
Iceland	59.4	41.4	32.1	39.8
United Kingdom	52.7	41.9	35.1	35.6
Czech Republic	19.3	46.8	37.5	37.7

Table 5.1 Comparative perspective on the size of the national debt (as a percentage of GDP)—cont'd

(i) OECD'S Fiscal situation

	General government gross financial liabilities		*Total tax revenue*	
	1995	*2003*	*1995*	*2003*
Slovak Republic	n.a	49.7	n.a.	31.1
Norway	40.5	50.4	41.1	43.4
Finland	65.1	52.0	46.0	44.8
Poland	n.a.	52.1	37.0	34.2
Spain	68.8	54.8	31.8	34.9
Denmark	77.6	55.5	49.5	48.3
Hungary	n.a.	58.1	42.4	38.5
Sweden	82.2	59.8	48.5	50.6
Netherlands	87.0	61.9	41.9	38.8
United States	74.2	63.4	27.9	25.6
Germany	55.8	64.6	37.2	35.5
Portugal	69.9	66.6	33.6	37.1
Austria	69.6	69.4	41.1	43.1
France	62.6	71.7	42.9	43.4
Canada	100.8	75.7	35.6	33.8
Belgium	135.2	103.2	44.8	45.4
Greece	108.7	108.8	32.4	35.7
Italy	125.5	121.4	41.2	43.1
Japan	87.0	154.0	26.7	25.3
OECD total	72.8	75.3	35.7	36.3

(ii)China's Fiscal Situation

	Debt-GDP(%)	*Revenue-GDP(%)*		
	2001	1995	2001	2007 estimate
Official data	16.4	10.7	16.8	21.6

	Revised debt-GDP ratio in 2001 after taking into account:	
	(a) 2nd recapitalisation costs	*(b) all contingent liabilities*
Citigroup (2002)	65.9	114.9
Fan (2003)	57.4	74.7

OECD data from: http://stats.oecd.org/wbos/viewhtml.aspx?QueryName=2&QueryType=View&Lang=en; China revenue data for 1995 and 2001 are from China Statistical Yearbook 2005, and revenue estimate for 2007 is from Deutsche Bank (2006).

Notes

1 Paper prepared for the conference '*Assessing the Power of China: Political, Economic, and Social Dimensions*' co-sponsored by the Institute for China Studies at Seoul National University, and the POSCO Research Institute (POSRI) in Seoul, South Korea, May 30–31, 2007. This paper has its origin in the *Debate on China's Economy* in the Reframing China Policy Debate Series of the Carnegie Endowment for International Peace; Available at: http://www.carnegieendowment.org/events/index.cfm?fa=eventDetail&id=929&&prog=zch

2 For a review of the debate on how to interpret China's high growth in 1978–2000 and why China, unlike the economies of the former Soviet bloc, did not experience a recession when it made the switch from a centrally-planned economy to a market economy, see Sachs and Woo (2000), and Woo (2001).

3 For example, in the preceding four aspects of the desired harmonious society, there is no highlighting of a prosperous society. This characterisation of the harmonious society is from 'CPC key plenum elevates social harmony to more prominent position,' *People's Daily* Online, October 12 2006.

4 'CPC Plenary session calls for developing the economy based on scientific concept,' *People's Daily* Online, October 12 2005; http://english.people.com.cn/200510/12/eng20051012_213891.html

5 The generation of these additional benefits is discussed in Woo (2005), and Woo (2006).

6 'Impromptu remarks reveal the party's pressure for reforms,' *South China Morning Post*, Monday April 16 2007.

7 To get a sense of how abusive the local leaders could be, the reader should consult Chen and Wu (2006) for documentation on five incidents in the 1990s in Anhui province that suggest that '[many] of China's underclass live under an unchanged feudal system.'

8 For example, in 2004, there were 74,000 'mass incidents' involving 3.7 million people compared to 10,000 such incidents involving 730,000 people in 1994; Minxin Pei, 'China is Paying the Price of Rising Social Unrest',' *Financial Times*, November 7 2005.

9 Tanner (2004) pointed out that the 'data demonstrate that unrest began rising rapidly no later than 1993–1995 when the rate of economic growth exceeded 10 per cent. Protests also show a ratchet effect, remaining quite high (and continuing to rise in at least two provinces) even as the rate of economic growth revived...'.

10 Tanner (2004).

11 For example, in the same meeting with the Trustees of Brookings Institution in October 2006, Premier Wen outlined a step-by-step extension of free election from the village level to the provincial level. While such a plan, if proposed, would most likely receive wide societal approval in 2006, it is possible that Chinese society in 2020 might have raised its expectations so that free elections should also be held at the national level.

12 If such escalations in social expectations are natural, then it is likely that regardless of whether or not the CPC defines 'democracy' the same way as the U.S. constitution (or the Taiwanese constitution), the form of the democracy that will finally emerge in China will be closer to the latter's definition. Perhaps this is why the former Party Secretary Zhao Ziyang warned his colleagues in 1986–1987: 'Democracy is not something socialism can avoid. The people's demand for democracy is a trend. We must meet their demand to the fullest extent.' (Zhao's remarks are quoted in Minxin Pei, 'How Far Has China to Go?,' *Financial Times*, January 18 2005.)

13 This sense of urgency explains why there is an explicit deadline of 2020.

14 '300,000 people die prematurely from air pollution annually, which is twice the number for South Asia, which has a roughly comparable population,' *Economy* (2004, p. 85).

15 *Economy* (2004, p. 69).

16 '... degradation has reduced China's grassland by 30–50 per cent since 1950; of the 400 million or so hectares of grassland remaining, more than 90 per cent are degraded and more than 50 per cent suffer moderate to severe degradation,' *Economy* (2004, p. 65).

17 I will not talk about air pollution in this chapter, however this should not be taken to indicate that it is not a serious problem. Of the 20 cities in the world identified by the World Bank as having the dirtiest air, 16 of them are located in China. It is shocking that lead and mercury poisoning are more common than expected, see 'China's economic miracle contains mercuric threat,' *Financial Times*, December 18 2004; and 'A Poison Spreads Amid China's Boom,' *Wall Street Journal*, September 30 2006.

18 'Top official warns of looming water crisis,' *South China Morning Post*, November 7 2006.

19 'China may be left high and dry,' *The Straits Times*, January 3 2004. The shortage is reported to be most acute in Taiyuan in Shanxi and Tianjin (Becker, 2003).
20 'Northern cities sinking as water table falls,' *South China Morning Post*, August 11 2001; and Becker (2003).
21 'Northern China sinking ... as the south rises,' *The Straits Times*, March 18 2002. 'Some 60 per cent of the land in Tianjin municipality is plagued by subsistence' (Becker, 2003).
22 'Chinese cities, including Olympic host Beijing, slowly sinking,' Agence France-Presse, July 23 2004.
23 'China may be left high and dry,' *The Straits Times*, January 3 2004.
24 'Top official warns of looming water crisis,' *South China Morning Post*, November 7 2006.
25 Examples of serious water pollution are 'Main rivers facing a 'pollution crisis',' *South China Morning Post*, June 6 2003; 'Booming cities polluting scarce water supplies,' *The Straits Times*, September 18 2003; 'Rivers Run Black, and Chinese Die of Cancer,' *New York Times*, September 12 2004; ''Cancer villages' pay heavy price for economic progress,' *South China Morning Post*, May 8 2006; and 'Rules Ignored, Toxic Sludge Sinks Chinese Village,' *New York Times*, September 4 2006.
26 'Quarter of land now desert – and Man mostly to blame,' *South China Morning Post*, January 30 2002.
27 This is average of the 3,800 square miles reported in 'Billion of Trees Planted, and Nary a Dent in the Desert,' *New York Times*, April 11 2004, and the 4,014 square miles reported in 'Quarter of land now desert – and Man mostly to blame,' South China *Morning Post*, January 30 2002.
28 The number of major sandstorms in China was five in the 1950–1959 period, eight in 1960–1969, 13 in 1970–1979, 14 in 1980–1989, 23 in 1990–1999, 14 in 2000, 26 in 2001, 16 in 2002, and 11 in 2003 according to Yin Pumin, 'Sands of Time Running Out: Desertification continues to swallow up "healthy" land at an alarming rate,' *Beijing Review*, June 16 2005.
29 'Billions of Trees Planted, and Nary a Dent in the Desert,' *New York Times*, April 11 2004.
30 'Quarter of land now desert – and Man mostly to blame,' *South China Morning Post*, January 30 2002.
31 'Ambitious canal network aims to meet growing needs,' *South China Morning Post*, November 27 2002.
32 'China approves project to divert water to arid north,' *South China Morning Post*, November 26 2002.
33 'Massive scheme aims to quench China's thirst,' *South China Morning Post*, May 12 2003; a lower estimate of 300,000 is given in 'China Will Move Waters to Quench Thirst of Cities,' *New York Times*, August 27 2002.
34 'China's river plan worries India,' *Times Of India*, October 23 2006.
35 'Massive scheme aims to quench China's thirst,' *South China Morning Post*, May 12 2003
36 'China Water Plan Sows Discord,' *Wall Street Journal*, October 20 2006.
37 'Chinese water plan opens rift between science, state,' *American-Statesman*, September 10 2006.
38 'China may be left high and dry,' *The Straits Times*, January 3 2004.
39 'Alert sounded over looming water shortage,' *The Straits Times*, June 10 2004.
40 'Water wastage will soon leave China high and dry,' *South China Morning Post*, March 8 2006.
41 'Alert sounded over looming water shortage,' *The Straits Times*, June 10 2004.
42 Menon *et al.* (2002), and Streets (2006).
43 See Bates (2005) for examples of African governments falling after removing food subsidies, and see Cooper (1971) for examples of government changes after currency devaluations. Soeharto of Indonesia was pushed out of office in May 1998, one month after raising fuel prices.

44 Of course, a strong fiscal position cannot overcome all challenges, e.g. when the challenger thinks that he can assume political power and hence take control of the fiscal mechanism, it will be very difficult to bribe him to go away.
45 http://stats.oecd.org/wbos/viewhtml.aspx?QueryName=2&QueryType=View&Lang=en
46 Except for Luxembourg which was excluded because of its atypical nature.
47 The Big Four are Agricultural Bank of China, Bank of China, China Construction Bank and Industrial and Commercial Bank of China.
48 The People's Bank of China established an investment company (Central Huijin Company) under the State Administration of Foreign Exchange to undertake this injection of capital. This gave Huijin 85 per cent of the ownership of China Construction Bank, and 100 per cent of Bank of China.
49 One should really use the consolidated debt of the state sector because it includes at least some part of the contingent liabilities (e.g., foreign debts of SOEs and SOBs, and unfunded pension schemes in the SOE sector) that the state might have to assume responsibility for when the state-owned units default on their financial obligations.
50 f has been above 1.5 per cent for the past seven years. r was 4 per cent in the past only because the interest rate was regulated. I think that the implementation of financial deregulation that is necessary for normal healthy development of the financial sector will render r to be at least 6 per cent because, one, according to Solow (1991), the stylised fact for the real interest rate in the United States is that it is 5 to 6 per cent; and, two, both the marginal rate of return to capital and the black market loan rate have been more than 20 per cent.
51 See Woo *et al.* (1994), and Woo (2001).
52 The asymmetry is from the absence of financial punishment when a loss occurs.
53 'China's poorest worse off after economic boom,' *Financial Times*, November 21 2006 reported a 2.4 per cent drop; and 'In China, Growth at Whose Cost,' *The Wall Street Journal*, November 22 2006 reported a 2.5 per cent drop.
54 Quoted in James Kynge, 'Modern China is facing an ecological crisis,' *Financial Times*, July 26 2004.
55 Pei, Minxin, 'China is Stagnating in Its "Trapped Transition",' *Financial Times*, February 24 2006.
56 Pei, Minxin, 'China is Stagnating in Its "Trapped Transition",' *Financial Times*, February 24 2006.
57 Except when the equation is an accounting identity.
58 Conceptually speaking, the error term changes from a white noise to a random walk during the duration that this atypical leader is in power. Since the outcomes are 'atypical' only during the term of this unusual leader, and the error term in this case does not affect the 'long-term' outcomes, i.e. there is a temporary regime shift.

References

Bates, R. (2005) Markets and states in tropical Africa: the political basis of agricultural policies, University of California Press.

Becker, J. (2003) 'The death of China's rivers,' *Asian Times Online*, August 26.

Chang, Gordon G. (2001) *The coming collapse of China*, New York: Random House.

Chen, Guidi and Wu, Chuntao. (2006) *Will the Boat Sink the Water? The Life of China's Peasants*, New York: Public Affairs. (Published in Chinese as *Zhongguo Nongmin Diaocha* by People's Literature Publishing House in December 2003.)

Citigroup (2002) *Greater China Insights*, June 14.

Cooper, R.N. (1971) *Currency devaluation in developing countries*, Essays in international finance, No. 86, Princeton, N.J.: Princeton University.

Diamond, J. (2005) Collapse: *How Societies Choose to Fail or Succeed*, New York: Viking Books.

Démurger, S., Sachs, J., Woo, W.T., Bao. S., Chang, G. and Mellinger, A. (2002) 'Geography, Economic Policy and Regional Development in China,' *Asian Economic Papers*, Vol. 1, No. 1, Winter, pp. 146–97.

Economy, E.C. (2004) *The River Runs Black: The Environmental Challenge to China's Future*, New York: Cornell University Press.

Fan, G. (2003) 'China's Nonperforming Loans and National Comprehensive Liability,' *Asian Economic Papers*, Vol. 2, No. 1, Winter, pp. 145–52.

Keidel, A. (2006) 'China's Social Unrest: The Story Behind the Stories,' *Policy Brief No. 48,* Carnegie Endowment for International Peace, September.

Menon, S., Hansen, J.E., Nazarenko, L. and Luo, Y, (2002) 'Climate Effects of Black Carbon in China and India,' *Science*, Vol. 297, 27 September, pp. 2250–53.

O'Connor, J. (1973) *The Fiscal Crisis of the State*, New York: St. Martin's Press.

O'Neill, J., Wilson, D., Purushothaman, R. and Stupnytska, A. (2005) 'How Solid are the BRICs?' *Global Economics Paper No: 134*, Goldman Sachs, December 15.

OECD (2006) *Challenges for China's Public Spending: Toward Greater Effectiveness and Equity*, Paris: Organisation for Economic Co-Operation and Development.

OECD public debt and state revenue data. Available at: http://stats.oecd.org/wbos/viewhtml.aspx?QueryName=2&QueryType=View&Lang=en

Pei, M. (2006) *China's Trapped Transition*, Cambridge, Massachussetts: Harvard University Press.

Sachs, J.D. and Wing, T.W. (2000) 'Understanding China's Economic Performance,' *Journal of Policy Reform*, Volume 4, Issue 1, pp. 1–50.

Solow, R. (2000) 'Sustainability: An Economist's Perspective,' the 18th J. Seward Johnson Lecture to the Marine Policy Center, Woods Hole Oceanographic Institution; published in Robert N. Stavins, *Economics of the Environment: Selected Readings*, 2000, 4th edition, New York: W.W. Norton, pp. 131–8.

Streets, D. (2005) 'Black Smoke in China and Its Climate Effects,' *Asian Economic Papers*, Vol. 4, No. 2, Spring/Summer, pp. 1–23.

Tanner, M.S. (2004) 'China Rethinks Unrest,' *The Washington Quarterly*, Vol. 27, No. 3, Summer, pp. 137–56.

Woo, W.T. (2001) 'Recent Claims of China's Economic Exceptionalism: Reflections Inspired by WTO Accession,' *China Economic Review*, 2001, Vol. 12, No. 2/3, pp. 107–136.

Woo, W.T. (2005) 'China's Rural Enterprises in Crisis: The Role of Inadequate Financial Intermediation' in Yasheng Huang, Anthony Saich, and Edward Steinfeld (editor), *Financial Sector Reform in China*, Cambridge, Massachussetts: Harvard University Press, pp. 67–91.

Woo, W.T. (2006) 'China's Macroeconomic Imbalances: The Liquidity Tango Mechanism,' presented at the February 2006 meeting of the Forum of Debt and Development in The Hague, Netherlands.

Woo, W.T., Démurger, S., Sachs, J.D., Bao. S., Chang, G. and Mellinger, A. (1994) 'How Successful Has Chinese Enterprise Reform Been? Pitfalls in Opposite Biases and Focus,' *Journal of Comparative Economics*, June, Vol. 18, No. 3, pp. 410–37.

Woo, W.T., Li, S., Yue, X., Wu, H.X. and Xu, X. (2004) 'The Poverty Challenge for China in the New Millennium,' report to the Poverty Reduction Taskforce of the Millennium Development Goals Project of the United Nations.

6 Assessing the fiscal power of the Chinese state: assessing the central government's capacity to implement national policies[1]

Christine Wong

Introduction

Entering the twenty-first century, China has adopted a new development paradigm that emphasizes the building of a 'Harmonious Society' with more balanced development across regions and across sectors. The paradigm adopts a 'scientific view of the development process' (科学发展观) that emphasizes sustainable growth and 'putting people first' (以人为本). This is laid out in some detail in the Eleventh Five-Year Plan and also explained in Wen (2004). Under this new development paradigm, the government has substantially increased its commitment to pro-poor, pro-rural programs. This is reflected in numerous official statements,[2] and the many new programs introduced over the past few years.

This is a timely shift in policy to redress the large disparities that have emerged in the course of China's remarkable economic growth, especially over the past decade.[3] The greatest disparities are those between urban and rural residents. By virtually all estimates, the average urban income per capita is now more than three times that of the average rural income per capita, a gap that is among the largest in the world. In addition, rural citizens enjoy public services that are far inferior to those provided to their urban counterparts. Reducing these differences would be a critical step toward building a Harmonious Society that includes all citizens.

Whether intended or not, by adopting the goal of building a Harmonious Society, the Hu Jintao–Wen Jiabao administration has committed itself to a program of large increases in public spending and a huge agenda of reform of government and its institutions since, unsurprisingly, the Harmonious Society program has opened the door to calls to address the many current inadequacies in social services as well as the unfairness of their distribution. At a May 2007 conference on health care policy, for example, the Vice Minister of Health Wang Longde argued that, 'Without a fair and equitable system of health care, building a Harmonious Society is impossible.'[4] Earlier, Premier Wen Jiabao had promised to make rural compulsory education once again 'free of charge ... within the next 1–3 years.' Other announcements include providing a safety net for the rural populace under a rural minimum living stipend scheme to be set up in all counties by the end of 2007.[5]

This paper examines China's public finances to address the question of whether the government has sufficient 'fiscal power' to implement the Harmonious Society Program (hereafter HSP), whose achievement is intended to help create the bedrock foundation for supporting China's rise as an economic power in the twenty-first century. In this chapter I will focus on two interrelated aspects of public finance: first, whether the government has enough resources to meet the public expenditure needs of upgrading services in the rural sector sufficiently to meet the inclusive goals of the HSP. The second aspect concerns whether the central government has the capability to manage the effective use of these resources to achieve these goals.

The chapter is organized as follows: Section I presents a brief history of fiscal reform. Section II reviews the legacies of fiscal decline. Section III assesses the current Harmonious Society Program. Section IV presents a more fully funded HSP and assesses its affordability. Section V turns to the delegated system of policy implementation in China and the challenges in reaching the rural sector. Section VI concludes.

A brief history of fiscal reform

The transition from a planned economy to a decentralized, market-oriented economy has required a thorough revamping of the public finance system – from tax policy, tax administration, revenue sharing with local governments, expenditure assignments, to budgeting processes, treasury management, and the provision of public services. This process of building a new public finance system to support a modernizing, market economy has been a core part of the transition in all former Soviet-type economies.[6]

In China this process of reforming the system of public finance has lagged far behind other changes in the economy. Although many changes have been introduced over the past quarter century, the system is still in transition (Wong and Bird, 2008). Briefly stated, fiscal reforms to date can be divided into two phases: the first phase began with the transition in 1978 and continued through 1997, and was dominated by a steep fiscal decline, when budget revenues fell from about 35 percent of GDP to less than 11 percent in 1996 (see Figure 6.1). This was accompanied by a decentralization of revenues, when the central government's share slipped to 20 percent of the total.

Phase II began around 1998, and is marked by an upturn in several key indices – total revenues, central revenues, and discretionary central resources. This upturn was followed by a renewed effort at improving equalization, as well as the beginnings of efforts to reform public expenditure management.[7]

Phase I: Steep fiscal decline and dwindling central control

From the start of the transition in China, dismantling the planning apparatus led quickly to an erosion of the government's main revenue mechanism – SOE profits, and government revenues went into a steep decline. At the same time,

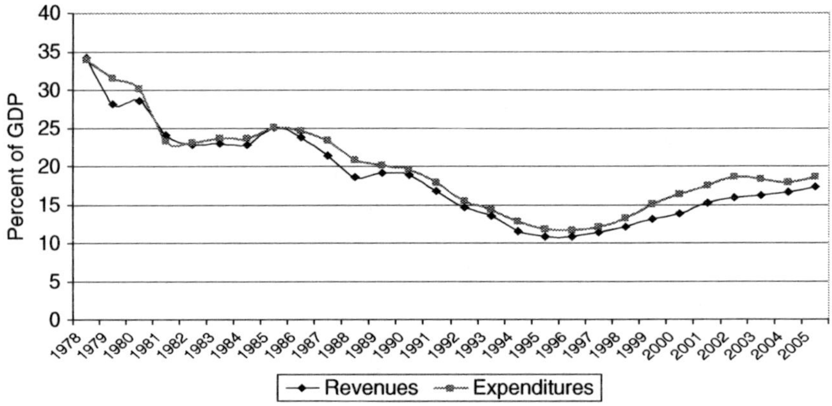

Figure 6.1 Trends in budgetary revenues and expenditures.
Source: CSY, with data adjusted to international definition.

decentralization had caused central revenues to fall as a proportion of total revenues, reinforcing the decline of central control over resources. At the trough, the central government controlled a budget amounting to just 3 percent of GDP (see Figure 6.2).

In 1994 the Tax Sharing System (TSS) reform was introduced, which fundamentally overhauled the revenue sharing system by shifting to tax assignments. By assigning the biggest tax, the value-added tax (VAT), as a shared tax and claiming 75 percent of its receipts, *nominally* the central government reclaimed a majority portion of total revenues.[8] The conventional view (including my own past work) has been that central revenues rebounded with the TSS. However, the government had committed to a program of tax rebates (税收返还), under which annually it returned to the provinces sufficient revenues to maintain their spending levels in the base year 1993, as well as a share of 'the growth' in VAT and the excise tax (a central tax). When tax rebates are netted out, the *discretionary*

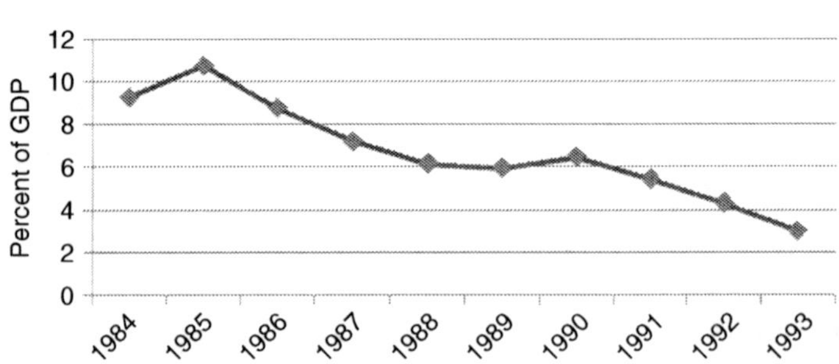

Figure 6.2 Central revenues as a share of GDP.
Source: CSY.

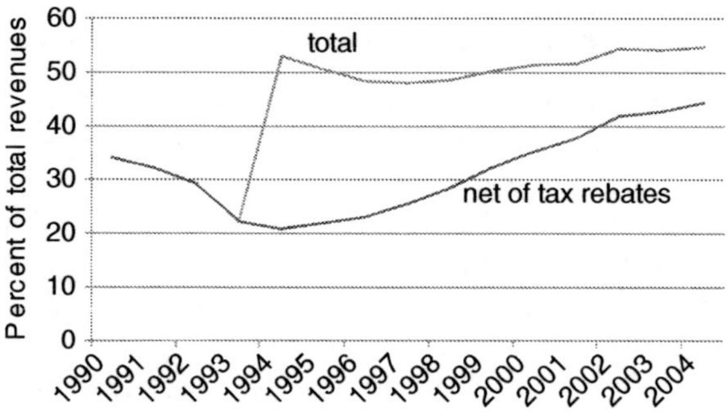

Figure 6.3 Central government share of revenues total and net of tax rebates.
Source: CFY and Li and Xu (2006).

revenues of the central government grew far more slowly (see Figure 6.3). Because of the large rebates in the initial years, the central share had in fact continued to decline through 1994 and 1995, rebounding only from 1996 onwards.

During this period, assistance to local governments in poor regions declined. This is shown in Figure 6.4, where discretionary transfers (defined to exclude tax rebates), fell to 1 percent of GDP in 1994 and remained at that level through 1997. In fact, this trend of declining support to poor regions had begun in the mid-1980s as central revenues dwindled (Wong 1997 and 2003). Moreover, the decline in transfers depicted in Figure 6.4 *significantly understates* the dramatic drop in redistribution, since the definition of transfers changed with the revenue-sharing system in 1994. Previously, most transfers were hidden under the system of negotiated revenue sharing, and what was called 'transfers' were only the additional injections to those poor provinces that could not meet minimum expenditure needs even after being assigned 100 percent of own revenues.

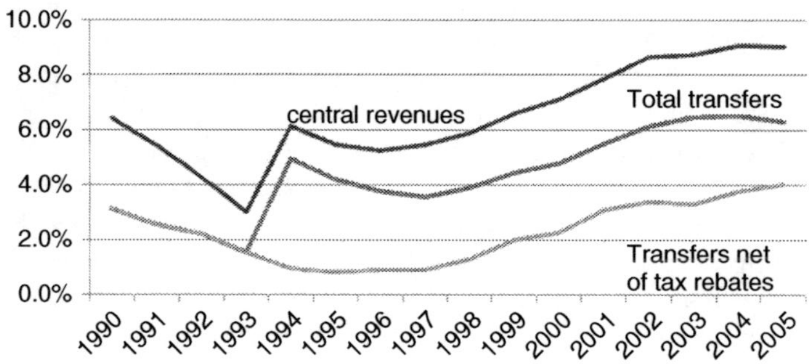

Figure 6.4 Trends in central revenues and transfers.
Source: CFY and Li and Xu (2006).

Phase II: Fiscal recovery, reform and increased effort at equalization

The TSS reform succeeded in rebuilding the revenue mechanism by introducing new tax types and strengthening tax administration and revenues began to rebound from the mid-1990s. Helped by buoyant economic growth, the budget is now reaching 20 percent of GDP – a level comparable to that in the 1970s when account is taken for the portion of capital investment spending that has been moved off the budget. Moreover, since social security is not included in Chinese budgetary data, this level of spending is not far below that in some OECD countries – especially those in East Asia, and is roughly in line with China's income level.

With fiscal recovery, the government began, belatedly, to undertake reform in public expenditure management, with changes to the budgeting and treasury management processes introduced in the late 1990s. However, progress has been slow, and some critical reforms have yet to be undertaken, most notably in revamping central-local fiscal relations, as well as clarification of the public role in the new economy. With the rebound in its own revenues, the central government also began to devote more resources to transfers, which grew to 4 percent of GDP in 2004. More effort also went into making the transfers more equalizing (World Bank 2007a).

Legacies of fiscal decline

The long period of fiscal decline had forced many adjustments on China's public finance, some with long-lasting and negative effects. Three of the most salient were a) the emergence of large horizontal fiscal disparities across regions, b) the growth of vertical imbalances, and c) the accelerated growth of extra-budgetary activities and commercialization of the public sector.

Growing horizontal imbalances

China's economic growth has been regionally unbalanced, with much higher growth rates in the coastal provinces than in inland provinces. This, by itself, would have exacerbated the already large income differences among provinces. As the shift to the TSS in 1994 had replaced the weakly redistributive system of revenue-sharing with tax assignments, without an offsetting transfer mechanism, the distribution of fiscal resources came to resemble more closely that of regional incomes, reinforcing the effect of income inequalities. The trend in Table 6.1 shows that disparities in fiscal resources grew across provinces through the 1990s. The trend may have been stemmed since 1998 but not reversed, even with some recovery in central transfers.

A more important problem is that the current transfer system is not equalizing. This is illustrated in Figure 6.5, which lists the 31 provincial level units by per capita GDP in a descending order, and shows their receipts of own revenues and

Table 6.1 Growing disparities in per capita budgetary expenditures by province*

	1990	*1994*	*1998*	*2002*	*2004*
Highest (1) Shanghai	609	1207	3337	5516	7875
Lowest (2) Henan	104	130	362	680	899
Ratio of (1) to (2)	5.9	9.3	9.2	8.1	8.8
Average	254	374	861	1684	2066
Absolute gap	505	1076	2976	4835	6977
Coeff. of variation	0.57	0.71	0.75	0.75	0.75

* Deflated to 1990 Yuan, and excluding Tibet.
Source: MOF Compendium of Local Fiscal Statistics, and CSY.

transfers in 2004 – transfers appear to have no discernible effect in alleviating fiscal disparities. This finding has been replicated with data on county level units (World Bank 2006b).[9]

Growing vertical imbalances

During the long fiscal decline, evidence suggests that higher level governments tended to 'grab' revenues and 'push down' expenditures, resulting in a

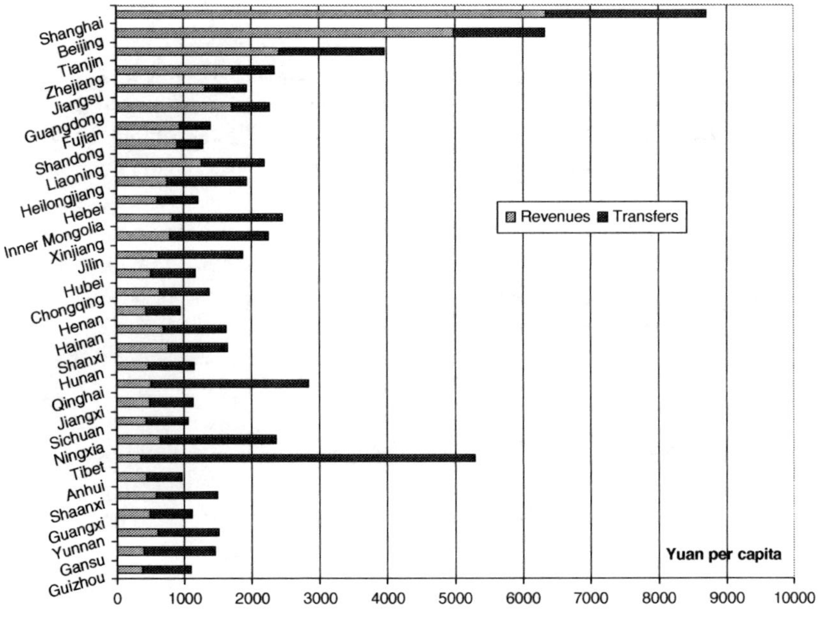

Figure 6.5 Fiscal resources by province 2004 (Yuan per capita).
Source: MOF Compendium of Local Fiscal Statistics and CSY.

Table 6.2 Fiscal trends differ for subnational governments

	1993	*1998*	*2000*	*2002*	*2004*
Revenues					
Central Government	22%	49.5%	52.2%	55.0%	54.9%
Provinces	13%	10.5%	10.7%	11.7%	11.2%
Municipalities	34%	19.7%	17.4%	16.3%	16.6%
Counties	19%	11.5%	12.0%	11.0%	12.0%
Townships	13%	8.8%	7.7%	6.1%	5.2%
Expenditures					
Central Government	34%	28.9%	34.7%	30.7%	27.7%
Provinces	11%	18.8%	19.1%	19.6%	18.7%
Municipalities	29%	24.1%	20.0%	21.0%	22.2%
Counties	16%	19.9%	18.9%	21.9%	25.2%
Townships	11%	8.3%	7.3%	6.8%	6.1%

Sources: Wong (1997), World Bank (2002), MOF Compendium of Local Fiscal Statistics, various years.

trend of growing vertical imbalances as revenues became increasingly concentrated at higher levels while expenditure trends went in the opposite direction (see Table 6.2).

Growing extra-budgetary activities and the commercialization of the public sector

As fiscal support to local governments and public services declined, especially in the 1990s, local governments and service providers were encouraged to 'diversify' their funding sources and levy user charges. As an incentive, they were allowed to retain a portion of their extra-budgetary revenues. Under generally lax management, the practice of supplementing staff salaries from 'self-raised funds' grew, and gradually came to be routinely accepted throughout the public sector.[10] With local governments and public service institutions behaving like revenue-maximizing enterprises, extra-budgetary activities grew rapidly (World Bank 2005 and Wong and Bird, 2008).

Social outcomes

Given that the TSS had recentralized revenues but left expenditure assignments unchanged, many local governments were left with inadequate resources for financing their expenditure responsibilities, and had little help from central transfers. As a result, many defaulted on their responsibilities and were unable to provide services mandated by law/regulation. Although the Education Law called for nine years of compulsory education for all children, for example, in 2004 some 17 percent of rural counties could not provide it, all of them in remote rural areas.[11] One scholar has estimated that during 1985–2000, as many as 150 million rural youths did not receive nine years of schooling, due to the combination of undersupply and the high fees that were often charged by schools.[12]

Likewise, the urban-rural gap in public services is large. For example, in 2003 the per capita recurrent expenditure on education is three times higher in city districts than in the rural communities, and health expenditures were almost three times as high in urban areas compared to those in rural (UNDP 2005). Figures for 2002 show the number of doctors per 1000 persons was 5.2 in urban areas, but only 2.7 in rural (MOH 2004). Similar urban-rural differences exist with respect to infrastructural services such as water, sanitation, roads, and information and communication technology. These urban-rural differences produced stark consequences for the rural population. For 2003, China's human development index was estimated to be 0.81 for urban and only 0.67 for rural areas. Aside from the differences in income, this reflects the lower life expectancy in rural areas, which, at 69.6, was 5.6 years less than in urban areas. It also reflects the differences in levels of education: the share of population between 15 to 64 years of age without any formal education was 8.7 percent in rural areas – more than three times the urban rate (Census 2000).

The current harmonious society program

The 11th Five Year Plan document lays out broad objectives for the HSP that include:

- Reducing inequalities across sectors and regions
- Strengthening the social safety net
- Improving public services, including environmental protection
- Strengthening the rule of law, etc.

The main thrust of the HSP is redistribution and rebalancing of the economy, aimed at reversing some of the inequalities that have emerged, addressing social grievances and relieving tensions.

In recent years senior officials have called for closing the gaps, and many new programs have been rolled out. Among them, free rural basic education, new cooperative medical insurance for farmers, building the 'new Socialist Countryside,' rural *dibao* (minimum living stipend), training and job placement support for rural out-migration, and social security schemes for farmers. These programs represent major steps forward in improving public services in the rural sector, with increased commitments of government support. Table 6.3 offers some details of the programs.

Under China's highly decentralized fiscal and administrative systems, all of these programs are to be implemented by county and township governments. To do so, they will need far more help than is provided by the current intergovernmental fiscal system. While the central government has injected additional funds into key programs, the level of funding provided to date is far short of what is needed.

Table 6.3 Key new programs for rural education and health

Program	*Launch Date*	*Policy Objective*	*Policy Content*
'Two exemptions and one subsidy'	2003	To reduce financial costs of schooling to families for nine years of compulsory education in order to expand access.	Government provides funding to replace revenues from the textbook and miscellaneous fees and provides a subsidy to boarding students from 'poor' families.
Free Rural Compulsory Education	2006–2007	To take on nine years of compulsory education financed by public resources; to reduce financial costs to families in order to expand access.	Government provides funding to replace revenues from 'miscellaneous fees' (*zafei*) at an average of RMB140 per student p.a. for all rural primary school students, and RMB180 per student p.a. for all rural junior middle school students. By 2007 this will cover 150 millionstudents.
New Rural Cooperative Medical Scheme (NCMS)	2005	To provide risk-pooling for major illnesses, to reduce the financial risks of farmers falling into poverty due to illness.	Designed mainly for in-patient services; run at the county level, scope of coverage and reimbursement rates are stipulated; participation is voluntary and on a household level; counties are permitted to set up a NCMS when 70 percent of households agree to participate. The minimum funding is set at RMB 50 p.a., with cost-sharing: Center RMB20; subnational governments RMB20–40 per participant toward the annual premium; RMB10 by the participant.
Rural Dibao (minimum living stipend)	2005	To provide income support to the poor	All households with incomes below the local stipulated minimum will receive a 'top-up' from the government. To be rolled out in all counties by year-end 2007.

Source: adapted from World Bank (2007b).

Initial experiences

The New Cooperative Medical Scheme is one of the principal components of the new HSP initiatives to which the central government has pledged support. The framework of how it is being implemented offers an illustration of some of the financial difficulties the program will face. Under the program, the central government calls for all rural counties to set up a community-based risk pooling system to provide medical care for their residents, whose participation is on a voluntary basis. It has set the minimum contribution at RMB 50 per person enrolled.[13] Of this, the central government contributes 20 yuan per participant, and asks provinces and municipalities to help with the 20 yuan 'local' contribution that is specified, leaving a personal contribution of only 10 yuan. Under this formulation, the program imposes a substantial burden – and perhaps even the majority portion, of financing costs on the counties, which bear the administration and collection costs as well as all of the financial risks of the program, in addition to some part of the 20 yuan local contribution.[14] To contain costs and avoid overspending, many county governments are designing very conservative plans that limit coverage and benefits, sometimes even adopting measures highly unfavorable to the people that the scheme is designed to help. In one county visited last November, we learned that the plan was so conservative that it had paid out in reimbursements only 40 percent of the collected funds during the first 18 months of the scheme. One county even decided to carve up the inpatient care fund among subordinate townships based on enrollment shares, and ask the townships and health institutions to share the costs in the event of overspending. The schedule was:

- The county would cover only up to 5 percent of overspending
- Overspending by 5–18% would be shared 20:20:60 among the county, township, and hospital
- Overspending in excess of 18 percent would be the sole responsibility of the hospitals.

In response, township and hospital officials reported that they planned to contain costs by transferring patients to hospitals at the county and municipal levels, where the reimbursement rates are lower.[15] In effect this pushes the financial risks right back to the patients (World Bank 2007a).

The free rural compulsory education program will face similar difficulties, as the central subsidy currently provided also covers only a portion of the revenue loss due to the abolition of miscellaneous and other fees, leaving large gaps to be filled by local governments – the central subsidy standard is RMB 140 p.a. per primary school student, and RMB 180 for junior middle school students, far less than the average levels of current collection.[16] The problem, moreover, is that the rural fiscal gap has grown in recent years as more and more new programs are being introduced, all of them representing partially funded mandates. Even though transfers have grown rapidly in total, they are not keeping up with increases in expenditure needs.

Is there enough money? Assessing central government financial capacity

Improving the delivery of public services to the rural populace is, and should be, a core component of China's strategy of building a Harmonious Society and a

'New Socialist Countryside.' Public services such as education, health care and social protection are essential to efforts to reduce the gap between urban and rural residents, by enabling rural citizens to acquire the human capital needed for participation in China's economic success. The financing needs of improving rural public services are huge given the enormous size of the rural population and the currently large deficits in rural services and service quality. As shown in the section above, however, the current level of funding provided by the central government is insufficient for achieving these objectives.

Rather than tackle the thorny issues of how much equalization is achievable or desirable in a huge country such as China, and even though top leaders have implied, if not outright called for, bringing rural services up to the level of urban services,[17] in this section I will focus on calculating the costs of remedying the critical shortfalls in just a few key rural services in the short-run.

These are five national programs already being implemented, albeit at varying levels of funding in different localities:

1. rural compulsory education
2. the new cooperative medical insurance scheme for farmers
3. the rural dibao (minimum living stipend) scheme
4. a village investment fund to support rural infrastructure, and
5. a training program to support rural out-migration.

Some estimates are presented in Table 6.4 of the costs of scaling up these programs to provide a more adequate level of funding for each. Based on modest assumptions, the estimates add up to RMB 205 billion yuan. This is an amount that is well within the financing capacity of the central government – equal to only 12 percent of central revenues of RMB 1.65 trillion yuan in 2005, or 16 percent of discretionary central revenues of RMB 1.25 trillion yuan after deducting for tax rebates. In fact, the net additional cost to the central budget would be substantially smaller, since most of the programs are already being funded, and other costs can be absorbed by revamping and replacing some of the current transfers of more than RMB 700 billion yuan annually (excluding tax rebates).

Not just a matter of money, but capability for policy implementation

Since the central government accounts for less than 10 percent of budgetary expenditures on social services such as education, health, and social relief, its control over social outcomes in the rural sector is at best attenuated, and compliance with central policies is not always assured at the local levels. Even when the central government injects resources to support local services, these resources pass through provinces and municipalities before reaching counties. Leakages can occur at each level, and at present the central government has few levers for holding local governments accountable.

Table 6.4 Cost estimates for a start-up HSP

	Assumptions	*Cost (billions RMB)*
Rural compulsory education	Provide funding to cover 2 times the gap in 2005 between total and budgetary expenditure in RCE for central and western provinces – to replace all fees and other non-budgetary revenues, and to provide a 20–25 percent increase in funding to improve teaching conditions	50
New Cooperative Medical Scheme	100 yuan subsidy per participant for rural population in the central and western provinces	65
Rural dibao (minimum stipend) living	Nationwide rural dibao line at dollar-a-day with 100% overhead	40
Village investment funds	100,000 yuan per village in 148,000 villages to help fund infrastructure	14.8
Support for labor transfer	20 million rural workers at 1750 per worker for basic training and job placement	35
Total cost		**204.8**
	As a share of central revenues	*12%*
	As a share of discretionary central revenues	*16%*

Source: author calculations and World Bank 2007b (poverty assessment).

Under China's highly decentralized systems of fiscal management and administration, the central government employs extensive delegation of authorities in a nested, hierarchical setting. The central government delegates authorities to the provinces, and depends on the provinces to carry out their responsibilities. The provinces in turn delegate to the municipalities, and depend on them to 'deliver' on their assigned responsibilities, and so on downward through the hierarchy (see Figure 6.6). This decentralized administration can be an asset for cost-effective service delivery, if local governments can be held accountable for performance. At present, though, the accountability relationships are weak at multiple levels, with the result that compliance with central policies is not always assured at the local levels, and central transfers are not always used as intended.

Central government → provinces

Provincial government → Municipalities

Municipalities → Counties

Counties → Townships

Townships → villages/farmers

Figure 6.6 Hierarchical delegation in China.

Likewise contributing to the often low effectiveness of public expenditures is the weak accountability relationship between service providers – which are mostly public institutions – and local governments. Just as the central government has few levers to enforce compliance by local governments, local governments often lack effective levers over service providers. Finally, the downward accountability of both service providers and local governments to citizens is also weak, and most services are provided without significant participation by citizens or communities.

These are in part legacies of the long fiscal decline, during which incremental reforms had focused narrowly on reviving revenue collection, especially central revenues. In the process revenue and expenditure assignments were de-linked, and the withering away of transfers led ultimately to a breakdown of the intergovernmental fiscal system – in the sense that decisions made at the top could not be implemented at the lower levels given the existing financial arrangements (Wong 1997 and 2007).

More importantly, they reflect the urgent need to repair the intergovernmental fiscal system. At present local governments are saddled with unusually heavy responsibilities, with neither sufficient assigned revenues nor a system of transfers to ensure the delivery of mandated services. Despite significantly increased transfers and improved equalization since 1998, underfunding remains a fundamental obstacle to the central-local accountability relationship today, as the intergovernmental fiscal system still does not ensure sufficient funding to counties and townships in the western and central provinces (World Bank 2007a). This is true for overall amounts as well as for specific programs, since the system still lacks mechanisms for ensuring that mandated services can be financed in poor counties. Moreover, the assignment of responsibilities across local governments is murky – with many programs requiring joint financing among the many levels but no clear divisions, and local governments do not have clearly articulated roles and functions against which they can be held accountable.

The accountability relationship with public service providers is similarly undermined by underfunding, as many of them are not adequately funded for their public service tasks. Instead, these providers are often expected to cross-subsidize their public service from money-making activities.

Weak accountability also stems from the weak information base for policy analysis in China, especially for rural public services, which undermines efforts to judge the performance of local governments and service providers. Even though a huge amount of information is routinely reported, China lacks a system for vetting and reconciling the data reported by the different ministries and agencies, and their figures can vary widely. For budgetary expenditures on rural compulsory education, for example, figures reported by the Ministry of Finance (MOF) are 10 percent greater than those from the Ministry of Education (MOE). Large discrepancies also exist for data reported by different levels of the administrative hierarchy. In 2004, for example, the sum of central and provincial expenditures on education exceeded the 'national consolidated' figure by 22 percent (CFY 2005). Data on social indicators and service outputs are weaker still – figures for school enrollments, hospital bed usage, etc. are widely considered unreliable.

Enforcement of public service delivery often is not clearly assigned to any level of government[18] and relies heavily on the personal responsibility system using the performance reviews of government officials. The system of personal responsibility has been effective in the past to enforce selected objectives such as economic development and family planning, and service-orientation is being included in the performance evaluations of local officials in some pilot reforms. However, personal responsibility cannot overcome systemic constraints: school principals cannot be personally responsible for improving school conditions if funds are not available, nor can teachers take 'personal responsibility' for preventing students from dropping out if their families cannot afford to pay fees.[19]

In sum, piecemeal reforms to the system of public finance over the past 25 years have repaired the revenue mechanism, but left expenditure management in substantial disarray. As a result, the central government faces significant difficulties in implementing social policies through the present system of delegated governance.

Conclusion

In Wong (2007) I had argued that rural interests tend to be left out in the competition for central transfers, so that Wen Jiabao's pro-rural policies will have an uphill struggle to get sufficient funding. In this chapter I have reviewed the new Harmonious Society policies being implemented, focusing not only on funding levels, but also policy implementation mechanisms to argue that because the government has delayed institutional reform in the public sector, the central government's capacity to achieve stated social objectives is weak. Under the current intergovernmental arrangements, on average, local governments do not have the wherewithal to implement the HSP, nor do they have unambiguous incentives for doing so. Under these circumstances, even though the central government has the will and the ability to provide funds, it will find it difficult to channel them toward delivering services at the grassroots levels of Chinese society. This inability of the central government to implement policies in support of the national vision of a Harmonious Society points to a fundamental weakness in the foundation on which China is building its hopes for the twenty-first century.

More worrisome is that the gap between government promises and its capacity to deliver is very large and growing rapidly on the many components of the Harmonious Society Program – on the environment, on health care and education reforms, and on 'tilting' toward the ethnic minority regions, etc. On every front, there are daunting institutional challenges. On the environment, the government will have to undertake large realignment of relative prices and significantly raise tax rates on energy resources, as well as tackle the issues such as giant SOEs including Sinopec, CNOOC, power companies capturing huge economic rents that keep resource regions impoverished and production methods which are backward and inefficient. To improve health care and education, provider incentives will have to be fundamentally altered, etc.

The challenges are great. The government has shown a willingness to acknowledge problems and seek solutions. The current piecemeal approaches, however, will unlikely suffice, especially since the central leadership remains stuck in the mindset that it can mandate policy changes, and spends too little effort building public support for its programs. The ratcheting up of promises by top leaders in the past 2–3 years carries significant political risks, since they are building expectations that the machinery of government will not be able to deliver.

Notes

1 This paper draws from work that was carried out under the World Bank studies *China: Public Services For Building The New Socialist Countryside* (2007); *China: Extending Public Finance to the Countryside* (2006); and *Reforming Intergovernmental Finance in China: a Study of the Northeast* (2007).

2 Since 2003, the first document issued by the State Council each year, popularly known as the 'Number One Document' where the top emphasis of the government is laid out, has been devoted to rural issues.

3 For recent studies of these disparities, see Ravallion and Chen (2004), Shue and Wong (2007), and World Bank (2007a).

4 'Grasping rules and regulations to guide the reform in health services,' speech given at the Westlake Forum on China's Health Policy, May 10–11 2007, Hangzhou.

5 'Chinese government decides to subsidize all rural poor,' 24 May 2007, Xinhua News Agency (English).

6 See, for examples, World Bank (2006), Wallich (1994), and Bird *et al.* (1995).

7 For an overview of China's budget reforms through the 1990s, see Wong (2005).

8 The VAT accounts for nearly half of all tax revenues in China. It is also a reliable tax whose revenues go up with GDP regardless of profitability, and thus less cyclical than income or profit taxes.

9 Other studies have also found that at the county level, low income is not a significant factor in attracting transfers (see, for example, Shih and Zhang 2007).

10 Until they were shut down under Zhu Rongji, all central ministries ran businesses to generate revenues for 'staff welfare' needs – MOF and SPC had large investment companies, the SPC owned the Xinhua Airline, etc.

11 Information from MOE.

12 Zhang Yulin, 'Fenji banxue zhidu xia de jiaoyu ziyuan fenpei yu chengxiang jiaoyu cha ju- guanyu jiaoyu jihui jundeng wenti de zhengzhi jixue tantao (The urban-rural gap under the system of schools run at separate levels of government ...)' Zhongguo nongcun guancha 2003 (1).

13 This standard was RMB 40 yuan initially.

14 Local governments are prohibited from using collected premiums to defray administrative costs.

15 World Bank, 2007a. The reimbursement rates for covered care in this county were 60 percent in the township hospital, 35 percent in the county hospital, and only 20 percent in the provincial hospital.

16 In one junior middle school visited, students had paid fees totaling nearly RMB 1000 p.a. before the new program was rolled out.

17 For example, at the National Conference on Health in January 2007, both Hu Jintao and Wen Jiabao called for building a health care system that 'covers both the urban and rural populace.' MOH website, January 30 2007.

18 Exceptions are made during national campaigns, such as the campaign to universalize nine years of rural compulsory education. Under this campaign, responsibility is assigned to the provinces and counties.

19 These are just some examples of the 'personal responsibility' assignments in schools today (World Bank 2007a).

References

Bird, Richard M. *et al.* (eds) (1995) *Decentralization of the Socialist State*. Washington, D.C: World Bank.

Li Ping and Xu Hongcai (eds) (2006) *China: Intergovernmental Fiscal Relations*. Beijing: China Public Finance Economics Press.

Ravallion, Martin, and Chen, Shaohua (2004) *China's (Uneven) Progress Against Poverty*. World Bank Policy Research Working Paper, No. 3408, September.

Shih, Victor and Qi, Zhang (2007) 'Who Receives Subsidies? A Look at the County Level in Two Time Periods', in Shue, Vivienne, and Wong, Christine (eds) *Paying for Progress in China: Public Finance, Human Welfare and Changing Patterns of Inequality*. London: Routledge.

UNDP (2005) China Human Development Report 2005. October.

Wallich, Christine (ed.) (1994) *Russia and the Challenge of Fiscal Federalism*. Washington D.C.: World Bank.

Wen, Jiabao (2004) 'Firmly Establish and Resolutely Implement a Scientific Development View,' closing speech at the specialized research course for provincial-level cadres on establishing and implementing a scientific development view, February 21.

Wong, Christine (2007) 'Can the Retreat from Equality Be Reversed? An Assessment of Redistributive Fiscal Policies from Deng Xiaoping to Wen Jiabao.' In Shue and Wong.

Wong, Christine (2005) 'Budgeting Issues in China' in OECD, Governance in China, China in the Global Economy, OECD, Paris.

Wong, Christine P.W. (ed.) (1997) *Financing Local Government in the People's Republic of China*. New York: Oxford University Press.

Wong, Christine and Bird, Richard (2008) 'China's Fiscal System: A Work in Progress' (with Richard Bird), in Brandt, Loren and Rawski, Thomas (eds) *China's Great Transformation: Origins, Mechanism, and Consequences of the Post-Reform Economic Boom*. New York: Cambridge University Press.

World Bank (2000) *China: Managing Public Expenditures for Better Results*. Washington, D.C.: Country Economic Memorandum.

World Bank (2002) *China: National Development and Subnational Finance—A Review of Provincial Expenditure*. Washington, D.C.: Poverty Reduction and Economic Management Unit. East Asia and Pacific Region..

World Bank (2005) *China – Deepening Public Service Unit Reform to Improve Service Delivery*. Poverty Reduction and Economic Management Unit. East Asia and Pacific Region: The World Bank

World Bank (2006) *World Development Report 1996: From Plan to Market*. New York: Oxford University Press.

World Bank (2006a) *China: Rural Public Finance for a Harmonious Society*. Washington, D.C.: The World Bank.

World Bank (2006b) *Reforming Intergovernmental Finance in China: a Study of the Northeast*. Washington, D.C.: World Bank.

World Bank (2007a) *China: Public Services for Building the New Socialist Countryside.* Washington, D.C.: World Bank.

World Bank (2007b) *China: poverty assessment.* Washington, D.C.: World Bank.

Zhang, Yulin, (2003) 'Fenji banxue zhidu xia de jiaoyu ziyuan fenpei yu chengxiang jiaoyu cha ju- guanyu jiaoyu jihui jundeng wenti de zhengzhi jixue tantao (The urban-rural gap under the system of schools run at separate levels of government...)' Zhongguo nongcun guancha.

Annual Budget Reports to the National People's Congress.

China Finance Yearbook (CFY).

China Statistical Yearbook (CSY).

Compendium of Fiscal Statistics for All Prefectures, Cities, and Counties.

Part 3

Assessing the international dimension of China's power

7 Assessing China's power reflected in foreign trade

Wei Zhang

Introduction

Opening up policy has been an important component of China's general economic reform. The direct goals of this policy are expanding China's international trade and attracting inflow of foreign investment, and thus promoting the economic growth and the improvement of people's living standards. The active participation in the international cooperation has led China to a fast track of the integration into the modern global economic system. After almost three decades since it began the opening up policy and economic reform in 1978, China has become a world trade power toady in terms of its trade share in the world total.

This paper aims to investigate the expansion of China's international trade, the driving forces behind such a development, and the possible future of this trend. The first section attempts to examine expansion and structural patterns of China's international trade; the second section focuses on some pre-conditions for China's fast trade expansion and some policy measures China's government has taken to foster the trade power; the third section discusses some main difficulties China is facing to continue to expand its trade power, mainly the constraints from the environment degradation, the intertwined relation between the internal imbalance and external imbalance, and the new challenges due to China's WTO obligation.

Expansion and structural changes of China's international trade

China's annual average growth rate of GDP from 1978 to 2006 reached 9.67 per cent, far above the world average growth rate of 3.3 per cent during the same period (Ma 2007). After almost three decades of fast economic growth, China has become the fourth largest economy in the world only after the United States, Japan, and Germany measured by the official exchange rate. If measured by Purchase Power Parity (PPP), it has surpassed Germany in 1987 and Japan in 1994, and now it is second only to the United States (World Bank, 2006). Although the per capita GDP of China is still at a relatively low level, its overall economic size would catch up with the United States by the end of 2025 if both countries continue the growth speed of the past decade or so.

GDP increased from 218.5 billion US$ in 1978 to 2225 billion US$ in 2005, per capita GDP increased from 228.8 US$ to 1720.9 US$ (see Table 7.1). The disposable income increased from less than 200 US$ to about 1500 US$ in the urban area and from about 70 US$ to about 490 US$. The countries' fiscal revenue also increased more than six times measured by the constant price.

Compared to the growth of GDP, the growth of China's international trade has been even more rapid. Total export and total import increased from 9.8 billion US$ to 762 billion US$ and from 10.9 billion US$ to 659.9 billion US$ respectively from 1978 to 2005, the compounded average annual growth rates

Table 7.1 GDP growth of China (1978–2005)

Year	*GDP*			*GDP per capita*	
	RMB billion yuan	*US$ billion*	*Growth %*	*US dollar*	*Growth %*
1978	367.9	218.5		228.8	
1979	409.5	263.3	7.2	272.0	18.9
1980	458.0	305.7	6.2	311.6	14.5
1981	493.1	289.3	5.8	291.0	−6.6
1982	536.9	283.7	9.6	281.6	−3.2
1983	601.9	304.7	11.0	298.4	6.0
1984	728.3	313.9	15.3	303.1	1.6
1985	912.4	310.7	12.7	295.7	−2.5
1986	1038.6	300.8	8.7	281.8	−4.7
1987	1218.1	327.3	11.3	301.7	7.1
1988	1520.9	408.6	10.7	370.8	22.9
1989	1724.5	458.0	4.0	409.3	10.4
1990	1890.9	395.3	3.9	348.3	−14.9
1991	2206.5	414.5	9.2	360.6	3.5
1992	2720.2	493.3	14.2	424.3	17.7
1993	3533.3	613.2	13.5	522.0	23.0
1994	4819.8	559.2	12.6	471.4	−9.7
1995	6079.4	727.9	10.5	607.6	28.9
1996	7117.7	856.1	9.6	707.8	16.5
1997	7897.3	952.7	8.8	780.4	10.3
1998	8440.2	1019.5	7.8	827.8	6.1
1999	8967.6	1083.3	7.2	872.2	5.4
2000	9921.4	1198.5	8.0	957.5	9.8
2001	10965.6	1324.8	7.7	1050.8	9.7
2002	12033.2	1453.8	8.6	1145.4	9.0
2003	13582.3	1641.0	9.9	1284.6	12.2
2004	15987.8	1931.6	9.8	1503.0	17.0
2005	18232.0	2225.0	10.1	1720.9	14.5

Both GDP and GDP per capita are measured in constant price of RMB or US$.
Growth Rate of GDP is measured in 1990 constant price of RMB.
Growth Rate of GDP per capita is measured in 1990 constant price of US$.
Source: The United Nations Statistics Division Economic Statistics, 2006. National Accounts Main Aggregates Database.

Table 7.2 Exports (1978–2005)

Year	*Total exports*		*Primary goods*		*Manufacturing goods*	
	US$ billion	*Growth %*	*US$ billion*	*Share %*	*US$ billion*	*Share %*
1978	9.8		4.9	50.4	4.8	49.6
1979	13.7	40.1	6.9	50.2	6.8	49.8
1980	18.1	32.6	9.1	50.3	9.0	49.7
1981	22.0	21.5	11.1	50.3	10.9	49.7
1982	22.3	1.4	11.2	50.4	11.1	49.6
1983	22.2	–0.4	11.2	50.5	11.0	49.5
1984	26.1	17.6	13.2	50.6	12.9	49.4
1985	27.4	4.6	13.8	50.6	13.5	49.4
1986	30.9	13.1	14.0	45.2	17.0	54.8
1987	39.4	27.5	15.7	39.8	23.7	60.2
1988	47.5	20.5	17.0	35.7	30.6	64.3
1989	52.5	10.6	15.1	28.7	37.5	71.3
1990	62.1	18.2	15.9	25.6	46.2	74.4
1991	71.9	15.8	16.1	22.5	55.7	77.5
1992	84.9	18.1	17.0	20.0	67.9	80.0
1993	91.7	8.0	16.7	18.2	75.1	81.8
1994	121.0	31.9	19.7	16.3	101.3	83.7
1995	148.8	23.0	21.5	14.4	127.3	85.6
1996	151.0	1.5	21.9	14.5	129.1	85.5
1997	182.8	21.0	24.0	13.1	158.8	86.9
1998	183.7	0.5	20.5	11.2	163.2	88.8
1999	194.9	6.1	19.9	10.2	175.0	89.8
2000	249.2	27.8	25.5	10.2	223.7	89.8
2001	266.1	6.8	26.3	9.9	239.8	90.1
2002	325.6	22.4	28.5	8.8	297.1	91.2
2003	438.2	34.6	34.8	7.9	403.4	92.1
2004	593.3	35.4	40.5	6.8	552.8	93.2
2005	762.0	28.4	49.0	6.4	712.9	93.6

Source: Data from 1978 to 1984 are based on Ministry of Commerce: Import and Export Statistics; Data from 1985 to 2005 are based on State Bureau of Statistics: *China Statistical Yearbook 2006*.

were 16.1 and 15.2 per cent respectively. They were about 6.4 and 5.5 percentage points higher than GDP growth rate, respectively. As a result, Chinese economy becomes much more openly measured by the index of export dependency, i.e. the ratio of the export to the GDP, which increased from 4.5 to 34.2 per cent (see Figure 7.1).

Faster expansion of international trade compared to general economic growth has been a phenomenal trend worldwide in the late twentieth century and the beginning of this century. However, the difference between the speeds of the trade expansion and the GDP growth in China has been even more significant than the world average. Consequently, China's export share in the world total has grown much faster than its GDP share in the world total. From 1978 to 2005,

Table 7.3 Imports (1978–2005)

Year	*Total imports*		*Primary goods*		*Manufacturing goods*	
	US$ billion	*Growth %*	*US$ billion*	*Share %*	*US$ billion*	*Share %*
1978	10.9		4.0	36.8	6.9	63.2
1979	15.7	44.0	5.4	34.2	10.3	65.8
1980	20.1	27.7	7.0	34.8	13.1	65.2
1981	22.1	10.0	6.7	30.2	15.4	69.8
1982	19.3	−12.4	4.6	23.6	14.7	76.4
1983	21.4	10.9	3.5	16.5	17.9	83.5
1984	27.4	28.1	4.0	14.6	23.4	85.4
1985	42.3	54.1	5.3	12.5	37.0	87.5
1986	42.9	1.5	6.1	14.3	36.8	85.7
1987	43.3	0.7	6.7	15.4	36.6	84.6
1988	55.2	27.9	9.7	17.6	45.5	82.4
1989	59.2	7.0	11.8	19.9	47.4	80.1
1990	53.4	−9.8	9.9	18.5	43.5	81.5
1991	63.8	19.6	10.8	17.0	53.0	83.0
1992	80.6	26.3	13.3	16.4	67.3	83.6
1993	103.9	29.0	14.2	13.7	89.7	86.3
1994	115.6	11.2	16.5	14.3	99.1	85.7
1995	132.1	14.2	24.4	18.5	107.7	81.5
1996	138.8	5.1	25.4	18.3	113.4	81.7
1997	142.4	2.5	28.6	20.1	113.8	79.9
1998	140.2	−1.5	22.9	16.4	117.3	83.6
1999	165.7	18.2	26.8	16.2	138.9	83.8
2000	225.1	35.8	46.7	20.8	178.4	79.2
2001	243.5	8.2	45.7	18.8	197.8	81.2
2002	295.2	21.2	49.3	16.7	245.9	83.3
2003	412.8	39.8	72.8	17.6	340.0	82.4
2004	561.3	36.0	117.3	20.9	444.0	79.1
2005	659.9	17.6	147.7	22.4	512.2	77.6

Source: Data from 1978 to 1984 are based on Ministry of Commerce: Import and Export Statistics; Data from 1985 to 2005 are based on State Bureau of Statistics: *China Statistical Yearbook 2006*.

China's GDP share increased from 1.86 to 5 per cent; while its export share increased from 0.72 to 7.34 per cent (see Table 7.4 and Figure 7.2). This fact demonstrates China's active participation in the economic globalisation, which means not only that its economy becomes more open to the world economy compared to its own past, but also the speed of its opening up to the rest of the world has been faster than most countries of the world. Measured by the total value of its international trade, China has become a trade power in the world. It is ranked both in the third place among the world leading exporters and the world leading importers of merchandise and services after Germany and the United States. If the intra EU trade is excluded, China is actually second only to the United States.[1]

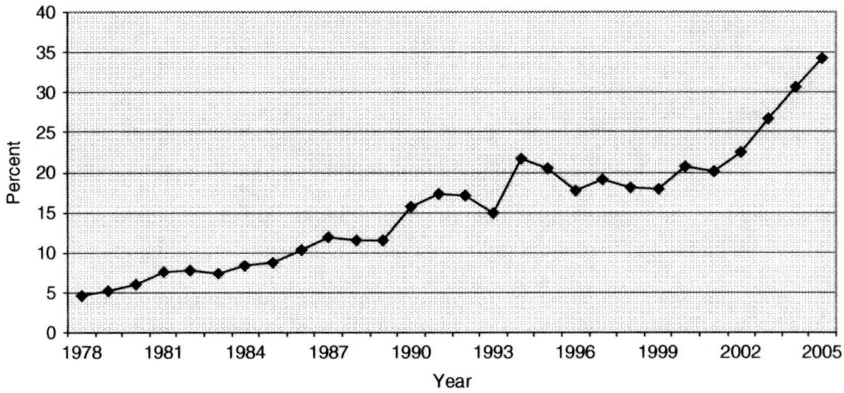

Figure 7.1 Ratio of exports to GDP (1978–2005).

China's international trade includes some clear features. Understanding those features is helpful to appreciate the directions of possible changes in its trade policies and resulting impacts on its main trade partners.

The first feature is a persistent and substantial size of the imbalance between exports and imports since the mid-1990s. Figure 7.3 shows the movement of China's trade balance during the period from 1978–2005. If we divide the whole period into two sub-periods, 1978–1993 and 1994–2005, two clearly different patterns in terms of trade balance in the two sub-periods can be seen. There was

Table 7.4 China's GDP and export shares in the world total (1978–2005)

Year	*GDP share*	*Export share*	*Year*	*GDP share*	*Export share*
1978	1.86	0.72	1992	1.75	1.95
1979	1.92	0.88	1993	1.77	2.19
1980	1.82	0.97	1994	2.07	2.65
1981	1.82	1.17	1995	2.42	2.75
1982	1.93	1.27	1996	2.76	2.69
1983	2.12	1.30	1997	3.05	3.13
1984	2.31	1.45	1998	3.24	3.16
1985	2.59	1.50	1999	3.27	3.26
1986	2.13	1.54	2000	3.47	3.73
1987	1.68	1.63	2001	3.81	4.11
1988	1.73	1.70	2002	3.97	4.82
1989	1.79	1.65	2003	4.20	5.65
1990	1.65	1.66	2004	4.66	6.51
1991	1.68	1.86	2005	5.00	7.34

Source: Calculated based on the data in World Development Indicators 2006 (World Bank, 2006).

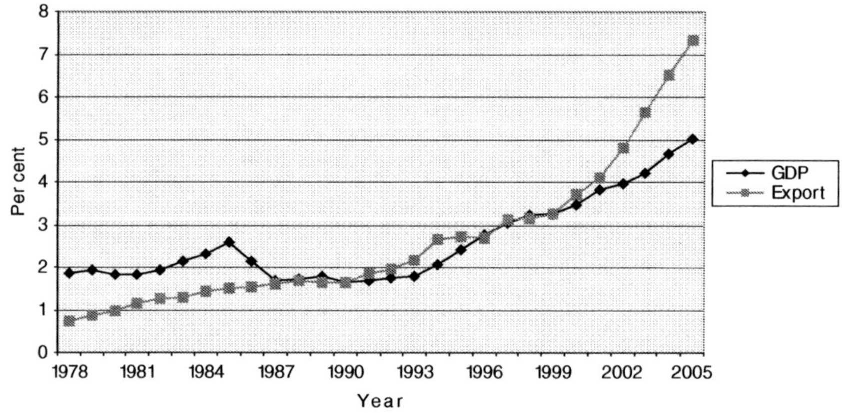

Figure 7.2 China's GDP and export shares in the world.

no obvious trade imbalance in the first sub-period. Balance of the current account had been fluctuating year by year, but it was balanced in general with a small amount of accumulated deficit over 16 years, which was only about 30 billion US$. However, the trade balance in the second sub-period demonstrated a very different pattern. It not only had trade surplus in every single year but also registered an upward trend in the size of the surplus. In 2005, China's total trade surplus reached 102 billion US$, accounting for about 13.4 per cent of its total export in the same year. The accumulated trade surplus in the second sub-section reached 384 billion US$. The trade surplus further increased by 74 per cent and reached 177.5 billion US$ in 2006.

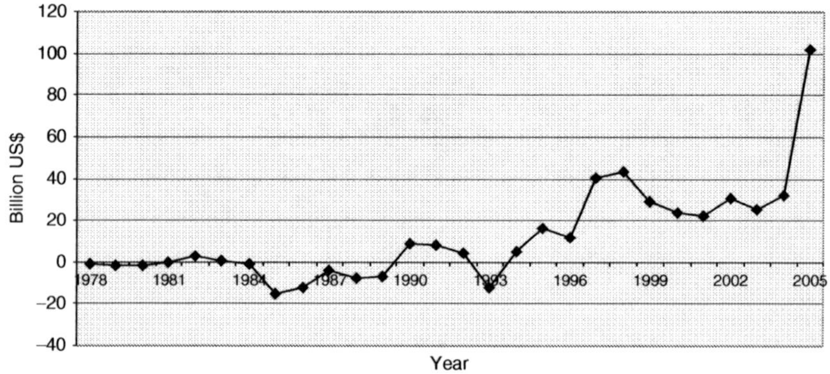

Figure 7.3 Balance of international trade (1978–2005).

The large size of the current account surplus has been, in addition to FDI and other forms of capital inflow, a main contributor to China's large foreign reserves. By the end of March 2007, already the world's largest, the country's foreign reserve exceeded 1200 billion US$. This number represents a 37.4 per cent increase on a year-on-year basis.

China's persistent and substantial size of trade surplus caused much tension between China and its main trade partners. Many countries regard it as a result of China's unfair trade policies and practice, such as various export subsidies, protective measures over the domestic markets, and the government intervention on RMB exchange rate. More and more WTO antidumping cases have been filed against China, and the pressures on RMB appreciation have also been consistently strong in recent years.

The second feature of China's international trade is a significant change in the structure of the traded goods, particularly a radical change in the structure of export products. Tables 7.2 and 7.3 detail the shares of primary goods and manufacturing goods in China's export and import respectively, which are based on 1-digit Standard International Trade Classification (SITC) code. The share of the manufacturing goods in total exports increased from 49.6 per cent in 1978 to 93.6 per cent in 2005; accordingly the share of the primary goods declined from 50.4 per cent to 6.4 per cent. During the same period, the share of manufacturing goods in total imports increased 63.2 per cent to 82.4 per cent and the share of the primary goods declined from 36.8 per cent to 17.6 per cent (see Figures 7.4 and 7.5).

These changes reflect the fact that the process of China's trade expansion has been a process of realising the comparative advantage in terms of the structure of factor endowment. China is a country with an abundant and cheap labour

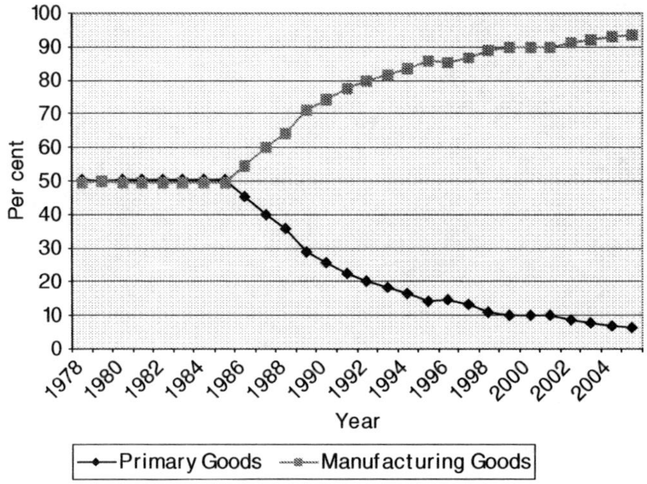

Figure 7.4 Changes in export structure.

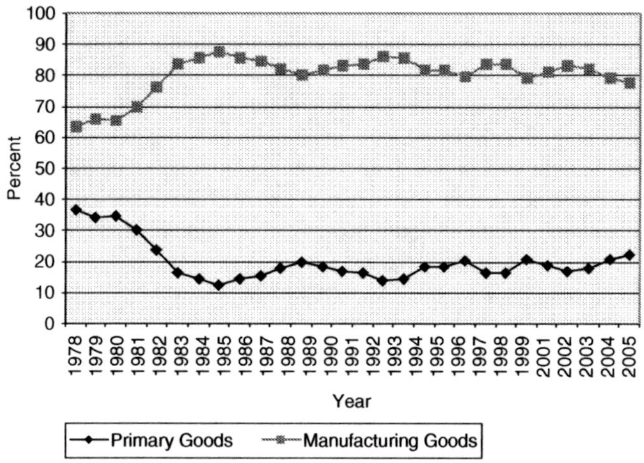

Figure 7.5 Changes in import structure.

supply but a shortage of natural resources (including mineral resources and land in per capita term). Giving full play to the comparative advantage by developing labour intensive export products has allowed China to maximise the benefit from the international trade. Due to this reason, the share of the processing goods in the total export has been kept very high. The share was approximately 52.7 per cent in 2005 (see Table 7.5).

Structural changes in export can be viewed even more clearly by investigating its export goods concentration. In 2005, China exported goods in 259 product groups among the total 260 product groups defined by the 3-digit SITC code. The value of the export goods in the top ten product groups amounted to 3053.0 billion US$, which accounted for 40.1 per cent of the total export in the same year. All of the ten product groups fall in the categories of 700s and 800s, which are mainly labour intensive industries or the labour intensive sector of capital/technology intensive industries (see Table 7.6). China's shares in the world

Table 7.5 Export by trading forms (2006)

Trade Form	*Value (US$ billion)*	*Share (%)*
Total value	969.07	100
Conventional trade	416.32	42.96
Processing trade	510.37	52.67
Processing trade with supplied material	94.48	9.75
Processing trade with imported material	415.89	42.92
Other trading forms	42.38	4.37

Source: Ministry of Commerce of PRC Comprehensive Department 2007.

Table 7.6 Top 10 export product group in SITC

SITC code	*Product group*	*Value US$ billion*	*Share in world %*	*Rank*
752	Automatic data-processing machines and units thereof; magnetic or optical readers, machines for transcribing data onto data media in coded form and machine	76.30	72.24	1
764	Telecommunications equipment, n.e.s., and parts, n.e.s., and accessories of apparatus falling within groups 761, 762 and 763	62.19	21.06	2
759	Parts and accessories (other than covers, carrying cases and the like) suitable for use solely or principally with machines falling within groups 751 and 7	29.70	19.97	3
845	Articles of apparel, of textile fabrics, whether or not knitted or crocheted, n.e.s.	23.50	27.84	4
894	894 – Baby carriages, toys, games and sporting goods	20.64	32.45	5
763	763 – Sound recorders or reproducers; television image and sound recorders or reproducers; prepared unrecorded media	20.43	32.96	6
776	776 – Thermionic, cold cathode or photo-cathode valves and tubes (e.g., vacuum or vapour or gas-filled valves and tubes, mercury arc rectifying valves and tubes)	20.41	25.15	7
851	851 – Footwear	19.05	30.91	8
778	778 – Electrical machinery and apparatus, n.e.s.	16.60	11.31	9
821	821 – Furniture and parts thereof; bedding, mattresses, mattress supports, cushions and similar stuffed furnishings	16.57	17.48	10

Source: International Trade Centre, 2006. *International Trade Statistics 2001–2005.*

total of those ten product groups are also noticeably high. The high degree of export products concentration reflects a high degree of specialisation of Chinese economy in the global economic system.

The third feature of China's international trade is a high concentration in export destinations and import origins. China's products exports to more than 190 countries and regions in the world. However, the share of export to the top five, top ten and top 15 largest markets in total exports were 57.6, 69.6 and 77 per cent, respectively. The share of imports from the top five, top ten and top 15 were 50.2, 62.7 and 71.4 per cent, respectively, in 2005 (see Tables 7.7 and 7.8).

Table 7.7 China's export country concentration (2005)

Country	*Value* *US$ billion*	*Share* *%*	*Rank*
United States	162.9	21.4	1
Hong Kong, China	124.5	16.3	2
Japan	84.0	11.0	3
Korea Rep.	35.1	4.6	4
Germany	32.5	4.3	5
The Netherlands	25.9	3.4	6
United Kingdom	19.0	2.5	7
Singapore	16.6	2.2	8
Taiwan, China	16.5	2.2	9
Russia	13.2	1.7	10
Italy	11.7	1.5	11
Canada	11.7	1.5	12
France	11.6	1.5	13
Australia	11.1	1.5	14
Malaysia	10.6	1.4	15
Top 5 countries	439.0	57.6	
Top 10 countries	530.2	69.6	
Top 15 countries	586.9	77	
Total	762.0		

Source: Calculated based on Table 18-8 Volume of Imports and Exports by Countries and Regions (Customs Statistics), in *Statistical Yearbook, 2007* (China State Bureau of Statistics, 2007).

Except for Malaysia, the 14 largest export markets are either G8 or EU countries or newly industrialised economies. There are a few more developing countries on the list of the 15 top largest import origins.

One of the immediate consequences of the export market concentration and import supply concentration is a concentration of trade surplus with a few export destination countries on one hand and a concentration of trade deficits with a few import origin countries. The three largest trade surplus sources in 2006 were the United States, Hong Kong and the Netherlands. Most of the surplus with Hong Kong is finally realised as extra surplus with the United States, because Hong Kong is mainly a transit port for Chinese export to the United States. China's total trade surplus with the top three reached 316 billion US$, about three times its total trade surplus. The three largest trade deficits sources in 2006 are Taiwan, Korea and Japan; the total trade deficits with the three regions were 175.5 billion US$.

For either the countries which provide big markets for China's export products or the countries for which China provides a big market, their economic relations with China become highly inter-dependent. The high concentration enables exporters to enjoy the economy of scale for their advantageous industries. On the other hand, it also produces a certain degree of vulnerability, because any changes in the market countries could cause significant shocks for the exporting countries thus affecting its domestic economic and political stability.

Table 7.8 China's import country concentration (2005)

Country	*Value US$ billion*	*Share %*	*Rank*
Japan	100.4	15.2	1
Korea Rep.	76.8	11.6	2
Taiwan, China	74.7	11.3	3
United States	48.6	7.4	4
Germany	30.7	4.7	5
Malaysia	20.1	3.0	6
Singapore	16.5	2.5	7
Australia	16.2	2.5	8
Russia	15.9	2.4	9
Thailand	14.0	2.1	10
Philippines	12.9	1.9	11
Saudi Arabia	12.2	1.9	12
Hong Kong, China	12.2	1.9	13
Brazil	10.0	1.5	14
India	9.8	1.5	15
Top 5 countries	331.2	50.2	
Top 10 countries	413.9	62.7	
Top 15 countries	471.0	71.4	
Total	660.0		

Source: Calculated based on Table 18-8 Volume of Imports and Exports by Countries and Regions (Customs Statistics), in *Statistical Yearbook, 2007* (China State Bureau of Statistics, 2007).

Main factors contributing to the expansion of China's trade power

The economic globalisation after the Second World War helped to rationalise economic activities across national boundaries through regional and global specialisation. It integrates nations into a more efficient system, which allows mobile resources to realise the comparative advantages in different locations. According to a research by the UNIDO (2002), there is clear evidence that some developing countries have enjoyed rapid and sustained export expansion, output growth, and employment increase by actively participating in globalisation.

On the other hand, some critics argue that developing countries will not necessarily benefit from globalisation because the main facilitator of globalisation in the new era is rapid innovation in information and communication technologies. As a result, cheap labour becomes less important than the previous epoch of globalisation (Bordo *et al.*, 1999). Lall (2002) also further explains why some developing countries cannot benefit from globalisation. His main argument is that an intense and rapid exposure to market forces can damage developing economies that suffer from market and institutional failures. This will affect their competitive response to global competitors and technologies thus preventing them from receiving the benefits from globalisation.

It is true that globalisation is only a necessary but not a sufficient condition for developing countries to expand their trade power and to develop their economies. In order to achieve these goals, they need to prepare themselves for a great exposure to strong international competitions. China could not take advantage of the economic globalisation until the late 1970s mainly due to its rigid planning economic system before the reform. However, since it started the opening-door policies in 1978, its economy has benefited greatly from the economic globalisation.

How has China taken advantage of the economic globalisation and grown up as a world trade power? There are at least three important factors to contribute to China's trade expansion in the past three decades.

China has been in a relative advantageous position in the latest round of the international labour division

China possessed three important advantageous conditions, which allowed it to gain huge benefits in the world economic restructuring:

1. vast and cheap labour supply has been a great attraction to foreign investment;
2. the pre-reform Stalin-Mao style planning economic system was extremely repressive and inhumane; however, it used state power to prepare China a basic industrial foundation which made it able to quickly play a role in world economic restructuring;
3. millions of overseas Chinese merchants the world over played a unique role in bridging China and rest of the world, which shortened the learning curve and lowered the cost for China to reach the international business standards.

China has a vast labour supply. In the event of the reform, among the 926.6 million population, 172.5 million lived in the urban area and 790.1 million in the rural area, which accounted for 17.9 and 82.1 per cent, respectively. There were at least 40 million and 250 million unemployed and surplus labour forces in the urban and rural areas, respectively. By the end of 2005, China's population increased to 1307.6 million, 562.1 million and 745.4 million in the urban and rural areas, which accounted for 43 and 57 percent, respectively (State Bureau of Statistics, 2006).

The absorption rate of the labour force has been approximately 1 million per percentage point of the GDP growth. Therefore, about 10 per cent average annual growth rate of GDP in the past 28 years brought about 280 million job opportunities, which is about 100 million less than the 381 million newly increased population during the same period. Even considering the factor of changes in longevity and age structure, China still has a similar size unemployment and surplus labour force as it had 30 years ago.

The vast pool of the surplus labour force has kept China's unskilled labour wage rate extremely low compared to those in both the developed countries and even those developing countries which are at a similar development level to China. Table 7.9 shows that the minimum wage rate of China in 2005 was not only lower than all of the developed countries and newly industrialised countries but also lower than those of India, Thailand, the Philippines and Mexico. This makes China an attractive destination for re-allocation of the labour-intensive manufacturing industries from the developed countries.

Of course, the wage rates of unskilled labour in many other developing countries, especially those in Africa, might be even lower than those of China. However, compared to those countries, China has a relatively ready foundation both in terms of industrial infrastructure and quality of labour force to absorb the transferred manufacturing industries.

From 1949–1978, China adopted a planning economic system. An important aspect of this system is to realise industrialisation by economic exploitation of the agricultural sector. Accordingly, there were also repressive political and social policies to serve this economic development strategy. The state forced farmers to sell their agricultural products to the state at a very low price level in order to accumulate the capital for the industrialisation. These policies kept the farmers' income just at or even lower than the subsistence level. At the same time, rural residents were forbidden to move to urban areas. The unfair economic policies and repressive political policies brought tremendous suffering to most Chinese people, especially the rural residents. It was these policies that caused the Great Famine in the early 1960s, which claimed the lives of more than 30 million people.

Table 7.9 Minimum wage comparison in selected countries

Country	*Lowest*	*Highest*	*%*	*Year*
China	0.19	0.48	1.00	2005
United States		5.15	10.73	2005
Hong Kong, China				
Japan				
Korea Rep.		2.71	5.65	2004
Germany		9.70	5.65	2004
The Netherlands		8.95	18.65	2004
United Kingdom		9.19	19.15	2005
Singapore				
Taiwan, China				
Russia				2006
Italy		7.04	14.67	2005
Canada	7.25	8.52	17.75	2005
France		9.96	20.75	2004
Australia				
Malaysia	0.23	0.38	0.79	2004
Mexico	0.53	0.56	1.17	2004
Thailand	0.44	0.57	1.19	2005
Philippines	0.40	0.78	1.63	2005
India	0.11	0.58	1.21	2005

Source: Calculated by the author based on ILO database 2007.

However, those inhumane policies at the same time effectively fostered a foundation of Chinese modern industry; they also provided a small portion of urban residents with some exclusive benefits in education, health care, pensions and other social welfare for the needs of modern industry. Although the share of industry in the national economy and educated urban residents in the total population were relatively small, given the giant size of the whole economy and population of the country, its industry and educated population are sizable in terms of the absolute amount. When China started to embrace economic globalisation in the 1980s, it already had a comprehensive industrial basis that produced a broad range of industrial products from aircraft to daily manufacturing goods. In 1985, the new student enrolments in universities, secondary technical schools and regular senior secondary schools were 619,000, 668,000 and 2.75 million respectively (Department of Comprehensive Statistics of National Bureau of Statistics, 1999). Adding those numbers together, there were approximately 4 million new enrolments in senior high schools and universities in total in a single year. All these prepared China with a basic industrial infrastructure and human capital for the international labour division, especially for the foreign investment and technological transfer.

A large population of overseas Chinese and their investment has been another significant favourable condition in helping China with attracting foreign investment and expanding the export power, especially in the first stage of China's reform period when many multinational corporations were hesitant to enter China due to the different political and legal systems and cultural environment.

There are about 60 million Chinese people living overseas. Among them more than half live in developed or newly industrialised countries or regions, including 2.9 million in North America, 1.6 million in Europe, 7 million in Hong Kong, 2.3 million in Singapore, and 23 million in Taiwan. Others are mainly concentrated in Southeast Asia. The overseas Chinese control a large amount of wealth. The estimate by the Overseas Chinese Committee of the Taiwan (ROC) of the floating assets of the overseas Chinese in the late 1990s is US$ 1.5 trillion and US$ 2 trillion by the Centre for Overseas Chinese Studies at Ohio State University (Peng, 2000).

The investment by the overseas Chinese has accounted for a significant share of total foreign investment in China. From 1978–2005, there were 510,000 foreign invested firms with a realised investment of US$ 570 billion, of which the number of firms and amount of capital invested by the overseas Chinese accounted for 70 and 60 per cent, respectively. Most of the products produced by those firms are for export (Li, 2006).

China's market-oriented economic reform, especially with regards to the foreign trade, helped to accelerate the formation of its trade power

The market-oriented reform in China since 1978 significantly improved the efficiency of the Chinese economy, especially the competitiveness of Chinese enterprises. This is a fundamental reason for the impressive expansion of China's international trade. Some special effective reform measures in the management and operation system of international trade further facilitated the rapid growth of the trade.

Among the general economic reform measures, ownership reform and price liberalisation played key roles in promoting economic efficiency. Allowing non-public sectors to grow and become the main part of the national economy provides the producers the motivation to improve micro economic efficiency and to make Chinese producers more competitive both in the domestic and international markets; liberalising the price control over most of the commodities makes a better allocation of resources and improves the macro economic efficiency.

China's fast growing non-public sector consists of foreign invested enterprises, self-employed individual industrial and commercial households and private enterprises. By the end of 2005, there were approximately 552,942 foreign invested enterprises (State Bureau of Statistics, 2006). By the end of September 2005, there were approximately 24.7 million registered self-employed individual and household businesses and 4.2 million private enterprises (World Trade Organization China Trade Policy Review Body, 2006).

As to the price liberalisation, by the end of the 1990s, 85 per cent of commodity transactions were realised through the market; more than 90 per cent of social retail consumer goods prices and around 80 per cent of production means and agricultural products prices were decided by the market without state intervention (Zhang, 1998).

Those market oriented reform measures have improved China's industrial productivity thus strengthening international competitiveness. According to a recent study by the author, the total factor productivity in all 37 main industrial sectors showed significant improvement during the period 1991–2002 (see Table 7.10). China's labour productivity in the industrial sector during the period 1988–1999 were also much higher than its neighbouring countries which are either China's important trade partners or export competitors (see Table 7.11) (Zhang, 2005).

In addition to the overall economic reform, China's reform on foreign trade also helped to strengthen China's international competitiveness and promoted China's trade power. Included among the main reform measures are decentralisation of trading rights, reduction of the scope of trade planning, depreciation of Chinese currency against the main world currencies, and reduction of import tariff.

Before the reform, there were only 12 monopolistic state-owned trade corporations that held the right of conducing international trade. This number increased to 1,200 trade companies by the end of 1986. By the end of 1994, there were 8,000 Chinese companies having trade rights, among which 30 per cent are manufacturers; there were also 174,000 foreign invested companies allowed to conduct export and import for their own materials and products. Now all legal persons in China have trade rights.

The plan of export and import has been decentralised. More than 97 per cent of exports and more than 90 per cent of imports were planned by the state before the reform. By 1986, they were reduced to 60 per cent of export and 40 per cent of import subject to the mandatory plan, and 20 per cent of export value and 30 per cent of import subject to the guidance plan. These numbers were further

Table 7.10 TFP Growth in industrial sectors (%)

	1992	*1993*	*1994*	*1995*	*1996*	*1997*	*1998*	*1999*	*2000*	*2001*	*2002*
Coal Mining and Dressing	16.99	40.06	−5.05	−1.62	21.03	6.94	6.56	10.98	6.02	5.83	4.26
Petroleum and Natural Gas	6.88	17.76	−2.66	−0.84	10.73	3.87	3.77	6.47	3.7	3.66	2.73
Ferrous Metals Mining	20.61	47.14	−5.65	−1.83	23.76	7.66	7.2	11.97	6.51	6.27	4.57
Nonferrous Metals Mining	16.55	39.16	−4.97	−1.6	20.67	6.84	6.47	10.84	5.95	5.76	4.22
Nonmetal Minerals Mining	12.73	31.15	−4.19	−1.34	17.26	5.88	5.61	9.48	5.27	5.13	3.78
Logging and Transport	34.99	71.49	−7.36	−2.43	31.68	9.6	8.86	14.51	7.71	7.35	5.3
Food Processing	8.19	20.87	−3.05	−0.96	12.35	4.39	4.25	7.27	4.13	4.06	3.02
Food Manufacturing	11.05	27.44	−3.8	−1.21	15.56	5.38	5.16	8.75	4.9	4.79	3.54
Beverage Manufacturing	9.13	23.09	−3.31	−1.05	13.47	4.74	4.57	7.8	4.4	4.33	3.21
Tobacco Processing	5.33	13.95	−2.16	−0.67	8.65	3.18	3.12	5.39	3.11	3.1	2.33
Textile Industry	9.31	23.49	−3.36	−1.06	13.66	4.8	4.63	7.89	4.45	4.37	3.24
Garments	8.4	21.38	−3.11	−0.98	12.61	4.47	4.33	7.39	4.19	4.13	3.07
Leather, Furs, Down	9.1	23	−3.3	−1.04	13.42	4.72	4.56	7.78	4.39	4.32	3.2
Timber Processing	14.81	35.58	−4.63	−1.48	19.19	6.43	6.1	10.26	5.66	5.5	4.04
Furniture Manufacturing	12.38	30.39	−4.11	−1.31	16.92	5.78	5.52	9.33	5.19	5.07	3.73
Papermaking Products	12.17	29.92	−4.06	−1.29	16.7	5.71	5.46	9.24	5.15	5.02	3.7
Printing	13.87	33.6	−4.44	−1.42	18.34	6.19	5.89	9.92	5.49	5.34	3.93
Cultural, Educational	9.77	24.54	−3.48	−1.1	14.18	4.96	4.77	8.13	4.57	4.49	3.33
Petroleum Processing	7.95	20.31	−2.98	−0.94	12.06	4.3	4.17	7.13	4.05	4	2.98
Raw Chemical Materials	9.76	24.52	−3.47	−1.1	14.17	4.95	4.77	8.12	4.57	4.49	3.33

Table 7.10 TFP Growth in industrial sectors (%)—cont'd

	1992	*1993*	*1994*	*1995*	*1996*	*1997*	*1998*	*1999*	*2000*	*2001*	*2002*
Medical	9.5	23.94	−3.41	−1.08	13.88	4.87	4.69	7.99	4.5	4.42	3.28
Chemical Fibres	10.39	25.97	−3.64	−1.15	14.87	5.17	4.97	8.44	4.74	4.64	3.43
Rubber Products	11.59	28.65	−3.93	−1.25	16.12	5.54	5.31	8.99	5.02	4.91	3.62
Plastic Products	9.23	23.32	−3.34	−1.05	13.58	4.77	4.61	7.85	4.43	4.35	3.23
Nonmetal Mineral Products	9.21	23.26	−3.33	−1.05	13.55	4.76	4.6	7.84	4.42	4.35	3.23
Pressing of Ferrous Metals	8.8	22.31	−3.22	−1.02	13.08	4.62	4.46	7.62	4.31	4.24	3.15
Pressing of Nonferrous Metals	10.61	26.47	−3.69	−1.17	15.1	5.24	5.03	8.54	4.79	4.69	3.47
Metal Products	8.74	22.17	−3.2	−1.01	13.01	4.6	4.44	7.59	4.29	4.22	3.14
Ordinary Machinery	10.12	25.35	−3.57	−1.13	14.57	5.08	4.88	8.31	4.67	4.58	3.39
Special Purpose Equipment	10.94	27.2	−3.77	−1.2	15.45	5.34	5.13	8.7	4.87	4.77	3.52
Transport Equipment	9.11	23.02	−3.3	−1.04	13.43	4.73	4.56	7.78	4.39	4.32	3.21
Electric Equipment	7.87	20.13	−2.96	−0.93	11.97	4.27	4.14	7.09	4.03	3.97	2.96
Electronic	7.99	20.41	−2.99	−0.94	12.12	4.31	4.18	7.16	4.07	4.01	2.98
Instruments, Meters, Cultural	12.38	30.38	−4.11	−1.31	16.91	5.77	5.52	9.33	5.19	5.07	3.73
Electric Power	8.58	21.79	−3.16	−1	12.82	4.53	4.39	7.49	4.24	4.18	3.1
Production and Supply of Gas	−19.72	−67.76	37.09	8.26	−97.29	NA	108.68	92.89	29.31	23.26	14.61
Tap Water	25.49	56.03	−6.34	−2.07	26.89	8.46	7.88	13.04	7.02	6.73	4.88

Source: Calculated by the author (Zhang 2005).

Table 7.11 Labour productivity in industry in selected countries (1995 US$)

Year	*China*	*HK*	*Japan*	*Korea*	*Malaysia*	*Singapore*	*Thailand*
1988	2,886	25,190	89,144	25,386	18,008		2,608
1989	2,924	26,032	92,163	25,550	17,486		2,959
1990	3,318	26,189	96,627	26,945	17,595		2,853
1991	3,046	26,299	96,815	28,506	16,854		2,650
1992	3,530	26,513	92,906	29,066	15,818		2,436
1993	4,030	27,279	89,175	31,129	15,710		2,422
1994	4,257	26,784	86,162	32,417	15,490		2,289
1995	4,530	27,540	86,058	34,207	18,467	48,799	2,211
1996	4,938	28,266	88,119	35,660	20,064	50,673	2,025
1997	5,385	28,196	89,142	38,113	20,256	59,229	1,966
1998	5,282	28,861	87,854	39,693	18,476	60,842	1,920
1999		30,629	87,589	43,201	20,577	61,768	2,010
Annual %	6.72	1.51	–0.16	4.97	0.29		–3.4

Source: Calculated by the authors based on data in *World Development Indicators 2003*.

reduced to about 15 per cent of exports and 18.5 per cent of imports subject to mandatory planning in 1992.

Reform on trade rights and trade planning systems has allowed more Chinese trade firms and manufacturers to be directly exposed to the international market, providing them with further information on market competition, management and technologies, thus further strengthening their competitiveness.

The depreciation of Chinese currency has been another important measure in promoting China's export. The continuous depreciation of RMB from 1985–1994 and a huge depreciation in 1994 made Chinese goods more competitive in terms of prices, which therefore promoted the expansion of the export of Chinese goods. Figure 7.5 shows the trend of depreciation of RMB against the US dollar

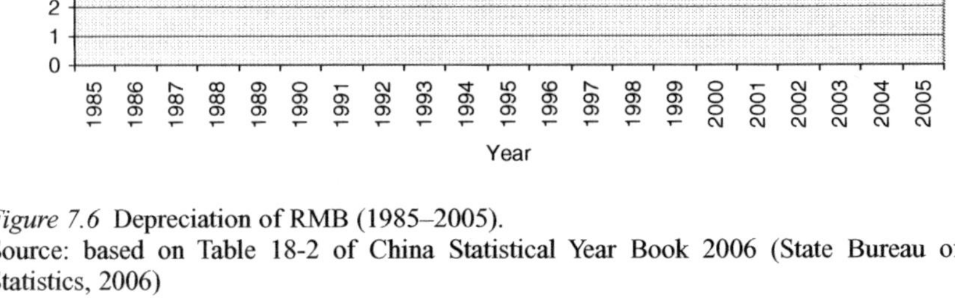

Figure 7.6 Depreciation of RMB (1985–2005).
Source: based on Table 18-2 of China Statistical Year Book 2006 (State Bureau of Statistics, 2006)

during the period 1985–2005. Before 1994, China's exports increased gradually along with the gradual depreciation of its currency. However, the Chinese government depreciated RMB against the US dollar by 50 per cent in 1994; that is the year when China started to have a continuous huge amount of trade surplus.

The reduction of import tariffs has also had positive impacts on China's trade expansion. This measure has had two-fold impacts. The reduction of import tariffs usually resulted from international negotiations, which helped China's export goods to gain better access to other countries' markets. Moreover, for its exports China needs to import huge amounts of raw materials, equipments, components and parts, as well as technologies. The reduction of tariffs allowed the export producers, especially those in the processing industries, to lower the cost of production thus becoming more competitive in the international markets.

The state implemented a series of preferential policies of attracting foreign direct investment to foster China's trade power

The growth of China's trade power has been largely promoted by foreign-invested enterprises. According to the statistics of Chinese custom, the foreign-invested enterprises produced 58.19 per cent of China's total export goods in 2006 (see Table 7.12). Actually this share only reflects the direct contributions of the foreign-invested firms to China's exports. There are also some indirect contributions through the close links between the foreign investment and Chinese indigenous firms.

Utilising the foreign investment to increase China's exports, increase employment and promote the domestic economic reform has been one of most important and consistent goals of China's economic reform. With constant efforts, China has been the largest recipient of foreign investment among all developing nations since the early 1990s (Fung, 2007), and it also became the world's third largest foreign direct investment recipient (UNCTAD, 2006). The accumulated foreign direct investment in China reached 662.4 billion US dollars during the period 1979–2005 (see Table 7.13).

A series of preferential policies to the foreign investment by the government has been an important driving force behind the surge of foreign direct investment

Table 7.12 Export by enterprise types (2006)

Type of Enterprises	*Value*	*Increase ±%*	*Share*
Total Value	969.07	27.2	100
State-Owned Enterprises	191.34	13.4	19.74
Foreign-Funded Enterprises	563.89	26.9	58.19
Other Enterprises	213.9	43.6	22.07
Collective Enterprises	41.09	12.5	4.24
Private Enterprises	170.74	52.1	17.62

Source: Ministry of Commerce of PRC Comprehensive Department 2007.

Table 7.13 Total FDI in China (1979–2005)

Year	*US$ (million)*
1979–1984	4,104
1985	1,956
1989	3,393
1990	3,487
1995	37,521
1996	41,726
1997	45,257
1998	45,463
1999	40,319
2000	40,715
2001	46,878
2002	52,743
2003	53,505
2004	60,630
2005	60,325
1979–2005	622,429

Source: State Bureau of Statistics, 2006.

and their contributions to China's export. Those policies cover financial support, land provision, market protection, taxation incentives and other industrial and trade polices. Creating various forms of special economic zones (SEZs)[2] is a demonstrative example of how Chinese central and local governments used state's power to attract foreign investment and promote the export.

In July 1979, the central government approved four SEZs in southern China. They are Shenzhen, Zhuhai and Shantou in Guangdong Province, and Huli (expanded to the whole island of Xiamen in 1984) in Fujian Province.[3] In 1984, encouraged by the initial success of the four SEZs, the central government decided to create 14 ETDZs. By the end of 2006, there were five SEZs and 1568 ETDZs; the planning area was 9949 square kilometres (Zhu, 2007). Among them, 222 were approved directly by the State Council.

The main preferential policies to encourage foreign investment in those zones are various forms of financial incentives. The income tax rate of foreign-invested enterprises located in the ETDZs was 15 per cent in the ETDZs, while it was 24 per cent in provinces of Guangdong and Fujian, and 30 per cent in the rest of the country. For the foreign-invested enterprises with an over-ten-year-term of operation, starting from the first year of profit making, their income tax for the first two years would be exempted and then for the next three years was only 7.5 per cent. If the foreign partner of a foreign-invested enterprise directly re-invested its profit into business in the ETDZs with an over-five-year term of operation, it could apply for a refund of 40 per cent of the paid income tax. If the foreign investor use its profit to set up or expand a export-oriented or technologically-advanced enterprise with an over-five-year term of operation, the income tax already paid shall be fully refunded.

In addition to those preferential policies given by the central government, many provincial and local governments also provide financial and other support for the foreign-invested firms located in these zones. Their support includes selling land to the investors at a price much lower than the market price, offering full rebates of local tax, and providing special treatments in services including electric power, water, telecommunication and others. There are also other preferential treatments provided by the state-controlled financial sector, such as loans with a lower interest rate.

With those special supports by the central government and local governments, foreign investment has flourished in the special economic zones. There is a lack of overall and comprehensive data on all of the different forms of special economic zones in the country. However, looking at the data of 54 national level ETDZs (thereinafter NETDZs),[4] the development of such foreign-invested zones and their contribution to the national economic growth, especially to the expansion of export are very impressive.

Table 7.14 shows that the GDP share of the 54 NETDZs in national total has reached 4.49 per cent in 2005, their GDP growth rate was 24.14 per cent which is 14.2 percentage points higher than the national level. The contribution of the NETDZs to the net growth of the GDP was 9.7 per cent.

The economic structure in the NETDZs shows a clear international orientation of the NETDZs economies thus reflecting the significant contribution of such zones to the trade expansion of China. The growth rates of the exports and imports were about 36 and 29 per cent, respectively, in 2005, and the shares of the NETDZs' international trade and foreign direct investment in that national total were three to four times that of their GDP share in the national total. Their contribution rates to the growth of the national export and FDI were also very high (Zhang, 2007).

The expansion of China's trade power is an interactive process of all the above-mentioned factors. There are some favourable conditions for China to join the international economic restructuring and labour division, the economic reform measures which aimed at promoting productivities of China's industries and strengthening their international competitiveness, and the state policies to

Table 7.14 Economic indicators of 54 NETDZs (2005)

	GDP RMB billion	*IVA RMB billion*	*Tax Rev. RMB billion*	*Export US$ billion*	*Import US$ billion*	*FDI US$ billion*
54 ETDZs	819.5	598.1	121.9	225.2	111.4	13.0
Growth (%)	24.14	23.18	30.68	35.51	29.72	–4.30
National	18,232.1	7,619.0	3,086.6	762.0	660.1	60.3
National (%)	9.90	16.40	20.00	28.40	17.60	–0.50
Share of 54 ETDZs	4.49	7.85	3.95	15.84	16.88	21.60
Contribution (%)	9.70	10.49	5.56	22.04	25.84	

Source: Department of Foreign Investment Management in Ministry of Commerce: NETDZ Development Report 2006.

promote the foreign investment and export. This analysis can partly explain why some other developing countries cannot achieve what China has achieved in the expansion of the trade; it also implies some inherent weakness of China's international trade development and the difficulties that China is facing.

Constraints and challenges to the further expansion of China's trade power

China has enjoyed rapid trade expansion over almost three decades; it has also successfully made foreign investment and resulting export-oriented industries a powerful engine for its fast economic growth. Can China continue this pattern of growth? If it could, what would be the cost it has to pay and how long is it going to last for?

There are still some positive factors for the continuous growth of China's trade and national economy. As mentioned, a large amount of labour surplus will exist for a long period, therefore China will continue to take advantage of relatively lower labour costs compared to both developed and some developing countries. Accumulated national wealth and improved economic efficiency over the past three decades will provide China with a good foundation for further development. The large size of the national economy will allow the countries to take advantage of positive externality of technological spill-over and industrial innovation. Plus well established manufacturing capacity and international market experience will provide China with self-enhanced international competitiveness in the field.

However, there are some serious constraints and challenges which China will have to face in its further efforts to expand export and to sustain economic growth in near future. Among those most important and urgent challenges, there are at least three factors which China cannot afford to ignore.

The first challenge is environmental degradation

As one of the world's main exporters of manufacturing goods, China has paid a very high cost of environmental degradation. China's main export-oriented industries (in particular textiles, chemistry, metallurgy and electronic components) are water or energy consuming and environment polluting by nature. Furthermore, the ruthless pursuit of minimum costs by the export-oriented producers and corruption of government officials made it extremely difficult for any serious environment protection efforts. As a result, the water and air pollution in China have reached an intolerant hazardous level.

According to recent research by the OECD (2007), one-third of the length of all China's rivers, 75 per cent of its major lakes and 25 per cent of all its coastal waters have been already highly polluted. Three hundred million people have no access to clean water; 190 million are suffering from water-related illnesses each year; and 30,000 children die from diarrhoea due to polluted water each year.

The air pollution has led to a high rate of lung diseases, including cancer, respiratory system problems and, therefore, high levels of work and school absenteeism

(World Bank, 2007). If it is not controlled, there will be 600,000 premature deaths in urban areas and 20 million cases of respiratory illnesses a year within 15 years (OECD, 2007).

The latest joint research by the World Bank and Chinese government estimates that the total cost of air and water pollution is as high as 100 billion US dollars, which is equivalent to about 5.8 per cent of the country's GDP (World Bank, 2007). An estimate by China's State Environmental Protection Agency is 200 billion US dollars, which is about 10 per cent of the country's GDP (*China Daily*, 2006). To the huge cost of environmental degradation, the export is a significant contributor. According to a former chief economist of Morgan Stanley Asia, 20–30 per cent of China's water pollution results from the manufacturing of goods that are exported (Spence, 2007).

Without any doubt, any efforts to protect the environment will inevitably increase the cost of the production thus increasing the cost of China's export goods at least in the short and medium term. Of course, due to the government control over the information flow and the repressive nature of the regime, China might continue to give priority to the trade expansion and income generation over the environment protection. However, along with the accumulation of the pollution cost, this growth pattern will be unsustainable in the long term. The increasing damage of public health will put huge pressures on the medical treatment and cause social discontent. At the same time, low environmental standards will also make people wary of buying Chinese goods, and the trademark 'made in China' a bad reputation. All of these will damage China's trade development.

The second challenge is intertwined internal and external imbalances of Chinese economy

China has successfully used expansion of international trade as a powerful engine to drive the national economic growth and increased employment. Direct trade-related jobs were approximately 80 million in 2005. The indirect impacts of international trade on the Chinese economy were actually much bigger than what this number represents (Yang, 2005).

As described in the first part of this chapter, China's external economic imbalance, demonstrated by its persistent and substantial trade surplus, has caused much tension between China and its main economic partners. China will not be able to simply run an ever-growing surplus and continue expanding its trade share in the world total.

This external imbalance has been tangled with China's internal structural problems (Woo, 2005) which are mainly low consumption rate and high investment rate. The increasing income disparity and lack of a social security network has depressed aggregate consumption propensity, thus impairing overall domestic demand. At the same time, the inefficient banking system, lower environment standard and immature capital market have also made the cost of capital too low, thus providing distorted investment incentives. As a result, there appears to be an over-capacity of production.

Owing to the very nature of China's gradualism reform, it has avoided tackling many fundamental economic structural problems. This strategy has even made the national economy very dependent on the export expansion. Now it is time for China to face both external and internal pressures simultaneously. To narrow down the income disparities amongst the rich and the poor and across the regions, to establish some basic social security network for the poor people, to increase domestic consumption demand will increase China's labour costs to a more reasonable level and channel more resources to domestic demands. This internal adjustment combined with the responsible reactions to the international pressures, including appreciation of RMB and other measures will inevitably slow down the expansion of the international trade.

The third challenge is to realise its commitment to the WTO

As analysed in section two, the Chinese government has used special investment incentives to attract foreign investment in promoting the export. However, there is an apparent contradiction between this practice and China's WTO obligations. Among all the agreements China committed itself to when it was admitted into the WTO, two agreements are particularly relevant to this practice: one is the Agreement on Subsidies and Countervailing Measures (SCM), and the other is Trade Related Investment Measures (TRIMS) Agreement.

According to the SCM Agreement, if the three elements are satisfied at the same time, any of the investment incentives provided by the government should be regarded as a subsidy. The three elements are:

1. a financial contribution by a government or any public bodies
2. a benefit is conferred, and
3. a subsidy specific to an enterprise, industry or group of enterprises or industries.

The SCM Agreement also specifies definition of financial contributions. It states that any one of the following actions means financial contribution:

1. a direct transfer of funds such as grants, loans and equity infusion, and potential direct transfers of funds or liabilities such as loan guarantees
2. if revenue otherwise due to government is foregone or not collected, i.e. fiscal incentives such as tax credit
3. if the government provides goods or services other than general infrastructure, or purchase goods, and
4. if the government carries out one of the above functions through a private body which would normally be vested in the government.

All subsidies under the SCM Agreement are categorised into two types of subsidies: prohibited subsidies and actionable subsidies. Export subsidy is one of two types of prohibited subsidies.

According to the definitions given by the SCM Agreement, many of the existing preferential treatments for the foreign-invested enterprises in various forms of special economic zones should be deemed as subsidies. For example, the Chinese government provides several forms of incentives such as lower enterprise income tax rate, the exemption of income tax for a certain period, a further reduction of income tax for export-oriented enterprises, the provision of basic services at a price lower than market prices, and so on.

Being aware of the inconsistency between its preferential polices to promote export and its commitments to the WTO, the Chinese government has been gradually changing some policies. The national congress passed a new enterprise income tax law in March 2007, which unifies the income tax between domestic firms and foreign-invested firms. That is a significant step towards eliminating the de factor subsidies to the exports by the foreign-invested firms.[5] Under the international pressures, China will move forward to reducing, and eventually eliminating, the pro-export subsidies and preferential treatment. This will also be a factor to slow down foreign investment inflow and China's expansion of export.

Concluding remarks

China's international trade has witnessed rapid growth and radical structural changes in the past three decades. There appear to be some important characteristics in this trade expansion, including a serious imbalance between its exports and imports since 1994, the radical structural shift from primary-goods intensive to manufacturing-goods intensive trade, and the very high market concentration of both exports and imports. Those features demonstrated China's achievement in realising its comparative advantages, on the other hand, some developments, in particular imbalanced trade structure and high market concentration, have also caused tensions between China and its main trade partners.

The rising of China's trade power is the result of interactions among some important factors. Among those factors, China's relative advantageous position in participating in international labour division and economic restructuring provided China with a favourable pre-condition; various measures of economic reform also play significant roles in promoting its productivity and thus international competitiveness; state policies are also an important driving force for the surge of foreign investment inflow and promote the rapid increase of international trade.

The further expansion of China's international trade is facing some serious constraints and challenges. Most important constraints will come from the environmental degradation, the intertwined relation between the internal imbalance and external imbalance, and the new challenges due to China's WTO obligation. All those factors will put pressure on China to increase investment in environment protection and social welfare, therefore inevitably increasing the cost of production and exports. The stoppage of state subsidies to foreign-invested export-oriented firms will also slow down the speed of expanding China's trade share in the world.

Notes

1 Based on Tables 1.5, 1.6, 1.7 and 1.8 in *International Trade Statistics 2006* (World Trade Organisation, 2006).

2 There are many different forms of the SEZs in China. Most of these zones can be divided into two main categories: one is 'Jingji Tequ' (SEZ); the other is 'Jingji Jishu Kaifaqu' (Economic and Technological Development Zones, EEDZ). The other forms of the special zones include Gaoxin Jishu Kaifaqu (High and New Technology Development Zones, HTDZs), Baoshuiqu (Free Tariff/Trade Zones, FTZs), Chukou Jiagongqu (Export Processing Zones, EPZs), and Bianjing Jingji Hezuoqu (Bordered Economic Cooperative Zones, BECZs).

3 The central government approved the fifth special economic zone, Hainan special economic zone in April 1988.

4 In China's official document, 54 ETDZs include 49 ETDZs and another five EDZs which enjoy the same preferential policies with the 49 state level ETDZs, they are Suzhou Industrial Park, Hainan Yangpu ETDZ, Shanghai Jinqiao Export Processing Zone, Ningbo Daxie ETDZ and Xiamen Haicang Investment Zone (Department of Foreign Investment Management in Ministry of Commerce, 2006). The economic size of the 54 NETDZs is estimated to account for about 73 per cent of all EDZs and about 86 per cent of all 222 national level EDZs.

5 However, some export promotion policies are still intact. China is going to give some new preferential policies to Tianjin New Coastal Area while keeping many preferential policies for Shanghai Pudong Area.

References

Bordo, M. D., Eichengreen, B. and Irwin, D.A. (1999) 'Is Globalisation Today Really Different from Globalisation a Hundred Years Ago?', *NBER Working Paper 7195*.

China Daily (2006) 'Pollution costs equal 10% of China's GDP', 6th June 2006, Beijing.

Department of Comprehensive Statistics of National Bureau of Statistics (1999) *Comprehensive Statistical Data and Materials on 50 Years of New China*. Beijing: China Statistics Press.

Fung, K. C., Iizaka, H. and Tong, S. (2002) 'Foreign Direct Investment in China: Policy, Trend and Impact', Paper prepared for an International Conference on China's Economy in the 21st Century, Hong Kong.

International Trade Centre (2006) International Trade Statistics 2001–2005.

Lall, S. (2002) 'The Employment Impact of Globalisation in Developing Countries', *QEH Working Paper Series – QEHWPS93*. Oxford.

Li, H. (2006) 'CAFTA fazhan yu huashang zuoyong yanjiu,' (Research on the Development of CAFTA and the Roles of Overseas Chinese Merchants) on the website of Overseas Chinese Affairs Office under the State Council, accessed as of 17 July 2007. Available at: http://www.gqb.gov.cn/news/2006/0207/1/1856.shtml

Ma, K. (2007) *China's Economic Development and Challenges*, A Speech to Economic Situation Conference in Beijing, Xinhua News Agency, May 4, Beijing.

Madani, D. (1999) 'A Review of the Role and Impact of Export Processing Zones,' *World Bank Policy Research Working Paper*, No. 2238. Washington D.C.: World Bank.

Ministry of Commerce of PRC Comprehensive Department, 2007, Statistics of Commerce, on the website of Ministry of Commerce of PRC, accessed as of 17 August 2007. Available at: http://zhs.mofcom.gov.cn/aarticle/Nocategory/200702/20070204344012.html

OECD (2007) Environmental Performance Review of China.

Peng, D. (2000) 'Ethnic Chinese Business Networks and the Asia-Pacific Economic Integration,' *African and Asian Studies*, Vol. 35, pp. 229–50, Brill Academic Publishers.

Spencer, J. (2007) 'China Pays Steep Price As Textile Exports Boom,' in *Wall Street Journal*, 22 August 2007; p. A1.

State Bureau of Statistics (2006) *Statistical Yearbook, 2006, China 18-8 Volume of Imports and Exports by Countries and Regions(Customs Statistics)*. Beijing: China Statistics Press.

State Commission of Science and Technology (1991) 'Gaoxin Jishu Chanpin Mulu (High-Tech Products Catalogue)', Beijing.

United Nations (1986) *Standard International Trade Classification Revision 3, Statistical Papers*, Series M, No. 34/Rev.3, New York: United Nations Publication.

United Nations Statistics Division Economic Statistics (2006) National Accounts Main Aggregates Database. Available at http://unstats.un.org/unsd/snaama/introduction.asp

Wang, G. (2004) 'Zhongguo Wuda Jingji Tqu Kechixu Fazhan Zhanlue Yanjiu (Research on Sustainable Development of China's Five Special Economic Zones)', Beijing: Jingjiguanli Chubanshe.

Woo, W. T. (2005) 'The Structural Nature of Internal and External Imbalances in China', *Journal of Chinese Economic and Business Studies*, Volume 4, Issue 1, pp. 1–19.

UNIDO (2002) *Industrial Development Report 2002/2003*, Vienna: UNIDO.

UNCTAD (2002a) *The Least Developed Countries Report 2002*, Geneva.

UNCTAD (2002b) *World Investment Report 2002: Transnational Corporations and Export Competitiveness*, Geneva.

UNCTAD (2006) *The World Investment Report: FDI from Developing and Transition Economies*, Geneva: Implications for Development.

World Bank (2006) *World Development Indicators 2006*, Washington, D.C.

World Bank (2007) *Cost of Pollution in China – Economic Estimates of Physical Damages*, Washington, D.C.

World Trade Organisation (2006) *International Trade Statistics 2006*.

World Trade Organization China Trade Policy Review Body (2006) 'Trade Policy Review Report: the People's Republic Of China', WT/TPR/G/16117 March 2006.

Yang, G. (2005) 'Jinchukou zonge guo wanyi meiyuan: yixiang shiji xinjilu,' (Export and Import Exceeded One Trillion, a Record of the New Century), jingji ribao. *Economic Daily*, 9th October 2005, Beijing.

Zhang, W. and Zhang, T. (2005) 'Competitiveness of China's Manufacturing Industry and Its Impacts on the Neighbouring Countries,' *Journal of Chinese Economic and Business Studies*, Vol. 3, pp. 205-30, Routledge, London.

Zhang, W. (2007) 'Stepping Stones to Market Integration: the Role of Economic and Technological Development Zones, in China: Linking Markets from Growth', edited by Ross Garnaut and Ligang Song, pp. 394-414, Asian Pacific Press: Canberra.

Zhang, Z. (1998) 'Zhongguo jingji tizhi gaige de zongti huigu yu zhanwang,' (Overall Review and Prospect of China's Economic Reform) Jingji yanjiu, (Economic Research) Vol, 3, Beijing.

Zhu, J. (2007) Quanguo Qingli Gelei Kaifaqu Chujian Chengxiao (Initial Achievement Has Been Made in Putting Various Development Zones in Order), Renmin Ribao, 23 April, Beijing: 1.

8 Assessing the diplomatic power of China

Zhongying Pang

Introduction: An analytical framework

Diplomacy is a major ingredient of power (Berridge 2005: 1). For the study of diplomacy and international relations, however, the relationship between diplomacy and power has been not clear cut. Power's 'relationship with foreign policy' has been neglected, 'partly because foreign policy has just been subsumed in general discussions about conflict and the rationale of the state' to quote an English writer (Hill 2003: 129). In the case of China's diplomatic source of power, it is difficult to see where the power actually comes from. This chapter, however, attempts to establish a relationship between China's diplomacy and its power.

The question of China's diplomacy power has not often been studied both inside and outside China.

Since the 1840s, many Chinese have firmly believed in this 'national lesson' or a common statement: 'China was a great but weak country that had no diplomacy' (弱国无外交). Diplomacy was simply excluded as a form of China's national power. The nation's power was popularly and largely perceived materially – that is, by modernized military might and by an industrialized, advanced economy and technology. The conception of 弱国无外交, as seen in the entire Chinese modern history and its interaction with the outside world, has deeply influenced Chinese thinking on the country's diplomacy. When experts thought of China's power, many of them, usually and naturally, expressed 'economic capacity' 经济实力, the developmental level of science and technology (科技实力), and military force (武力) as the major elements of China's power (Chu 2007: 107–18). Diplomacy power was hardly ever mentioned. Unfortunately, diplomacy as an element of China's power has been neglected and forgotten. Effective and skillful diplomacy, however, was particularly and extremely important to China as a powerless but large state. Such a radical misunderstanding on diplomacy should have never been accepted.

The Chinese military played a central role in China's diplomacy. Chinese diplomats with military background were asked to behave like military men and women. The late Premier Zhou Enlai (周恩来), PRC's first Foreign Minister and the founding father of its Ministry of Foreign Affairs, required Chinese diplomats, in the 1950s, to act as 'a group of the People's Liberation Army (PLA) in civilian clothes.' The first generation of PRC diplomats mainly came from the PLA.

In other words, the PLA generals and soldiers played a crucial role in PRC's early diplomatic build-up. Is it enough then to assess China's diplomatic capability (in the real sense of the word) from this simple perspective of evaluating diplomacy power? Unfortunately, diplomacy is not military. Military men and women are not necessarily diplomats.

In China's social sciences, the popular study of China's 'overall (national) strengths'(整体实力) or 'comprehensive power'(综合实力), in the 1980s, began to include a key assessment of China's 'diplomatic capabilities' (外交实力). It was a knowledge contribution. Related researches had been mainly done by scholars without foreign policy or international relations credentials. These were certainly not adequate, as they used very traditional concepts of power with a dominant Chinese interpretation – physical power (实力). The term 'strength' (i.e. 'power' in Chinese) here lacked meaningful theoretical definition. In most cases, this was too narrowly on a par with the country's material and perceived capabilities, which were equally deemed as China's 'hard power', such as the economy, technology and military.

This chapter's focus veers away from those doctrines or theories of 'overall strength' or 'comprehensive power.' By discussing a relationship between power and diplomacy, the author attempts to develop and to define the meaning of diplomacy power.

The concept of 'diplomacy power'

Diplomacy is a major means of implementing a nation's foreign policy.

Diplomacy as an institution is a (national) power, at least in peace time. Adam Watson, a British scholar-diplomat and one of the founding members of the 'English School' of international relations theory, wrote that diplomacy is 'the process of dialogue and negotiation by which states in a system conduct their relations and pursue their purposes by means short of war' (Watson 1982: 11).

Diplomacy can be seen as a 'normative power' in international relations terms.

> States that are aware that their domestic policies are affected by 'every thing that happens' outside, are not content merely to observe one another at a distance. They feel the need to enter into a dialogue. This dialogue between independent states – the machinery by which their governments conduct it and the networks of promises, contracts, institutions, and codes of conduct which develop out of it – is the substance of diplomacy.
>
> (Watson 1982: 14).

To better understand the power-diplomacy relationship, we must return to America's Hans Joachim Morgenthau, who wrote that, in international politics, the quality of diplomacy is the most important element of national power. He asks these key questions: 'What are the factors that make for the power of a nation vis-à-vis other nations?' and 'What are the components of what we call national power?'

(Morgenthau and Thompson 1985: 127). He identifies 'the quality of diplomacy' as one of eight 'elements of national power,' to wit:

> Of all the factors that make for the power of a nation, the most important, however unstable, is the quality of diplomacy. All the other factors that determine national power are, as it were, the raw material out of which the power of a nation is fashioned. The quality of a nation's diplomacy combines those different factors into an integrated whole, gives them direction and weight, and awakens their slumbering potentialities by giving them the breath of actual power. The conduct of a nation's foreign affairs by its diplomats is for national power in peace what military strategy and tactics by its military leaders are for national power in war.
>
> (Morgenthau and Thompson 1985: 158–59).

In understanding power, Morgenthau was an extreme exception. Many others apparently wrote little about diplomacy as an element of (national) power or have thought little about the relationship between diplomacy and power.

The concept of power has been debated around the world, without consensus on its meaning. But in the late twentieth century, the understanding of power has achieved progress in two prominent areas.

First, the concept of 'soft power' was coined and defined for the first time. America's Joseph Nye contributed much to the development of this concept. However, in the author's view, Nye's concept of soft power, to some extent, is misleading as he regarded many other resources as a country's soft power. For example, Yao Ming, a Chinese basketball star who plays with the Houston Rockets in the American NBA (National Basketball Association), was seen ridiculously as among China's soft power (Nye 2005). This risks his concept losing the powerful explanation in the study of diplomacy; and it was also imprecise as its distinction from 'hard power' is obscure in many cases.

Second, the relatively new field of the study of international political economy (IPE) distinguished 'relational power' from 'structural power.' Scholars such as Britain's Susan Strange, a distinguished theorist of international relations,[1] saw 'structural power' as more fundamental and important than 'relational power' in diplomacy. By using her multi/inter-disciplinary approach to IPE (Strange 1991: 33–49), she proposed an insightful framework:

> in the notion of enveloping structures that ... set the agenda and determined the range of options within which states, and other groups and individuals, contested all the major who-gets-what issues of politics, both within the state and in the world economy.
>
> (Strange 1991: 34)

Strange defined these as 'structures of power' and as an important determinant of power relations among people, groups or states. For her, there are primary structures such as 'security,' 'production,' 'finance,' and 'knowledge' structures.

In the competitive environment of world political economy, 'structural power' is more decisive than 'relational (bargaining) power.' Relational power is the power of a state or a non-state actor to get another to do something it would not otherwise do; whereas structural power is the power that shapes and determines the structures of world political economy within which the states, institutions, groups or individuals have to operate. In other words, structural power is that which determines how things shall be done. It is the power that shapes frameworks in which states, institutions, and individuals are interrelated (Strange 1988: 23–42). As differentiated from mere economic or political power, structural power becomes the organizing engine of its respective structural domains (security, finance and the like) for longer periods. It thus becomes more decisive than the outcome of relational power, in which the actors' choices are determined by the structure and limited to a particular social-economic and political context. For instance, in the issue of energy, China basically has no structural power to safeguard its 'energy security.' It has no direct influence on the global energy structure, which was decided by both the major energy producers (OPEC countries and Russia) and the major energy consumers (the West and Japan).

Structural power, on the other hand, does exist in every primary structure. In Strange's framework, power does not stem from only one source but can be found and derived from a number of structures. A state can exercise power (or control) in any one or more power structures, while it might not be able to do so in others. Accordingly, whoever or whatever exercises control over the security of people – over the mode of production; over determining what is produced by whatever combination of labor, capital, land and technology, and by what production methods; over the supply and distribution of credit; over the accumulation, storage and communication of respected knowledge, etc. Such a state, group or individual will exercise structural power over the others. In real life, these power structures are not independent from one another and, in fact, overlap with each other. This means whoever or whatever exercises control over any one of those structures might be able to exercise power over the other structures.

Chinese literatures show how some scholars quickly experienced, learned, accepted, and used the concept of 'soft power' and 'structural power.' Furthermore, some began to think that diplomacy as a (national) power can be understood as both 'soft power' and 'structural power.'

China's diplomacy power: an assessment

In the following section, the endeavor to link China's diplomacy with China's power with these four points:

China's diplomacy as a (national) hard power

As stated above, diplomacy is definitely part of a nation's 'hard power.' A retired Chinese ambassador realized that China should develop its 'diplomatic hard power.' In his policy bill to the CPPCC (Chinese People's Political Consultative

Conference, perhaps China's Upper House of the Parliament or China's Senate) in 2007, he said the leadership of the country's diplomacy – including its foreign policy decision-making, diplomatic activities or practices done by the President, Premier and his ministers, appointed ambassadors and other diplomats – is the hard power of a nation. He added among the list of hard power: the nation's international influence and results (benefits), major diplomatic presences bilaterally and multilaterally, international organization memberships, and so on (Zhang 2007).

A modern, efficient, and adaptive department of foreign affairs is a major indication of a country's diplomatic hard power. Organizationally or institutionally, China now runs a similar ministry of foreign affairs (MFA) as other large countries in the West and Asia. China's Central Government is still the largest government in the world. Its Other Government Ministries or Departments (OGDs) (Berridge 2005: 11) and other parts of the state machinery (Hill 2003: 138), such as the Ministry of Commerce and the Ministry of Defense[2] or every other office and agency, also have their own important international (foreign) sections (departments, divisions or bureaus) for implementing related foreign policy and dealing with their own foreign affairs. Apart from the MFA, the International Department under the Chinese Communist Party (CCP) conducts China's 'political party diplomacy.' Few foreign scholars have written on the role of party departments, such as the CCP's International Department, but David Shambaugh states:

> No ruling party or government in the world mounts anywhere near as extensive an effort to maintain links with domestic political parties, groups, and personages as does the CCP/ID. In recent years, it has also played important roles in managing relations with DPRK (North Korea) under the new circumstances, in assessing the causes and consequences of the collapse of the former Soviet Union and other communist party-states, and has also been a key conduit in relations with Asian, European and Latin America parties and NGOs.
>
> (Shambaugh 2007: 26–54)

CCP/ID has played a central role in China's foreign policymaking because it has provided extensive, valuable, and reliable information based on good analyses of global, regional and country affairs. Apart from the CCP International Department ID, the party and the state's other branches also conduct their own international exchanges, among them China's 'parliamentary diplomacy' conducted by the National People's Congress (perhaps China's House of Representatives) and the CPPCC and China's 'military diplomacy' conducted by the PLA.

As a great power, China has a big diplomatic global network operating its international missions (embassies, consulates and delegations as well as offices) around the globe. See the following tables.

China has invested financially to conduct its public diplomacy with Chinese characteristics. (In many cases, it does not necessarily use the term 'public diplomacy'.) Public diplomacy is starting to take on more significance, however, especially in

Table 8.1 China's global network of diplomatic missions (diplomatic machinery of government)

The Chinese Embassies and similar missions:
In Asia:
Afghanistan, Bangladesh, Brunei, Cambodia, DPRK (the Democratic People's Republic of Korea), East Timor, India, Indonesia, Japan, Laos, Malaysia, Maldives, Mongolia, Myanmar, Nepal, Pakistan, ROK (the Republic of Korea), Singapore, Sri Lanka, Thailand, Philippines, Vietnam

In Western Asia (Middle East) and North Africa:
Algeria, Bahrain, Egypt, Iran, Iraq, Israel, Jordan, Kuwait, Lebanon, Libyan, Mauritania, Morocco, Oman, Palestine, Qatar, Saudi Arabia, Sudan, Syria, United Arab Emirates, Tunisian, Turkey, Yemen

In Africa:
Angola, Benin, Botswana, Burundi, Cameroon, Cape Verde, Central Africa, Chad, Comores, Congo, Coted'lvoire, DR Congo, Djibouti, Equatorial Guinea, Eritrea, Ethiopia, Gabon, Ghana, Guinea, Guinea-Bissau, Kenya, Lesotho, Liberia, Madagascar, Mali, Mauritius, Mozambique, Namibia, Niger, Nigeria, Rwanda, Senegal, Seychelles, Sierra Leone, South Africa, Tanzania, Togo, Uganda, Zambia, Zimbabwe

In Europe and Central Asia (former Soviet Union states):
Armenia, Azerbaijan, Belarus, Georgia, Kazakhstan, Kyrghyz, Moldova, Russia, Tajikistan, Turkmenistan, Ukraine, Uzbekistan

In Europe:
Albania, Andorra, Austria, Belgium, Bosnia and Herzegovina, Bulgaria, Croatia, Cyprus, Czech Republic, Denmark, Estonia, Finland, France, Germany, Greece, Hungary, Iceland, Ireland, Italy, Latvia, Lithuania, Luxembourg, Macedonia, Malta, Norway, Poland, Portugal, Romania, Serbia, Slovak, Slovenia, Spain, Sweden, Switzerland, Netherlands, United Kingdom

In North America and Oceania:
The United States of America, Kiribati (Care-Taking Group in), Australia, New Zealand, Papua New Guinea, Canada, Fiji, Micronesia, Samoa (United States of America), Tonga, Vanuatu, Delegations from China and the U.S. met on Counterterrorism

In Latin America:
Grenada, Antigua and Barbuda, Argentine, Bahamas, Barbados, Bolivia, Brazil, Chile, Colombia, Costa Rica, Cuba, Dominica, Ecuador, Guyana, Jamaica, Mexico, Peru, Suriname, Trinidad and Tobago, Uruguay, Venezuela

Chinese Consulates General
In Asia:
Laoag(Philippines), Cebu (The Philippines), Chiangmai (Thailand), Chongjing (DPRK), Fukuoka (Japan), Ho Chi Minh City(Viet Nam), Karachi (Pakistan), Kuching (Malaysia), Mandalay (Myanmar), Mumbai (India), Nagasaki (Japan), Osaka (Japan), Pusan (ROK), Sapporo (Japan), Songkhla (Thailand)

In Western Asia and North America:
Aden-Yemen (Yemen), Alexandria (Egypt), Dubai (United Arab Emirates), Istanbul (Turkey), Jeddah (Saudi Arabia)

(Continued)

Table 8.1 China's global network of diplomatic missions (diplomatic machinery of government)—cont'd

In Africa:
Cape Town (South Africa), Douala (Cameroon), Durban (South Africa), Johannesburg (South Africa), Lagos (Nigeria), Tamatave (Madagascar), Zanzibar (Tanzania)

In Russia and Ukraine:
Khabarovsk, St. Petersburg, Odessa

In Europe:
Manchester (United Kingdom), Milano (Italy), Barcelona (Spain), Constanta (Romania), Edinburgh (United Kingdom), Firenze (Italy), Frankfurt (Germany), Gdansk (Poland), Gothenburg (Sweden), Hamburg (Germany), Marseille (France), Munich (Germany), Podgorica (Serbia and Montenegro), Strasbourg (France), Zurich (Switzerland)

In North America and Oceania:
Auckland (New Zealand), Calgary (Canada), Chicago (America), Houston (America), Los Angeles (America), Melbourne (Australia), New York (America), Perth (Australia), San Francisco (America), Sydney (Australia), Toronto (Canada), Vancouver (Canada)

In Latin America:
Santa Cruz (Bolivia), Barranquilla (Colombia), Guayaquil (Ecuador), Rio De Janeiro (Brazil), Sao Paulo (Brazil), Tijuana (Mexico)

In 2004, China's Ministry of Foreign Affairs created a Department of External Security Affairs (涉外安全司) for the first time.

Strengthening China's consular protection service of its overseas organizations and citizens, in order to address its growing concerns over the security of its nationals all over the world, China recently set up the Consular Protection Center in Beijing, on 23 August 2007. (This was formerly a smaller division for consular protection under the MFA.)

Chinese missions to the international organizations and the European Union

- The Mission of the People's Republic of China to the European Union
- Permanent Mission to the United Nations Economic and Social Commission for Asia and the Pacific (ESCAP)
- Permanent Mission to the World Trade Organization (WTO) in Switzerland
- Office of Commercial Development in Haiti
- Permanent Missions to the Organization for the Prohibition of Chemical Weapons
- Permanent Mission to the United Nations Office at Geneva and Other International Organizations in Switzerland
- Permanent Mission to the United Nations and Other International Organizations in Vienna
- Permanent Mission to the United Nations
- Office of Commercial Development in Panama
- Permanent Mission to the International Sea Bed Authority

Source: Mainly from the Chinese Ministry of Foreign Affairs' English Website. Available at: http://www.mfa.gov.cn.

Table 8.2 China institutions of research and education in diplomacy or international studies

State-sponsored and owned research institutes:

- At least six research institutes for world affairs and key area studies at the Chinese Academy of Social Sciences (CASS) including the World Economy and Politics, American Studies, Asia-Pacific Studies, Japan Studies, Western Asian and African Studies, European Studies, East European and Russian Studies, Latin American Studies
- Research institutes under the State Council, MFA, and other OGMs (such as China Institute of International Studies, China Institutes of Contemporary International Relations, etc.)
- Prestigious (national) universities. Three top universities of Peking, Renmin, and Fudan have conducted their international studies.
- The Chinese Communist Party's system of the Party School (for example, the Institute of International and Strategic Studies at the CCP Central Party School)

State-owned education institutions for foreign studies:

In the 1960s, under the direction of Mao Zedong and Zhou Enlai, China's Ministry of Higher Education built several international studies departments and institutes at major universities. The field of international studies has, since the 1990s, become an unprecedented boom area. Statistically, after the above-mentioned three top universities' schools of international studies, more than 70 new schools or departments of international studies have been created in China's university system so far.

trying to create China's positive image or to repair its negative image (国家形象). Currently, with Beijing having hosted the Olympic Games in 2008, China attaches more importance to its national image building. It published its first English newspaper, *China Daily*, in 1981 and opened an English channel at the Central Television Station (CCTV) in 2000. In support of the foreign universities' efforts of Chinese language studies, China had launched by the end of 2006 at least 120 Confucius Institutes, including Confucius Schools and Confucius Classes in approximately 50 countries and regions.[3]

China's diplomacy as a (national) soft power

There are many Chinese scholars of international studies who are interested in the question of soft power and how to develop the nation's soft power (Su 2007). However, few analysts clearly see or realize diplomacy as a soft power.

By entering into the world bodies, China boosts its influence in international institutions. Some Chinese scholars argue that a country's influence in international institutions is a soft power. To cite one argument:

> China has not only maintained its activeness in the international political organizations, but also expanded its connections with international economic, trade and financial institutions; not only kept interests in political, economic and cultural affairs but also managed to enter the field of arms control and disarmament.
>
> (Wang 2003: 26)

China has obtained representative status in nearly all important universal intergovernmental organizations. China's relatively belated multilateral diplomacy has therefore contributed to the nation's 'soft power' by negotiating China's full accession to international organizations.

By introducing China to the world, its diplomacy also contributed to the nation's attractiveness to the world. For example, many countries in the developing world have been interested in China's development experiences and even in its development models. Many African countries want to learn methods of poverty relief from China. Some scholars in the West have summarized China's lure to the developing world as the 'Beijing Consensus' (Ramo 2004) or 'China's charm' (Kurlanzick 2006).

Some of China's foreign policy principles have translated into China's soft power in the world, particularly among the developing countries, as China and the other developing countries still share these principles. China has long been a firm supporter of the basic principles of international relations, including sovereignty and its equality. Its foreign policy represents the basic principles of the developing world. From Southeast Asia to South Asia, from Asia to Africa, the developing world has maintained the principles of sovereignty and non-interference in the internal affairs of other countries. Even at the end of the Cold War, both the African Union and ASEAN began to embrace new norms and principles such as human rights, good governance, and human security as well as conditional international intervention in their regional cooperation charters. The principles of independence, sovereignty and others are still not regarded as outdated. In the 1950s, China was a leading country in helping build such principles in other newly independent countries such as India and Indonesia. Since the 1960s, China has shared these principles with most of the Asian and African countries. The Five Principles of Peaceful Co-existence, commonly created by China, India and other countries in the first Afro-Asian Conference in Bandung, Indonesia, in 1954, served as a bedrock principle in conducting relations with the developing world and beyond. China has committed to peaceful resolution of conflict with foreign countries, especially China's neighboring countries in Asia. For example, regarding the fundamental improvement of its relations with Southeast Asian countries, China was the first non-ASEAN country to sign the Southeast Asia's Treaty of Amity and Cooperation (TAC) on 8 October 2003. In fact, the nation's policies or principles of sovereign equality and non-interference have better served China's interests in the developing world. In its current engagements with Asia, Africa and Latin America, the principles of non-interference in political relations and non-political conditional aid helped increase China's influences there.

China's diplomacy as a (national) relational power

China's deepened or widened economic connections with the world significantly helped expand its relational power in the world. Since the late 1970s, China has forged closer and more complex economic relations with most of Asia, the West, and other developing countries. China's huge 'buying power' – that is, its long 'economic diplomacy' to the West and its aid policy to the developing world – for instance, strengthened China's relational power. It has conducted so-called '(business) contract diplomacy' in the West and Russia. To name a few examples: Chinese and Russian companies signed contracts worth over $4.3 billion during President Hu Jintao's state visit to Russia on March 26 to 28, 2007;[4] China and Australia signed a new $35 billion liquid natural gas supply contract during Hu Jintao's visit to Australia on September 6, 2007.[5]

It began to negotiate the first free trade agreement (FTA) with ASEAN in 2000. After that, China and several key economic partners in the Asia-Pacific region attempted to work out their FTAs. The FTA negotiations with Australia and New Zealand separately are being push forward. The country has also been exploring possibilities of FTA relations with Japan, South Korea, India, Pakistan and others.

China has become an important donor in international development assistance to the developing world. To maintain and further develop China's relations with the developing world, it has conducted 'aid diplomacy' in Africa, Asia, Latin America, and the Pacific Region. In 2005, at the UN Summit, Chinese President Hu Jintao committed to increasing China's development assistance to poor countries at the UN Summit.[6] Symbolically, China became a new donor in the World Bank's International Development Association (IDA) for the first time. But in 2000 China was still a recipient of IDA aid.[7]

In short, China's diplomacy in the era of 'reform and opening up' is mainly about economic diplomacy; its relational power in the world mainly comes from its economic engagements worldwide.

China's diplomacy as a (national) structural power

For the first time in modern world history, China's influence in managing global political economy is rising significantly, at both global and various regional levels. The Chinese nation is now, institutionally, an indispensable and constructive member of the current international system.

In global security, China has played its prominent part. Symbolic of a great/global power or not, its veto power at the UNSC is one of the nation's key structural sources of diplomacy power.

In particular, its role in the management of the global economy has been increasing. China began to receive support from international economic institutions for its economic reform and development (especially poverty relief efforts) in the 1980s, when China smoothly joined the International Monetary Fund (IMF) and the World Bank (WB). Almost 20 years later, China has evolved into an economic giant in terms of size. Its role in global economic management has changed substantially. Several times, it was the elected member at the IMF and WB's executive directors. China belatedly gained access, after a hard process of negotiation, to the World Trade Organization (WTO) in 2001. As the largest 'emerging economy', its influence in these pillars of global economic order has been steadily and inevitably increasing. China was granted a quarter more votes in the IMF, in September 2006, as an acknowledgment of its growing economic importance. Of course, with less than 4 percent of votes on the IMF board of governors, compared to almost 17 percent for the United States, China still lags far behind the United States and others (Altman 2007).

By reaching the world through its engagements with the non-UN and the non-Asian institutions, China's structural power in the world has also been boosted. It has built close relations with the European Union (EU). In 2003, China's first regional policy paper, *China's EU Policy,* was released. It has maintained good contacts with the West-dominated institutions, such as the Group of Eight (G8). China has even explored an emerging working relationship with NATO (Zhang 2002a). In Latin America, the Organization of American States (OAS) accepted China as a permanent observer in 2004. China's new role in Africa has been widely noticed by the West. For making clear China's goals and motives in the world's second continent, China released its second regional policy paper, *China's Africa Policy,* in 2006. So far, the nation has established successfully the 'strategic partnership' with many regions, particularly with the EU and the African Union. Since 2003, Chinese President Hu Jintao, together with other leaders of big developing countries, has been invited three times to attend the G8 Outreach Summits.

China borders with almost every sub-region in Asia. At the sub-regional levels, since the end of the Cold War, it has gradually achieved many diplomatic successes in regional, multilateral institution-building. Its relations with the Association of South East Asian Nations (ASEAN) have improved in the past 15 years, as acknowledged by the first China-ASEAN Summit on October 2006 in Nanning, China. By economic integration with the Asian region, the basis of China's international structural power has been strengthened.

Table 8.3 China's memberships in inter-regional, sub-regional and regional institutions

At the inter/trans-regional levels:
Asia-Pacific Economic Cooperation (APEC, 1989)
Asia-Europe Meeting (ASEM, 1996)
China-EU Summit (1998)
China-Africa Summit (2006)
At the regional levels:
East Asia Summit (2005)
Shanghai Cooperation Organization (SCO, 1996)
At the sub-regional levels:
In Southeast Asia, the ASEAN Regional Forum (ARF, 1996), the ASEAN + China, Japan and Republic of Korea, and the ASEAN + China (1997)
In Northeast Asia, the Six-Party Talks (2003)
In South Asia, the South Asian Association for Regional Cooperation (SAARC, observer, 2005)

Finally, regarding China's structural power, several important developments should be mentioned, as the country is now an emerging major international state actor:

- China changed its attitude towards UN peacekeeping and peace-building missions, and began to play a larger role in promoting world peace and stability. Chinese peacekeepers are now present in Africa, Latin America, and Asia. Its participation in peacekeeping and post-conflict peace-building means China is exploring more flexibilities of foreign policy, in order to adapt to global changes. China is a member country of the newly created international body, UN Peace Building Commission (PBC).
- China's role in other global agendas is increasing. For example, it is a major stakeholder of international arms control norm-building. It plays a key role in the negotiation of global climate change diplomacy. China has firmly supported a post-Kyoto Protocol climate change negotiation. In such 'non-traditional security' fields, its diplomatic role might continue to increase.
- China is realizing the importance of so-called 'agenda settings' in influencing international institutions and conferences (talks). In other words, its international role began to go beyond the universal norms compliance. Together with other developing countries, e.g. Brazil, Egypt, India and South Africa, it has played a key role in inter-governmental organizations, such as the Group of 20 (G20). It played a leading role in forming the Shanghai Cooperation Organization (SCO), which has already become a central regional grouping in Central Asia.
- China's structural diplomacy power comes from its unchanged identity with the developing world. The nation's leaders and analysts repeatedly say that 'China is still a developing country' or 'China is the largest developing country' (Wen 2007). Such expressions apparently have helped secure China's relations with many developing countries. The developing world has long been regarded as China's 'foothold' for its foreign policy.

The question of China's quality of diplomacy

The quality of its diplomacy must not be overlooked, as China's real diplomacy power depends on it. In this regard, first, China's forms of diplomacy should be studied. Diplomacy includes many forms, such as the use of hard power (coercive diplomacy) and the use of soft power (non-coercive diplomacy, for instance, 'cultural diplomacy'). In general, in most cases, China's diplomacy used forms such as sanctions and other coercive means. Second, the role of China's negotiations in its diplomacy or the quality of China's negotiations must also be considered. Negotiation, as the most important function of diplomacy in the West, has evidently been relegated to a relatively lesser important place in China's diplomacy. Third, poor or not, qualified diplomats decide another country's quality of diplomacy. Here, this paper focuses on the issue of China's diplomatic professionalism, a relatively new topic to China. Comparatively, Chinese ambassadors and other diplomats were, for many reasons, not necessarily well-trained in terms of negotiation. For example, Chinese ambassadors were not doing commercial work in the past, unlike their counterparts in other industrial countries (Liu 2001). Fourth, attention must be paid to China's foreign policy system, currently the system is not so modernized. Finally, the relationship between its foreign policy education system (and think tanks) and its diplomacy is a decisive factor in promoting or improving China's quality of diplomacy.

- European old powers and the US have developed and used 'carrots-and-sticks' foreign policymaking and implementation. As a non-Western and still 'socialist' country, China's diplomacy has employed little 'coercive diplomacy' such as expulsions and subversion, which are used by the old established powers. China keeps a principle of 'non-interference' in the internal affairs of others. As its economic power increases, in international disputes, it still hardly uses economic sanctions (which the US frequently resorts to) against others.
- One interesting finding is that, in most of China's diplomacy textbooks at major universities, the section on the 'art of negotiation' barely occupied several pages; while, in the West, this is apparently the core of most textbooks on the study of negotiation. Of course, China's diplomats have their own style of negotiation. Many China affairs experts and diplomats in the West have published books on Chinese negotiation. In reality, however, China's diplomats have lacked good training in the modern art of negotiation.
- In theory, today's top Chinese diplomats and ambassadors were appointed or promoted principally from China's career diplomats. The new Foreign Minister Yang Jiechi is an experienced diplomat and a British-trained scholar. The Personnel Department of China's MFA has increasingly depended on the normal channels to recruit its staff from university graduates. It is a positive sign of development of its diplomatic professionalism that China appointed some highly qualified female ambassadors, who by themselves are a form of 'soft power' in diplomacy. For example, China's current ambassador to the UK, Fu Ying, has been a successful diplomat in her key posts (the general director of Asian Affairs at MFA and Chinese ambassador to Philippines and Australia, separately). The MFA began to recruit Chinese who hold degrees from overseas universities to join the foreign ministry and the overseas missions. In the mid-1990s, according to reports, China finally abandoned its long-established prohibition on locally engaged staff in overseas missions (Berridge 2004).
- China's current foreign policy system was built in the 1950s, when the PRC was just born; then Soviet Union's foreign policy system was basically transplanted. Today, the nation comprehensively enters into the West-dominated and the US-centric international system. With the evolution of globalization and regionalization, China needs to reform an old and, at least partially, outdated foreign policy system in order to adapt to the sea changes in the world diplomatic system. There is so far no clear road-map showing how to do so, however.

- After the end of the Cultural Revolution, from the early 1980s, China's universities began to supply more and more talents to the foreign policy system. The official think tanks and scholars have increasingly assisted China's improvements in foreign policy decision-making, by providing more accurate, balanced and scholarly analyses on the contemporary world. Apparently, China's diplomacy (decision-making and policy implementation) will continue to depend on the country's improvement of its system of higher education and social sciences.

China's diplomacy with multinational companies (MNCs)

Again, in the pioneering study of 'dimensions of diplomacy' undertaken by Susan Strange, the 'state-firm' relationship was mentioned to refer to 'diplomacy between governments and firms.' Strange points out that 'governments have had to increasingly to bargain with firms.' She defines that the government's negotiation with firms (including multinational companies) is also diplomacy (Strange 1991: 43).

China is now called 'the largest receiver of foreign direct investment (FDI)' which is a result of its long pro-foreign investment policy. In the past 30 years or so, Chinese top leaders conducted their relations singularly or in groups with most of the world's top multinational companies. China's practice of de facto state-firm diplomacy strongly confirm Strange's concept of 'new diplomacy' (Strange 1993, 1997). Unfortunately, however, many orthodox diplomacy scholars still refuse to pay attention to this unorthodox 'new diplomacy.'

This paper not only raises this point, but also poses a further question: Does China's multinational company diplomacy or 'FDI diplomacy' strengthen or weaken its power?

Today, more and more Chinese scholars begin to worry about the country's over-dependency on 'foreign investments.' They cite that the Chinese economy is almost dominated or controlled by the global multinational companies. In most cases, the so-called 'China's exports' or 'productions' are actually foreign exports from China or foreign productions in China. Former Commerce Minister Bo Xilai famously said: 'The trade between China and the United States is with the surplus going to the Chinese and the profits flowing to the Americans.'[8] Professor Zhang Youwen of the Shanghai Academy of Social Sciences wrote that, discounting the proportion of FDI contributions to its economic growth and exports, China's real national strength is still limited. Some Chinese scholars have pointed out a striking phenomenon: China's economic growth also means the growth of poverty (Zheng 2007).

Along with the emergence of China's economic nationalism, in this process of China's diplomacy with multinational companies, critics observe that some of the government's economic departments 'have not necessarily served China's interests but seriously damaged China's national interests.' For instance, China's Ministry of Railways has been condemned as a 'department of selling the country' by becoming a department of imports.[9]

Thus, many people around the world are talking about 'the rise of China.' Whether the argument of China's rise is true or not, these things are certain: American power in China is rising; European power in China is rising; Japanese power in China is rising; Korean power is rising, etc.

Robert Cox points out that the relationship of production is an important determinant of power relations (Cox 1987). China has not determined the global finance structure, which means 'the system under which credit is created, allocated, and put to use' (Strange 1991). This is due to China's long FDI absorption policy, its unconvertible currency, its limited overseas investment, and its perhaps bad-managed state-owned banking system as well. Beijing is a service government for MNCs, which partially explains why Beijing cannot use its huge foreign reserves to deal with the US administration effectively. However, it has to buy US bonds, US goods and services. In the China-U.S. 'Strategic Economic Dialogue' (SED), China always was in a defensive position to face America's pressures. A consequence of this place is clear, for China's power, as Wang Yizhou writes: 'China still has no generally dominant power in the world' (Wang 2005).

The limits of China's diplomacy power

The question of China's multinational company diplomacy leads to another central question, the core concern of this paper: What are the limits of China's diplomacy power?

First, the authority of China's central government has been challenged by both internal and external factors. Internal factors are China's local and department leaders, the industrial sectors, and the emerging groups of interests, etc. Deng Xiaoping stressed in 1988 that 'The Central must have authorities' (Deng 1988). The authority issue of the Central is once again raised and noticed, recently, as China's policy measures of 'macroeconomic control' were not fully implemented at the local level. External factors, in fact, whether acknowledged or not, multinational (foreign) companies from around the globe and their home governments.

This author considers that the Chinese state also experiences a process of 'The Retreat of the State' (Strange 1998). China's diplomacy power has thus been weakened by above-mentioned internal and external factors. For example, it has been studied by some scholars, such as Chen Zhimin of Fudan University and Fang Changping of Renmin University (Chen 2001; Fang 2005), that China's local governments have been conducting so-called 'under-central diplomacy' ('次中央外交') – a Chinese style 'para-diplomacy.'

Second, being a big and great country demographically, territorially and technically, China exposes some signs of a rising power. However, it is still an indispensable part of the developing/South/Third World. Mao Zedong declared China belonged to the 'Third World,' due to its closeness and socialism; but it had relatively few characteristics of a Third World country, as describes by the classic development economics and politics in the West. It is correct to say that the current leaders acknowledge China still belongs to the 'developing world' (and not just for reducing the international perception and argument of the 'China threat').

As many indications have shown, it is moving quickly towards being a very real developing country with more developing country characteristics. It has possibly further become a typical Third World country by now. Being a developing country, like the others, China's diplomacy power has many features typical of a developing country.

Third, China's external relations, so far, especially its relations with the West, have been oriented or based on interests. It has been taking advantage of its reputation as a key 'emerging market or economy.' At the same time, the outside world has been building its relations with China to fully develop its potential in the booming market. The country now uses its foreign reserves to buy or invest in the world's markets. But this so-called 'China's buying power' does not necessarily mean China's real power, as many domestic economists point out. This is because its purchasing activities around the world are not necessarily for home grown sectors, but are for international productions in China. As the world's workshop, China very much needs energies and other natural resources. China's top leaders, just like the CEOs of the assembled companies, have visited all over the world to assist in the world's workshop's demands for energy. This 'energy diplomacy' is not only about China but also about the world. Therefore, such buying power might be difficult to translate into China's diplomacy power. This is why China has been reluctant to use its economic engagements with Tokyo to deal with a remilitarized Japan.

China lacks values-based diplomacy with the world. The growth of its soft diplomacy power has been restricted by its current disadvantages in values-oriented diplomacy. Since Deng Xiaoping, China has claimed that its foreign policy would 'go beyond the political and ideological differences' with others, particularly with the West. In other words, shared values or ideologies are no longer used as a foreign policy standard (Li 2007). The 'going beyond political and ideological differences' has unfortunately been replaced gradually by so-called 'value(s)-free' policy. In recent years, as China has done 'energy diplomacy' in Africa, Asia, and elsewhere, both the Chinese and the outside China-watchers agree that the nation is pursuing a 'values-free diplomacy' or 'ideologies neutral' policy. In fact, it never conducts any values-oriented diplomacy. In other words, according to this summary, China as a big power surprisingly has no values-oriented diplomacy. Of course, in some eyes, its values free 'strategy' was wise in a West-dominated or US-hegemonic world, after the collapse of the Soviet Union. However, as Wang Yizhou wrote, a modern country or a world power should not depend only on material (hard) power. Such dependency is unlikely to last or to make China alluring (Wang 2005).

Fourth, due to many complex political considerations (i.e. it does not want intervention into Taiwan and Tibetan affairs by the West and others; it still needs to maintain the traditional principles of state sovereignty and non-interference in others' internal affairs), China has repeatedly stressed that it has maintained its long policy of non-(international) interference (intervention). International intervention is a major form and content of the established powers in the West, and even in emerging powers like India. In the foreseeable future, this author believes

China will still not play a big international intervention role in major international conflicts and crises. In the issue of the North Korean nuclear program, China has played an organizer role in the management of the nuclear dispute between the DPRK and the USA, as a key stakeholder since 2003, although it hosted the Six-Party Talks in Beijing. Mediation is only a minimum or limited intervention. Even small and neutral powers in the world can perform such diplomacy. However, in today's world of many threats and challenges, China's diplomacy is clearly in a dilemma over how to tackle international problems, crises and disputes such as a proliferation of WMD and humanitarian crises.

Fifth, China's real NGOs, or civil society forces, or individuals in diplomacy have been underdeveloped. They have played a poor role in China's diplomacy (Su 2007). Clearly, the development of China's diplomacy power is still state-driven.

Finally, on the issue of China's ability of international 'agenda setting,' it has no choice but to continue to be a custodian or maintainer of the existing international system rather than a challenger to it. It has played little role in international initiatives. This is because China is relatively a latecomer in the Westphalia or post-Westphalia international system, and most of the universal international institutions are still West-dominated. Particularly since the end of the Cold War, China's foreign policy has been guided by Deng Xiaoping's 'low key' philosophy (韬光养晦), which has been only for managing to stabilize China's external relations or reduce unnecessary international pressures. For example, except for some statements of abstract principles,[10] China has initiated or sponsored little in concrete action plans on the reform of the UN system.

The future of China's diplomacy power

Generally speaking, a rising China very much needs a diplomacy that is commensurably modern, skillful and active, as well as strong. However, there is still a long way to go before such diplomatic power emerges in the world.

From the foreign policy-power perspective, China's diplomacy faces big and deep challenges.

- In solving its differences and disputes with others, China increasingly relies more on diplomatic negotiations than on other means. It also wants to see many pressing and thorny international issues settled or managed by talks or negotiations.
- As its interests and individuals have been consistently growing and going global, how to secure China's overseas interests and lives has been debated in the country.
- Its sovereign and legitimate interests including development interest has been sporadically internationally challenged .
- It is necessary that China re-builds its values-based relations with the world in order to improve its relations with the West and other political and ideological different countries.

- The West, especially the US and the EU, will continue to pressure China, as a part of the international system, to undertake more international responsibilities on global issues. China's capacity in tackling global challenges, such as environmental protection, climate change and sustainable development, will have to be strengthened.

Even as the 'low key' foreign policy continues, China's diplomacy has to explore how to be a key international state actor. Its diplomacy has been turning active, since the Asian financial crisis in 1997, with more actions, more reactions and more interactions in the world.

But there are many uncertainties in its diplomacy power. This paper wishes to raise several key questions about China's diplomacy power:

- Does China understand the relationship between diplomacy and power?
- As an emerging power, can China also conduct 'coercive diplomacy' like other powers in the future and add its choices of diplomatic instruments?
- Can China have a good command of modern and post-modern diplomacy, especially improving bargaining and negotiating skills and strengthening capabilities of negotiation?
- Can China develop a modernized system of foreign policy decision-making and implementation by reforming the 'machinery' – foreign ministry and overseas diplomatic representation?
- Is China politically and strategically aware of effective approaches to update China's art of diplomacy?
- By using China's development experiences, will China really enjoy a 'Beijing Consensus' in its relations with the developing world as a whole?
- Are there possibilities of China's efforts to promote more democratic international rules and institutions?
- Will China, as a major participant, continue to help build regional institutions in Asia and trans-regional cooperation between Asia and other world regions?
- Will China having more memberships in non-UN and non-Asian international/global institutions enable better management of globalization and security?
- How will China revise and demonstrate more flexibility in its attitudes towards international principles of non-intervention?

Concluding remarks

China's diplomacy power is a large but often neglected topic. A major purpose of this paper is to address the issue. It is difficult to define the meaning of power. In this chapter, referring to China's case, power means both instruments and ends. The author briefly examined the four overlapping dimensions of China's diplomacy power: namely, its 'hard power,' 'soft power,' 'relational power,' and 'structural power.' The overlapping questions such as China's quality of diplomacy and

China's new diplomacy with global business have been raised. It is true that China's diplomacy power is rising. It has learned quickly in the world diplomatic system. It is now a well-noted, emerging international state actor. However, there are many problems in the process of an emerging modern diplomacy for an emerging world power. Thus, particularly and purposefully, this author poses many questions about China's diplomacy power. These questions might be more important than a pure 'assessment' of its diplomacy power, as they help to understand and define what China's diplomacy power has been, and how it would be developed in the future.

Notes

1 'Susan Strange 1923–1998: a great international relations theorist', *Review of International Political Economy*, Volume 6, Number 2, 1 May 1999, pp. 121–32 (12).
2 The current ministries and commissions under the State Council of China (China's Administration) total 28. See http://english.gov.cn/links/statecouncil.htm.
3 Data from The Office of the Chinese Language Council International (Han Ban). Available at: http://www.hanban.edu.cn/en_hanban/content.php?id=2519
4 *People's Daily*, 22 March 2007.
5 *Sydney Morning Herald*, 6 September 2007.
6 'Promote Universal Development to Achieve Common Prosperity', the written statement by President Hu Jintao of China at the High-Level Meeting on Financing for Development at the 60th Session of the United Nations, New York, September 14 2005.
7 'China pushes World Bank aid pledges to record high', AFP news from Berlin, 15 December 2007.
8 Bo Xilai's remarks at the National People's Congress (China's current parliament) Press Conference, 12 March 2007, Beijing.
9 '*The railway department: an imports department or a department of selling the country*' (《铁道部是进口部还是卖国部?》), Beijing: Dajun Economic Watch and Research Center (北京大军经济观察研究中心), 18 April 2007, Available at: http://www.dajun.com.cn/tiedaobu.htm.
10 *Position Paper of the People's Republic of China on the United Nations Reforms*, Beijing, 8 June 2005.

References

Altman, D. (2007) 'Managing Globalization: Two economic giants, how many votes?', *International Herald Tribune,* 3 April.

Berridge, G.R. (2004) 'Book review on Xiaohong Liu, Chinese Ambassadors: The rise of diplomatic professionalism since 1945'. Seattle: University of Washington Press, 2001. Available at: http://www.grberridge.co.uk/booknote_reviewed_1.htm#liu.

Berridge, G.R. (2005) *Diplomacy: Theory and Practice*, 3rd edn. London: Palgrave Macmillan.

Chen, Z.M. (2001) *Ciguojia zhengfu yu duiwai shiwu (The Under Central Government and Foreign Affairs)*. Beijing: Long March Press.

Chu, S.L. (2007) '*Quanmian jianshe xiaokang shiqi de zhongguo waijiao zhanlue (China's Diplomatic Strategy in the Constructing a Well Off Society Period)*', in Niu, J. (ed.) *China's Diplomacy*. Beijing: New World Press.

Cox, R.W. (1987) *Production, Power and World Order*. New York: Columbia University Press.

Deng, X. (1988) 'Zhongyang yao you quanwei (The Central Must Have Authorities)', in *Selected Works of Deng Xiaoping (in Chinese)*, vol. 3. Beijing: Foreign Languages Press.

Fang, C.P. (2005) 'Zhongguo duiwai zhengce de guonei zhengzhi:yixiang yanjiu yicheng (The Domestic Politics in China's Foreign Policy: A Research Agenda)', *Journal of Teaching and Research (in Chinese)*, Renmin University of China, No. 11.

Hill, C. (2003) *The Changing Politics of Foreign Policy*. London: Palgrave Macmillan.

Li, A.S. (2007) 'Transformation of China's Policy towards Africa', working paper, Hong Kong: CCTR, UST. Available at: www.cctr.ust.hk/articles/pdf/WorkingPaper20_LiAnshan.pdf.

Liu, X.H. (2001) *Chinese Ambassadors: the Rise of Diplomatic, Professionalism since 1945*. Seattle and London: University of Washington Press.

Kurlantzick, J. (2006) 'China's Charm: Implications of Chinese Soft Power', *Policy Brief*, No. 46. Washington DC: Carnegie Endowment for International Peace.

Morgenthau, H. and Thompson, K. (1985) *Politics among Nations*, 6th edn. New York: McGraw-Hill.

Nye, J.S.J. (2005) 'The rise of China's soft power', *The Wall Street Journal Asia*, 29 December.

Ramo, J.C. (2004), *The Beijing Consensus*, London: The Foreign Policy Centre.

Shambaugh, D. (2007) 'China's Quiet Diplomacy: the International Department of the Chinese Communist Party'. Singapore: *China An International Journal*, Vol. 5, No. 1.

Strange, S. (1988) *States and Markets*. London: Pinter Publishers.

Strange, S. (1991) 'An eclectic approach', in C.N. Murphy and R. Tooze (eds) *The New International Political Economy*. Boulder: Lynne Rienner Publishers.

Strange, S. (1997) 'The Erosion of the State', *Current History*, Vol. 96, November.

Strange, S. (1998) *The Retreat of the State: The Diffusion of Power in the World Economy*. Cambridge: Cambridge University Press.

Strange, S. and Morgan, R. (1993) *New diplomacy in the post-cold war world: essays for Susan Strange*. New York: St. Martin's Press.

Su, C.H. (2007) 'China's soft power: the case of international institutions and China', Shanghai: *Journal of International Review*, No. 2.

Wang, Y.Z. (2003) 'Briefing multiple perspectives on relations between China and international organizations', in Y.Z. Wang (ed.) *Construction within Contradiction: Multiple Perspectives on the Relationship between China and International Organizations*. Beijing: China Development Publishing House.

Wang, Y.Z. (2005) 'Renshi dangdai zhongguo de san ge shijiao (Three Perspectives on Contemporary China)', *China and the World Affairs*.

Watson, A. (1982) *Diplomacy: the Dialogue Between States*. London: Methuen.

Wen, J.B. (2007) 'Guanyu shehui zhuyi chuji jieduan de lishi renwu he woguo duiwai zhengce de jige wenti (Our Historical Tasks at the Primary Stage of Socialism and Several Issues Concerning China's Foreign Policy)', *Xinhua News Agency*, 26 February 2007.

Zhang, H.X. (2007) 'Jianyi dazao woguo waijiao ruan shili (Suggestions for Building China's Diplomatic Soft Power)', the CPPCC Annual Assembly, Beijing, March 2007.

Zhang, Z.Q. (2002) 'Beijing calling', *NATO Review*, No. 3, Autumn 2003.

Zheng, B.W. (2007) 'Zhongguo xu fangzhi zengzhangxing pinkun (China Must Alleviate Poverty from Economic Growth)', *China Securities News*, 13 April 2007.

Part 4

Party-state-society relations and sustainability

9 Globalization and the state power in China[1]

Alvin Y. So

Introduction

In the 1990s, a new mode of governance was said to be emerging because of globalization. Due to the rapid expansion of information technology, global production, global finance, and the massive flow of capital/products/people/information in and out of state border, the old territorial mode of governance by the nation-state was no longer viable, i.e. the territorial nation-state was no longer able to implement, monitor, and enforce its regulations over the citizens within the confine of its territory. Subsequently, researchers talked about 'the retreat of the nation-state', 'the end of the nation-state,' and 'the eclipse of the state' (Strange 1996; Ohmae 1995; Evans 1997). According to these accounts, the nation-state was portrayed as a helpless victim to the forces of globalization; the nation-state was said to be in crisis and was destined to decline, demise, and disappear.

A decade later, however, this nation-state death news has largely disappeared. Researchers began to realize that although the Westphalian notion of nation-state sovereignty might have become outmoded, new forms of sovereignty have emerged to fit post-statist conditions. Large-scale globalization, for example, has encouraged a new *polycentric* (multi-site and networked) mode of governance (Scholte 2005: 185; Jessop 2002). There are four significant shifts in the character of the nation-state as a result of its response to such global issues as electronic finance, transworld production, ecological change, and human rights.

First, governance is shifted '*upward*' to suprastate organizations and networks such as WTO, the World Bank, IMF, WHO, UN, OCED, UNDP, EU, ASEAN + 3, the Commonwealth, etc. The WTO, for example, has 140 membership states, addresses not only cross-border exchange of merchandise but also such matters as trade in service, intellectual property rights, electronic commerce, and competition policy. The Trade Policy Review Body of WTO conducts periodic surveillance of member government's commercial measures; states which violate WTO rules are subjected to punishment.

Second, governance may be shifted '*downward*' to substate institutions. Provincial and county government can be better suited to handle matters like the provision of infrastructure for global companies, the control of transworld infectious diseases and transworld crime. Moreover, the devolution from central state to substate institutions has often come with the blessings and financial support from suprastate agencies like the EU or the multilateral development banks.

Third, governance can be shifted '*sideways*' to develop cross-border links with the adjacent nation-states or with suprastate agencies. These 'cross-border connections' have often unfolded without intermediation by central state governments, as many provincial and municipal governments have developed their own departments of foreign affairs.

Last, governance can also be shifted '*outward*' from the public sector to the private sector in the economy and society. Under the calling of neo-liberalism, Western states were urged to scale back their public welfare measures in the 1980s/1990s in order to transform itself into a competitive state in the global economy. Thereafter, responsibilities for the provision of education, health care, housing, pensions, and the like, have tended to shift from the state to such non-state actors as the NGOs and the families. The society and the marketplace are asked to regulate themselves without bothering the state.

In short, governance under conditions of large-scale globalization has become polycentric, involved not just the nation-states but also other state institutions like the supra-states, the substates, the cross-border institutions, and private agencies. The trend is from statism to polycentrism by shifting the focus from the central state to a multi-scalar, multi-site diffuse governance apparatus.

The aim of this chapter is to examine how such forces of globalization have transformed the Chinese state. Has the Chinese mode of governance been diffused from the central government to other sites 'above' (to the supra-states), 'below' (to the substate institutions), 'sideways' (to the border provincial governments), or 'outward' (to the private sectors), leading to de-centering and fragmentation? This chapter will examine these 'upward,' 'downward,' 'sideways' and 'outward' movements one by one. It will also explore the implications of these state transformations for state capacity and state power, and discuss whether the Chinese state has been weakened (or strengthened) by these forces of globalization.

Upward shift of governance to suprastate organization?

Since the late 1970s, China has joined many suprastate organizations and has entered into many global regimes in the areas of global trade (like The WTO, The IMF, The World Bank, The World Customs Organization, and The World Intellectual Property Organization), and in the areas of environmental protections, human rights and arms control (Wang 2007: 167).

In the area of environment, for instance, the Chinese state signed 28 protocols, conventions, memos, or joint declarations with 24 states on environmental cooperation between 1980 and 1999 (Zhang and Wang 2001: 14). In the 1990s, China signed 25 international treaties and entered into a large number of bilateral and multilateral projects dealing with environmental issues (Chan 2004a: 72).

In the area of global trade, China was finally allowed to join the WTO (World Trade Organization) in 2001. China's membership of the WTO carries heavy duties and responsibilities laid down in a legal document some 900 pages long. In essence, China has committed (Chan 2004b: 53):

- To provide non-discriminatory treatments to all WTO members.
- To eliminate dual-pricing practices as well as differences in treatment accorded to goods produced for sale in China in comparison to those produced for export.
- To remove price controls for protecting domestic industries or service providers.
- To implement the WTO Agreement in an effective and uniform manner by revising some of its domestic laws and enacting new legislation fully in compliance with the WTO Agreement.

According to Hsu and Arner (2007: 54), these WTO commitments have induced the Chinese state to develop a legal system that is supreme over the state and the CCP. Inevitably, China's domestic laws and principles have to harmonize with international standards. By the end of 2000, a year before China's entry to WTO, the state had reviewed over 1400 laws, regulations and other similar documents, including six statutes, 164 State Council regulations, and 887 ministry regulations (Nan 2001).

These administrative law reforms will result in making the Chinese state move towards 'greater public input, transparency, and accountability.' Ostensibly, 'the implementation of international laws in liberalizing trade and regulating financial institutions is *de facto* depriving the leadership of the CCP' (Hsu and Arner 2007: 54).

Despite the massive legislative efforts to ensure fair competition in accordance with the WTO rules, Western trading partners are still skeptical and they have tried hard to monitor China's compliance with the WTO rules. The US, for example, has monitored China's WTO compliance through two agencies. First, there is an inter-agency group called the Trade Policy Staff Committee (TPSC). The TPSC, chaired by the US Trade Representative Office's Deputy Assistant, brings together representative from some 20 different agencies in the US government, including the Department of Treasury, Commerce, State, Agriculture and Labor. The TPSC is required to submit annual reports to the US government on China's WTO compliance. Second, the US Embassy in Beijing has established a WTO Implementation Coordination Committee to track and analyze changes in Chinese laws and regulations, and to meet regularly with members of the private sector and other diplomatic missions to assess progress and to identify possible problems (Hsiung 2003).

Aside from US agencies, the US can also rely on WTO's Transition Monitoring Mechanism (TRM) and WTO's Dispute Settlement Mechanism to get redress from China if it fails to comply. The TRM is an unprecedented instrument that requires China to provide detailed information to WTO and to give them the opportunity to raise questions about Chinese compliance with its WTO commitments. China's trading practices are to be reviewed annually, in terms of its laws, regulations and programs, in the first eight years after its accession to the WTO (Chan 2004b).

In sum, China's WTO experience illustrates that China is experiencing a silent legal revolution to revise old laws/regulations and to design new ones in meeting the WTO requirements, and its Western partners are closely monitoring China's trading activities with special agencies. As other suprastate organizations (like the WHO and UN Commission on Human Rights) would impose similar activities on China when China joins their organizations, the power of the Chinese nation-state is inevitably constrainted by all these suprastate memberships.

Nevertheless, it is highly misleading to portray the Chinese state as a helpless victim to these suprastate organizations. This paper argues that the Chinese state, because of its historical specificity, is also able to expand its power and influence in joining the suprastate organizations. On this issue, James Hsiung (2003: 95) also points out that after taking into account China's pariah status following the Tiananmen Square tragedy of 1989, China's membership in suprastate organizations confers outright 'a windfall of power' and symbolizes 'an implicit lift in its international status.'

In addition, after becoming a fully fledged voting member in such a suprastate organization as the WTO, China now can speak for the developing world within the WTO inner council. This ability could expand considerably China's prestige among the developing world. According to Pascal Lamy, the European Trade Commissioner, China's entry into the WTO sparked off a major shift in the balance of power within the global trade body. The US and the EU have been the dominant players in the WTO, with Japan and the developing world competing to get the issues on the agenda for discussion. This sort of four-corner power game has changed to a five-corner game with the inclusion of China (Chan 2004: 48).

Moreover, China is a fast learner and has quickly learned how to play the rules of the game of the global trade to its advantages. In 2002, for instance, China won its first-ever antidumping case in the US. According to the lawyers for the Chinese firms, the Chinese state will resort to more frequent use of WTO rules for the protection of Chinese firms in future antidumping cases. Thus, a Chinese state official remarked that post-WTO China is now a player of 'equal footing' on the global economic stage. China can now appeal to the WTO if it fails to get relief from the US in bilateral antidumping disputes (Hsiung 2003: 97).

Furthermore, China has adopted a pro-active approach to multilateral organizations. For example, China is instrumental in setting up the Shanghai Cooperation Organization (SCO), a new regional organization in West Asia which would manage the region's common interests in terms of security, economic exchange, and cultural interaction. The inclusion of Uzbekistan – which does not border with China – in the SCO indicated the formal regionalization of the process. The Secretariat of the SCO was opened in Beijing in January 2004, with the former Chinese ambassador to Russia appointed as its first head (Wang 2007). Similarly, the hatching of an ASEAN + 1 (China) free trade area helps to eclipse the long-brewing ASEAN + 3 (Japan, Korea, and China) and strengthen the influence of China in the Southeast Asian region (Hsiung 2003).

David Shambaugh (2002) observes that the Chinese leaders are now more informed and better skilled in conducting global affairs because of the growth and the maturity of the China's international think tanks. Over the past two decades, a new generation of think tank specialists has emerged from those who were educated abroad, and ministerial-level officials have increasingly turned to their affiliated think tanks for policy research, expert advice, and information/intelligence gathering. David Lampton (2007) also adds that 'China's leaders are relentless travelers and spend substantial time with foreign dignitaries; China diplomats are capable, experienced, and language proficient and they increasingly understand their host societies.'

Downward shift of governance to substate institutions?

Jean Oi (1992) argues that in China, local states use their political authority single-mindedly to promote *local* industrial development. In Zouping, for example, local (township and village) leaders raised the initial capital for new enterprises and closely supervised and assisted in their subsequent growth. Using their political authority they mobilized capital for investment, arranged and allocated credit, and provided market information and technical expertise well in excess of what was initially present in the locality. In the above process, local states have taken on many characteristics of a business corporation with local state officials acting as the equivalent of a board of directors. Thus Oi (1997) coins the term '*local state corporatism*' to capture this merger between state and economy in the local setting.

This new local institutional development is a product of fiscal decentralization in the reform era. In the mid-1980s provinces, municipality, county, and township governments were subject to a bottom-up revenue-sharing system that required localities to submit only a portion of the revenues to the upper level, and then they were allowed to retain all, or at least most, of the reminder. This fiscal decentralization made local states become independent fiscal entities that had the unprecedented right to use the revenue that they retained (Oi 1992).

As such, the local state officials have a personal interest in promoting local development. Those who prove themselves to be successful economic administrators are rewarded with higher bonus payments, given greater leeway in decision making, and are likely to be promoted to a higher level in the Party and the state (Sargeson and Zhang 1999).

Since local economic development depends to a large extent on the degree to which local states can obtain preferential treatment in the form of loans and financial subsidies from the central state, various local states competed fiercely and they frequently utilized corruption to attain their goals. 'Running red lights,' i.e. bribing those responsible for inspection and/or implementation of regulations and 'Seeking money from ministries' ('*Pao Bu Qian Jin*') has become an unwritten and successful measure for advance local economic development, while the bribery of public officials by other public officials for public, rather than private interests ('*Gong Hui*') was an open secret as a means for seeking funds and other favors from the central government (He 2000).

In sum, fiscal decentralization and local state corporatism are commonly believed to have weakened the power of the central state and shift the mode of governance downward to local state institutions. Wang Shaoguang and Hu Angang (2001) had argued that fiscal decentralization has considerably weakened the central state's extractive capacity. The Chinese state is unable to control the extra-budgetary funds of the local governments, and its relative share of tax revenues has decreased to the extent that the central state has lost effective control over China's economic life.

The failure of local leaders to abide by the regulations issued by the central state and the rampant corruption incurred at the local levels seem to indicate that the central party-state is unable to monitor its lower-level agents and to regulate central-local relations (Pei 2002).

Maybe in response to fiscal decentralization, local state corporatism, and rapid local economic development, there is also a rise of localism in Chinese society. Starting in the 1980s there is a publishing boom of books, journals, and articles devoted to local culture and history, local dignitaries, local grammar and local language (Goodman 2007).

In sum, during the first stage of the reform in the 1980s, there were indeed indicators to show the downward shift of the governance to the local states through fiscal decentralization, local state corporatism, and the rise of localism in Chinese society. Nevertheless, at a later stage of the reform during the 1990s/2000s, the strong party-state is able to re-assert itself and shift the governance back to the center.

First, in the 1990s, a new 'cadre responsibility system' (*ganwei zerenzhi*) is instituted by the central party-state to strengthen its control over the evaluation and monitoring of local leaders. County party secretaries and township heads sign performance contracts, pledge to attain certain targets laid down by higher levels, and are held personally responsible for attaining those targets. There are different contracts for different fields, such as industrial development, agricultural development, tax collection, family planning, and social order. The Chinese party-state has the capacity to be selective, i.e. to implement its priority policies, to control the appointment of its key local leaders, and to target strategically important areas (Oi 1989). Thus Maria Edin (2003: 36) argues that 'state capacity, defined here as the capacity to control and monitor lower-level agents, has increased in China, and that the Chinese Communist Party is capable of greater institutional adaptability than it is usually given credit for.'

In addition, in 1994 the central party-state introduced a 'Tax Sharing Scheme' (TSS) to redress the centre-local imbalance in fiscal matters (Yep 2007). The TSS is aimed to improve the center's control over the economy by increasing 'two ratios' – the share of budgetary revenue in GDP and the central share in total budgetary revenue.

It seems that TSS did succeed in raising the 'two ratios' (Loo and Chow 2006), thus helping to arrest the decline of fiscal foundation of the center and increase the extractive capacity of the central party-state. Zheng (2004: 118–19) argues that the TSS has shifted fiscal power from the provinces back to the center, so 'now, it is the provinces that rely on the central government for revenue.'

Furthermore, the rise of localism over the past two decades certainly doesn't mean the rise of ideology of separatism or some form of cultural and political fragmentation. In the era of globalization, local identities are not constructed as exclusive identities separate from or opposed to other identities, local or national. On the contrary, they are now seen in terms of multiple and overlapping identities. Goodman (2007) insightfully observes that the new local identity was explicitly structured by the central party-state within a hierarchy of pace and identity that reached down to and interacted with the more local levels of county and village, as well as up to the national level. Thus, local identity politics are also likely to reinforce integration with the rest of China. Indeed, Goodman (2007: 17) argues that 'it was China as a whole that remained privileged, in popular culture as much as within the politics of the party-state, rather than the provincial or the local.'

Sideways shift of governance to border provincial governments?

In China, the combination of globalization with decentralization has led to a very uneven pattern of spatial development, with rapid economic growth taking place mostly along the eastern coastal seaboard of China from Macao in the South to the Bohai rim in the North (Breslin 2000). Chen (2005:11) locates the following four subregions that have extensive transborder links but without a formal integration of entire national economies through inter-state treaties or agreements:

- The Greater Tumen Subregion which comprises of three areas: the southeastern border region of China's Jilin province, the northern border area of North Korea, and the Khasan region of the Russian Far East.
- The Bohau/Yellow Sea Subregion consists of the coastal zones of China's Liaoning and Shandong provinces plus Beijing and Tianjin, South Korea's west coast, and Japan's Kyushu region.
- The Greater Southeast China Subregion covers China's Guangdong and Fujian provinces, Hong Kong, Taiwan, and Macau.
- The Greater Mekong Subregion extends over China's Yunnan province, Myannmar, Lao, Thailand, Cambodia, and Vietnam.

The above subregions are characterized by an *'extrovert'* economy, i.e. their economies are driven by foreign direct investment (FDI) and export-led industrialization, and their economic growth relied upon their integration with the global commodity chains. For example, with regard to the commodity chain of athletic shoes, the 1990s observed the trend that transnationals (such as Nike and Reebok) moved their factories from their subcontractors in Taiwan to Dongguan in Guangdong and Putian in Fujian. Most of the raw materials were shipped from Taiwan, and the shoe factories in Guangdong were run by Taiwanese resident managers. The commodity chain of toys is similarly structured: toys were designed by Hong Kong, assembled in Guangdong, often with a Taiwan-made chip for talking dolls, and finally packaged and shipped from Hong Kong to the world markets (Chen 2005).

It is misleading to describe the above subregions as *natural* economic territories (Scalapino 1995). It is nothing 'natural' if we consider how much infrastructure and financial incentives that the local provincial, municipal, and township governments have to put in. Not only do they have to build roads and bridges, reduce land prices, offer long factory leases, cut utilities charges to foreign investors, but they also have to provide special services to foreign investors in processing entry and exit travel documents, clearing traded goods, settling economic disputes, maintaining public order, plus children's education (Chen 2005). In Central China, the local county-level Kunshan government is never shy to admit that it acts as foreign investors' 'running errands' (*paotui*) and never afraid to bypass rules and regulations in order to minimize costs for foreign capital (Po and Pun 2007).

Since the developmental spillovers of FDI have been nowhere near as large as the Chinese leadership expected when they embarked on opening China, and since these subregions appear to be more integrated with the global economy than with the Chinese national economy, Breslin (2007) is critical of the developments of these subregions because they may have to reconfigure the interests of local governments to the global economy.

In addition, a new form of regional governance arrangement is emerging in these subregions to handle such affairs as human and cargo traffic flows across the border, cross-border pollution problem, and the spread of infectious disease like SARS across the borders, and cross-border smuggling and crimes (Lee 2002). These cross-border matters cannot be dealt with solely by the local governments, but have to be handled through a joint effort between the local governments and the adjacent states. For example, a 'Hong Kong-Guangdong Cooperation Joint Conference' was established in March 1998 to develop closer economic integration in the Pearl River Delta (Shen 2004).

The 'extrovert' nature of the economy and the very close linkages to the adjacent states are usually seen as factors to induce the border governments to challenge/resist central policy. Thus, Cai and Treisman (2006) tell a story that the reformist governor of Guangdong (Ye Xuanping) felt so confident by the economic success of his province that he dared to oppose Premier Li Peng's attempt to recentralize budget revenue.

Again, the stories of Ye's 'Provincial rebellion' and the 'fragmentation of national economic space' are overdrawn. There are little indications that the central government has lost control over the border provinces. First, central authorities had little trouble removing regional leaders on many occasions and imposing its policies on them. The provincial governors that did manage to challenge central policies did do by exploiting vertical ties to patrons at the center rather than by mobilizing horizontal organizations of other governors or coordinating a common response (Cai and Treisman 2006).

Second, the central government had the capacity to weaken the economic and political power of the subregions. In the initial stages of the reform, only four special economic zones (SEZs) were established in Guangdong and Fujian provinces, giving these two provinces an undue edge over other places to attract foreign investments and to promote export-led industrialization. However, this preferential SEZ policy was later expanded to other types of zones – 'coastal open areas,' 'coastal open cities,' 'economic and technological development zones,' 'hi-tech development zones,' 'border open cities,' etc. (Chung 2001). With so many different types of zones existing in China, they now need to compete fiercely with each other for FDI as well as for the center's preferential treatment, making them less willing to challenge the central state.

Finally, the central state has the capacity to change the speed of regional integration as it sees fit. For example, not satisfied with the slow rate of integration between Hong Kong and mainland China, even after Hong Kong has become a Special Administrative Region (SAR) of China, the Central government has taken a more active role in managing cross-border affairs (Shen 2004) in recent years:

- When the Hong Kong SAR government and the Guangdong government could not reach agreement on the issue of extending opening hours for border crossings in 2001, the State Council intervened and agreed to provide more funding for the cross-border operation on the Shenzhen side.
- When the Hong Kong SAR government and the Macao SAR government could not reach an agreement on the location and the route of the Hong Kong-Zhuhai/Macao Bridge, and when the bridge plan appeared to be falling apart, the Central government intervened and gave the go-ahead signal for the bridge to pass through both Zhuhai and Macao.
- When the Hong Kong government failed to recover from the Asian economic crisis and the SAR crisis, the Central government agreed to an 'individual traveler's' scheme (previously mainland tourists have to come as a group to Hong Kong on official tours) in order to give a much needed boost to Hong Kong's tourist industry.

In addition, the Central government also can change the scope of regional integration. In 2003, it induced the Hong Kong and Guangdong governments to sign the CEPA (Closer Economic Participation Arrangement). In 2004, it inaugurated the Pan-Pearl River Delta (Pan-PRD) Regional Cooperation and Development Forum between Hong Kong and Macao plus other nine provinces (Guangdong, Guangxi, Yunan, Guizhou, Sichuan, Human, Jiangxi, Fujian and Hainan), an arrangement so-called '9 + 2' (Yeung 2005; Chiu 2006). The CEPA and the Pan-PRD projects are aimed at expanding the scope of regional integration from coastal Guangdong to other inland provinces.

Outward shift of governance to the market and society?

Up until the early 2000s, the Chinese state had been faithfully carrying out the policies of neo-liberalism in its globalization drive (Harvey 2005). Since the Chinese economy was completely dominated by the state in the Maoist period, the aim of the post-Mao reforms was to liberate the market from the state so the Chinese economy could be invigorated and compete in the world economy. The state carried out the following policies over the past several decades:

- *Marketization* policy to restore/expand the market. For example, a new labor market was introduced to the Chinese economy in the late 1980s to create a flexible labor force that is responsive to the ups and downs of the market. After a labor market is created, the state enterprises are no longer required to provide life-long employment to their workers, and they were given the autonomy to hire and fire workers.
- *Privatization* policy to cut the size of the state sector and to increase the size of the private sector. In the 1990s the state enterprises (SOEs) were undergoing corporatization so they are no longer dependent on the state for funding, and they have to operate independently in the market. After corporatization, the SOEs are asked to operate the same as an independent private profit-making enterprise and to go bankrupt if they are losing money (So 2006).
- *Commodification of human services*. Whereas the Maoist state provided human services (like housing, health care, welfare, education, pension, etc.) on a need basis and free of charge to all citizens, the post-reform state treat human services as a commodity to be distributed to people on market principles. Beneficiaries now have to pay a part of the costs for the services in most welfare fields. Such changes can be seen in social insurance (pension, medical care and the newly created unemployment insurance), higher education, and many personal services (Guan 2000).
- *Socialization of social welfare.* What this term means is that in welfare matters, people should eschew dependence on the state. Instead, all strata of society – local communities, mass organizations, families, and individuals – must be actively involved. Citizens should take part in service provisions and management, and they should share in the finance of services. For example, community care is supposed to be the answer to help enterprises to shed their welfare burden. Amenities run by street offices and residents' committees – old people's homes, nurseries, support groups for the elderly, work therapy stations for mental patients – have grown rapidly after the corporatization drive in the 1990s (Wong and MacPherson 1995).

Through the above processes of marketization, privatization, commodification, and socialization, the state was moving toward the 'neo-liberal' doctrine of reducing the state's role in welfare and human services provision. It seems that the Chinese state was working hard to download its welfare functions and shift its governance to market and society.

The above observation, however, may have been outdated by the recent policy of the Hu-Wen leadership. Secretary-General Hu Jintao and Premier Wen Jiabao reestablished their credentials as champions of those who have not fared so well from reforms. In 2006, they presented a new policy of 'building a new socialist countryside' and a 'harmonious society' to the Sixth Plenum (Saich 2007).

The 'socialist countryside' policy is significant because it could signal a change of ideological orientation of the Chinese state (Kahn 2006). Whereas the pre-2006 Chinese state endorses a neo-liberal orientation which could be called 'GNPism', the Hu-Wen policy is moving toward a more balanced orientation between economic growth and social development. While market reforms would continue, this 'socialist countryside' policy indicates that the state would take a more energetic role in moderating the negative impacts of marketization. In the new policy, the state should include 'the people and environment' in its developmental plan and should not just focus narrowly on GNP indicators and economic growth.

Thus the new policy advocates a transfer of resources from the state to strengthen the fiscal foundation of the countryside. Not only has the agricultural tax been abolished to help relieve the burden on farmers, there is a 15 percent boost in rural expenditure (to $15 billion) to bankroll guaranteed minimum living allowances for farmers, and an 87 percent hike (to $4 billion) for the health-care budget (Liu 2007). These policies indicate a massive infusion of funding from the state onto the peasants and rural areas.

In addition, there is a de-commodification of human services. Rural residents would no longer have to pay many of the miscellaneous charges levied by schools; fees at primary school will be abolished as part of a nationwide campaign to eliminate them in the countryside for the first nine years of education. The state is also going to increase the subsidies for rural health cooperatives that will be available in 80 percent of the rural counties by 2008. For now rural residents have to pay market rates at the village's private clinic and most of them do not even have medical insurance and will have to spend more than 80 percent of their cash on health care (Liu 2007).

Furthermore, the 'socialist countryside' policy is aimed at reducing social inequality, especially the widening gap between the countryside and the city. Thus, pensions are to be made available for everyone, not just those enjoying the privileged status of registered urban residents. Over the past two years, the state has also been promoting the spread of Minimum Living Standard Assistance (MLSA) for the rural population. This could be a highly significant development, opening up for the first time the real possibility of instituting a social safety net that covers the whole of the population, whether urban or rural (*The Economist* 2006; Hussain 2005).

Why did the Chinese state suddenly want to reverse its policy toward market liberalization? Studying the New Deal policy in the United States, Karl Polanyi (1944) puts forward an explanation that when the effects of market liberalization have caused massive harm to the society, a counter-movement will emerge from the society to tame the market so as to minimize its damages. If we apply Polanyi's framework to the Chinese case, then the mounting insurgency of labor in the urban area (So 2007), the spread of farmers' protests in the countryside (Li and O'Brien 1996), the growing activism of the NGOs and the civil society (Zhang 2003), and the growing vocalism from a new generation of 'New Left' in the academic circle (Hook 2007) could be seen as counter-movements that prompt the Chinese leaders to adopt 'reform from the above' to contain these resistance movements before they grow out of hand.

Since the above pro-welfare policies only started in 2006, it is obviously too early to tell whether they will have a long-term structural impact. Nevertheless, the fact that these pro-welfare reforms existed has already indicated that the Chinese state had second thoughts about the neo-liberal policies and it may not want to download all of the welfare function to the market and society.

Conclusions and remarks

Like the socialist states in Eastern Europe, China has faced the challenges of globalization when it decided to re-engage the world-economy in the late 1980s. Subsequently, its mode of governance has shifted '*upward*' to suprastate organizations when it joins such organizations as the WTO and WHO, has shifted '*downward*' to substate organizations when it carried out the policy of fiscal decentralization, has shifted '*sideways*' to border governments when subregion economies have sprung up along the coastal areas, and shifted '*outward*' to market and society when it carried out neo-liberal policies to download welfare obligations.

However, unlike the socialist states in Eastern Europe, China is able to handle the challenges of globalization very well. For the '*upward*' challenge, China is able to seize the opportunity to expand its power and influence in suprastate organizations, to learn how to play the rules of games to take advantage of them, and even able to initiate its own macro-regional organizations (like the SCO and the ASEAN + 1). For the '*downward*' and '*sideways*' challenges, China is able to turn them into motive forces of economic development while still maintaining full control over the substates and the border governments. For the '*outward*' challenge, China is also able to re-regulate the market and contain the harms done by it.

In sum, the Chinese state is able to manage the globalization process very well. It is not threatened by globalization and is definitely not a victim of the forces of globalization. As such, what is the implication of all these transformations on the power of the Chinese state?

If power is defined as the capacity to restructure actual situations, then the power of the Chinese state has increased during its re-engagement with the world economy. First, its *extractive capacity* of the Chinese state has increased. Although fiscal decentralization in the early stage of reform has weakened the state's extractive capacity, the Tax Sharing Scheme (TSS) in 1994 is able to redress the center-local imbalance in fiscal matters. In fact, the central state is now so rich that it could afford to allocate massive funding to the countryside to improve its infrastructure on education and health.

Second, its *adaptive capacity* has increased. The Chinese state is able to design new policy or to modify old policy when a new situation arises. For example, it could propose fiscal re-centralization to strengthen the center's finance; it could accelerate the speed or expand the scope of cross-border integration between

Hong Kong and mainland China (through the CEPA and Pan-PRD project) when Hong Kong is unable to overcome the Asian financial crisis and the SAR crisis on its own.

Third, its *legitimacy capacity* also seems to be functioning well. Despite the growing number of protests in urban areas and the countryside, these protests are generally small-scale, short duration, compartmentalized, mostly targeted at the local institutions, and stay within legal limits (So 2007). The Chinese state is thus able to blame the local officials for causing the protests and maintain a moral high ground. Despite the emergence of localism and local identity, the Chinese national symbol and national identity remain very strong.

The above observations tend to support the view that the Chinese nation-state have been strengthened and has more capacity during its re-engagement with the world economy. If this is the case, why is China able to do so while other states are failing at their attempts?

The Chinese nation-state is no ordinary state because it has a *Leninist party-state* structure, with the communist party and the state bureaucracy closely intermingled with each other. Before the 1978 reform era, the Chinese Leninist state was so strong that it was able to penetrate deeply into economy and society to carry out such revolutionary programs as the Land Reform, the Great Forward, and the Cultural Revolution.

Although the Leninist party-state has the capacity to make structural transformations, its ideology has served to preclude it from promoting any capitalist economic development. In fact, the Leninist party-state was fond of attacking the 'capitalist roaders' who are found to have deviated from the official socialist policy. In the 1950s/1960s, this ideological rigidity is reinforced by the Cold War, whose line of conflict was drawn between capitalism and communism. The US tried every means to contain Chinese communism from spreading to other places (like setting up an economic blockade, dividing the Chinese nation into a free (Taiwan) and a 'non-free' one, starting wars along the China's border: the Korean War and the Vietnam War, and preventing the communist party-state from joining the UN). Therefore, before the era of globalization in the 1980s, China was forced to withdraw from the capitalist world economy due to the strong hostility of the anti-communist front.

Then why would China re-enter the world economy? The Chinese Leninist party-state had to wait until the Cold War and the Cultural Revolution to subside as well as wait until the old generation of communist revolutionaries passed away in the late 1970s before it had a chance to clear up the ideological barrier. Moreover, China is situated in East Asia, a region which experienced very rapid economic growth after the Second World War. Observing the remarkable economic success of its East Asian neighbors (Japan, South Korea, Taiwan, Hong Kong, and Singapore) must have convinced the Chinese state to drop the socialist ideology and follow the band wagon of export industrialization (So 2003a). Since ideology is the main barrier to prevent China from promoting capitalist development, the clearing of an ideological barrier would provide the Chinese Leninist party-state with an opportunity to fully realize its capacity to promote structural transformations.

In sum, the success of China's management of the globalization process is explained through its legacy of the Leninist party-state. This paper argues that a strong Leninist party-state had provided China with the capacity to meet the challenges of globalization. In the Maoist period, it was due to this ideological blind spot that China was prevented from realizing its potential. Once this ideological barrier is cleared away, the post-ideological Leninist party-state could quickly promote capitalist development and handle the challenges of globalization.

Of course, this doesn't mean the road will be completely smooth for Chinese development from now on. After going through the first stage of '*opening up*,' China now needs to face a different set of challenges of '*rising up*' like the following:

- The challenge of continued economic growth. China has attained a truly remarkable economic growth over the past three decades, but there are signs that China is running out of resources, is having difficulties catching up with technological innovation and will have to move up the value-added hierarchy in the commodity chain.
- The challenge of hegemonic struggle. The global search for raw materials (especially energy), market, talents, and capital will inevitably bring China into conflict with major powers of the world. US pundits and politicians have already speculated how to prevent or to delay the rise of China.
- The challenge of changing class structure and the power base of the party-state. Rapid economic growth has resulted in the expansion of both the capitalist class and the new middle class, undermining the traditional socioeconomic support of the party-state (So 2003b).
- The challenge of distribution of power in China. So far, the party-state has focused on economic development while avoiding making any changes on the political structure. Given the growing unrests in the civil society, it seems that the party-state can no longer prolong the issue of political restructuring.

Although this paper argues that the Leninist party-state has successfully met the challenges of '*opening up*' in its initial encountering with the forces of globalization, there is no guarantee that it will be so successful at meeting the above challenges of '*rising up.*' This is because in the second stage of 'rising up,' the issues will be more complicated as they involve structural changes, the stake involved will be higher, and the conflict will be more acute. For example, Pei (2006) is quite pessimistic and talks about the possibility of political decay and a 'trapped transition.' How China handles the above challenges will determine its historic fate in the twenty-first century.

Note

1 The author wants to thank Keun Lee and other conference participants for their critical comments on the chapter.

References

Breslin, S. (2000) 'Decentralization, Globalization and China's Partial Re-Engagement with the Global Economy', *New Political Economy,* 5(2), pp. 205–25.

Breslin, S. (2006) 'Impact of Globalization on State Agency in China', paper presented at the International Conference on State Capacity of China in the 21st Century, City University of Hong Kong, 19–20 April 2007.

Cai, H.B. and Treisman, D. (2006) 'Did Government Decentralization cause China's Economic Miracle?', unpublished manuscript, Department of Political Science, UCLA.

Chan, G. (2004a) 'China's Compliance in Global Environmental Affairs', *Asian Pacific Viewpoint,* Vol. 45, pp. 69–86.

Chan, G. (2004b) 'China and the WTO: the Theory and Practice of Compliance', *International Relations of the Asia-Pacific*, Vol. 4, pp. 47–72.

Chen X.M. (2005) As Border Bend: Transnational Spaces on the Pacific Rim. Lanham: Rowman & Littlefield.

Chiu P.Y.W. (2006) 'CEPA: A Milestone in the Economic Integration between Hong Kong and Mainland China', *Journal of Contemporary China,* 15 (47), pp. 275–95.

Chung, J.H. (2001) 'Reappraising Central-Local Relations in Deng's China: Decentralization, Dilemmas of Control, and Diluted Effects of Reforms', in B.J. Dickson (ed.) *Remaking the Chinese State*, pp. 46–75. New York: Routledge.

The Economist (2006) 'Asia: Dreaming of Harmony; China', *The Economist*, 21 October 2006, 381 (8500): 76.

Edin, M. (2003) 'State Capacity and Local Agent Control in China: CCP Cadre Management from a Township Perspective', *The China Quarterly,* Vol. 173, pp. 35–42.

Evans, P. (1997) 'The Eclipse of the State? Reflection of Stateness in an Era of Globalization', *World Politics,* 50 (October), pp. 62–82.

Goodman, D.S.G. (2007) 'Localism and State Capacity: Economic Growth and the Construction of Space', paper presented at the International Conference on State Capacity of China in the 21st Century, City University of Hong Kong, 19–20 April 2007.

Guan X.P. (2000) 'China's Social Policy: Reform and Development in the Context of Marketization and Globalization', *Social Policy and Administration,* Vol. 34, pp. 115–30.

Harvey, D. (2005) *A Brief History of Neo-Liberalism.* Oxford: Oxford University Press.

He, Z.K. (2000) 'Corruption and Anti-corruption in Reform China', *Communist and Post-Communism Studies*, Vol. 32, pp. 243–70.

Hook, L. (2007) 'The Rise of China's New Left', *Far Eastern Economic Review,* April pp. 8–14.

Hsiung, J.C. (2003) 'The Aftermath of China's Accession to the World Trade Organization', *The Independent Review,* 8 (Summer), pp. 87–112.

Hsu, B.E.C. and Douglas W.A. (2007) 'WTO Accession, Financial Reform and the Rule of Law in China', *The China Review,* Vol. 7, pp. 53–81.

Hussain, A. (2005) 'Preparing China's Social Safety Net', *Current History*, 104 (683), pp. 683–722.

Jessop, B. (2002) *The Future of the Capitalist State*. Cambridge: Polity Press.

Kahn, J. (2006) 'A Sharp Debate Erupts in China Over Ideologies', *New York Times*, 12 March 2006.

Lampton, D.M. (2007) 'The Faces of Chinese Power', *Foreign Affairs*, 86 (1): 115.

Lee, Y.S.F. (2002) 'Tackling Cross-border Environmental Problems in Hong Kong', *The China Quarterly*, pp. 986–1009.

Li, L.J. and O'Brien, K.J. (1996) 'Villagers and Popular Resistance in Contemporary China', *Modern China*, Vol. 22, pp. 28–61.

Liu, M. (2007) 'Beijing's New Deal', *Newsweek*, 26 March 2007.

Loo, B. and Chow, S.Y. (2006) 'China's 1994 Tax Sharing Reforms: One System, Different Impact', *Asian Survey*, Vol. 46, pp. 215–37.

Nan, X. (2001) 'WTO: Fa de chongxin goujia (WTO: the restructuring of law)', *Nanfang Zhoubao* (Southern Weekly). 25 October, quoted in Statement made by Donald C. Clarke before the US-China Commission's Public Hearing on WTO Compliance and Sectoral Issues, 17 January 2002.

Oi, J. (1989) *State and Peasant in Contemporary China: The Political Economy of Village Government*. Berkeley: University of California Press.

Oi, J. (1992) 'Fiscal Reform and the Economic Foundations of Local State Corporatism in China', *World Politics*, Vol. 45, pp. 99–126.

Oi, J. (1997) 'The Evolution of Local State Corporatism', working paper, *The Social Sciences*, no. 8, Division of Social Science, Hong Kong University of Science and Technology.

Ohmae, K. (1995) *The End of the Nation State*. New York: Harper Collins.

Pei, M.X. (2002) 'Beijing Drama: China's Governance Crisis and Bush's New Challenge', *Policy Brief*, No. 21, November 2002.

Pei, M.X. (2006) 'The Dark Side of China's Rise?', *Foreign Policy*, March/April 2006.

Polanyi, K. (1944) *The Great Transformation*. Boston: Beacon.

Po, L. and Pun, N. (2007) 'Taiwanese Capital and the Formation of the Kunshan Export Processing Zone', unpublished manuscript.

Sargeson, S. and Zhang, J.(1999) 'Reassessing the Role of the Local State: A Case Study of Local Government Interventions in Property Rights Reform in a Hanzhou District', *The China Journal*, Vol. 42, pp. 7–99.

Scalapino, R.A. (1995) 'Natural Economic Territories in East Asia – Present Trends and Future Prospects', in Korean Economic Institute of America (ed.) *Economic Cooperation and Challenges in the Pacific*. Washington, DC: Korean Institute of America, pp. 99–109.

Scholte, J.A. (2005) *Globalization: A Critical Introduction*. New York: Palgrave.

Shambaugh, D. (2002) 'China's International Relations Think Tanks: Evolving Structure and Process', *The China Quarterly*, Vol. 171, pp. 575–96.

Shen, J. (2004) 'Cross-border Urban Governance in Hong Kong: The Role of State in a Globalizing City-Region', *The Political Geographer*, Vol. 56 (4), pp. 530–43.

Saich, T. (2007) 'Focus on Social Development', *Asian Survey*, Vol. 47, pp. 32–43.

So, A.Y. (2003a) 'Rethinking China's Developmental Miracle', in Alvin Y. So (ed.) *China's Developmental Miracle: Origins, Transformations, and Challenges*. Armonk: M.E. Sharpe, pp. 1–26.

So, A.Y. (2003b) 'The Changing Pattern of Class and Class Conflict in China', *Journal of Contemporary Asia*, Vol. 33 (3), pp. 363–76.

So, A.Y. (2007) 'The State and Labour Insurgency in Post-Socialist China', in Joseph Y.S. Cheng (ed.) *Challenges and Policy Programmes of China's New Leadership*. Hong Kong: City University of Hong Kong Press, pp. 133–50.

So, B.W.Y. (2005) 'Privatization', in C. Tubilewicz (ed.) *Critical Issues in Contemporary China*. New York and London: Routledge, pp. 50–79.

Strange, S. (1996) *The Retreat of the State*. Cambridge: Cambridge University Press.

Zhu, T.B. (2003) 'Building Institutional Capacity for China's New Economic Opening', in L. Weiss (ed.) *States in Global Economy: Bringing Domestic Institutions Back In*. Cambridge: Cambridge University Press, Chapter 7.

Wang, G.G. (2007) 'Conditionality for China's Peaceful Rise,' in J.Y.S. Cheng (ed.) *Challenges and Policy Programmes of China's New Leadership*. Hong Kong: City University of Hong Kong Press, pp. 153–77.

Wang, S.G. and Hu, A.G. (2001) *The Chinese Economy in Crisis: State Capacity and Tax Reform*. Armonk, NY: M. E. Sharpe.

Wong, L. and MacPherson, S. (1995) *Social Change and Social Policy in Contemporary China*. Aldershot: Ashgate.

Yep, R. (2007) 'Tax Assignment Reform and its Impact on County Finance: Enhancing Regulatory Capacity for the Central State?', paper presented at the International Conference on 'State Capacity of China in the 21st century', City University of Hong Kong, 19–20 April 2007.

Yeung, Y-M. (2005) 'Emergence of the Pan-Pearl River Delta', *Geography Annals*, 87 B (1): 75–9.

Zhang, K. and Wang, C. (2001) 'China's Sustainable Development Strategy and International Cooperation on Environment,' in Z.H. Tao and R. Wolfrum (eds) *Implementing International Environmental Law in Germany and China*. London: Kluwer Law, pp. 1–20

Zhang, Y. (2003) 'China's Emerging Civil Society', unpublished manuscript.

Zheng, Y.N. (2004) *Globalization and State Transformation in China*. New York: Cambridge University Press.

10 Can the Communist Party sustain its rule in China?

Yongnian Zheng

> The modern prince, the myth-prince, cannot be a real person, a concrete individual. It can only be an organism, a complex element of society in which a collective will, which has already been recognised and has to some extent asserted itself in action, begins to take concrete form. History has already provided this organism, and it is the political party . . .
>
> Antonio Gramsci: *Prison Notebooks*

Introduction

'Is Communist Party Rule Sustainable in China?' This was the title for the first debate of *Reframing China Policy*, organised by the Carnegie Endowment for International Peace, a Washington-based think tank.[1] In the debate, two leading China experts in the United States, Roderick MacFarquhar (from Harvard University) and Andrew Nathan (from Columbia University), presented rebuttals to each other's position, with MacFarquhar arguing that the Chinese Communist Party (CCP) will not be able to sustain itself and Nathan taking the opposite view.[2] Whilst each presented plenty of evidence to support his case, none of it is convincing. One can reasonably argue that it will be a difficult, if not impossible, enterprise to answer such a big question; but exactly because it is a big question, both the scholarly community, and policy circles as well, have tried to answer it, and the amount of attention being paid to it seems to be justifiable. It is widely believed that the rise of China has presented one of the most important global challenges facing all major powers this century. As the only ruling party, the CCP's sustainability is apparently legitimate to be questioned.

It has not been easy for the scholarly community to answer this question. Indeed, immediately after the crackdown on the pro-democracy movement in 1989, MacFarquhar (1991) predicted that the days of the CCP in China were numbered, and he was not alone at that time in making such a prediction. Of course, contemporaneous arguments were that the CCP would go back to a very traditional and highly centralised rule after the crackdown. No one predicted that the late Deng Xiaoping would make a southern tour and initiate an ever more radical movement of decentralisation, which fundamentally altered the direction of change in China. On reaching the post-Deng era, the question at issue has been repeatedly raised.[3] At the other end of the spectrum from MacFarquhar, optimists are beginning to view China as a model for other parts of the world.[4] Still others have made efforts to go beyond simply pessimistic and optimistic positions to reach a more balanced view on China's future.[5]

Among many uncertainties about China, the key is undoubtedly the CCP. Once deemed the vanguard of the Chinese State, the CCP's failing ideological appeal, its equally unattractive and clumsy structure, and its disillusioned party cadres are increasingly making the Party's sustainability problematic. China's 'open door' policy and the rapid globalisation process in the post-Cold War era have generated increasingly high pressure for changes in the leadership of the CCP. To sustain its rule, the CCP now needs to review its continued relevance to the ongoing and fast-changing economic, social and political climates in China. Party reform appears to be the most logical and urgent choice, and whilst the CCP leadership has engaged in various forms of this, there is no clear direction given for the Party's transformation.

Although there is a fast-growing body of literature on China's development and its future, the CCP has been marginalised in the scholarly community. More often than not, when scholars attempt to examine the development and future of China, they tend to focus on some other factors rather than the CCP itself, even though they realise its importance. Most arguments have centred on China's economic development and the impact of that on other aspects of development, including the CCP. In recent years, there have been some efforts to bring the CCP back in;[6] nevertheless, it remains under-studied.

In an attempt to answer the question of whether the CCP rule is sustainable, this chapter focuses on the Party itself. It is divided into three parts: the first one discusses the nature of the CCP; the second examines how the CCP has transformed itself; and the third explores the relations between the CCP and global capitalism. Finally, there will be an assessment of the sustainability of the CCP, from all of these perspectives.

The nature of the CCP

To answer the question of whether the CCP rule is sustainable, it is important to look at the nature of the CCP; strictly speaking, it is not a 'political party' by Western standards.

The term 'political parties' emerged in the nineteenth century with the development of representative institutions and the expansion of the suffrage in Europe and the United States (Sartori 1976) and the expression initially referred to those 'organizations whose goal was the capture of public office in electoral competition with one or more other parties' (Schlesinger 1968: 428). Perceptions of what constituted a party also differed; in continental Europe, scholars often regarded the party as the instrument of its membership and thus put an emphasis on party structure. This is especially reflected in the works of the scholars Robert Michels, from Germany, and the French Maurice Duverger. Based on his study of the German Social Democratic Party, Michels (1962) formulated the 'iron law of oligarchy'.

It seemed to him that nothing could prevent the party leaders' ambitions for office from superseding the membership's ideals. In the same vein, but one step further, Duverger (1964) argued that the entire electorate would inevitably be incorporated into parties. On the other hand, in the Anglo-Saxon tradition, the party is often perceived as primarily responsive to the electorate. Scholars have also focused on different aspects of the party (Schumpeter 1975; Downs 1957). Eckstein points out that study of the party in the West is organised around two major facets, i.e. the study of party 'units' vs. the study of party 'systems'. The former involves the characteristics of political parties as discrete entities – their various social bases, histories, goals and appeals, formal organisations, and actual power structures, while the latter involves the competitive interaction patterns between party units (Eckstein 1968: 436).

It has almost become an absolute truth that where there are no elections, there is no democracy. Scholars have regarded the existence of competitive elections between parties as a necessary condition of democracy. This is also true in the case of China. When scholars talk about democratisation in China, more often than not they refer to the birth of the multiparty system and the attendant competitive elections. In democratic settings, political parties are often narrowly defined as an interest-integrating or interest-representing mechanism for social groups. Whilst there is nothing wrong with this definition, it is deficient in explaining the party system in China (and also other East Asian states). Political parties were the product of Western political development, which then spread to the rest of the world. When parties came to East Asia, they began to play a role radically different from that played by parties in the West.

In late-developing countries, including China, political parties are often dominant over states. But this is not the case in the advanced West, especially Western Europe and North America. Before the birth of modern political parties, modern states were already developed in the West. From the twelfth to fourteenth centuries, when the modern state began to form, to the nineteenth century, when it became mature, the state was under constant transformation (Poggi 1978). The political party was a later product of this long genesis. Whilst the birth of the political party radically transformed the modern state, the political party *per se* is hardly relevant to its origin. It is reasonable to argue that parties were developed to rationalise the state by democratising the political process; the development of democracy in the West went through various stages, as did the development of political parties, which was associated with the rise of parliaments (LaPalombara 1969).

Max Weber divided the historical evolution of political parties into three stages: aristocratic cliques, small groups of notables, and plebiscitarian democracy. In the early stage, although political parties aimed at participating in the political process, they were actually 'clubs' and only a small portion of social elites were eligible to join. The first group of social 'elites' was comprised only of aristocrats; democracy implied power-sharing amongst this group exclusively, and had nothing to do with other types of social elites. With rising demands for political participation from other social groups, these clubs expanded their social bases to include a wide range of social elites in its membership. Political parties became a mechanism for different types of social elites to share power. But only when parties reached the stage of plebiscitarian democracy and when competitive elections became widely accepted did modern parties reach maturity (Weber 1958).

Most scholars have pointed to the fact that parties were the most effective means of coping with a political crisis resulting from political development. Amongst others, the main forms of crisis in the West included legitimacy, integration and participation. All of these crises provided opportunities for the rise of parties, which in turn helped with the resolution of all of these crises (Binder *et al.* 1971). In modern democracies, democracy means partisan politics and is realised via elections, which are organised by political parties. Schumpeter (1975), on this basis, regarded democracy as a process in which political elites competed for political power via elections; the rationale of political parties was embedded in elections. If effective elections were to materialise, there must be organisations and forums, and political parties came to perform these functions.

When examining the development of political parties in China and other East Asian countries, it will be found to be necessary to go beyond the narrow definition of 'parties as electoral machines'. Simply speaking, while 'no political parties, no democracy' remains true in China and East Asia, the existence of political parties is not only, and merely, for the development of democracy, but also for state building. Though the evolution of political parties in the West went through different stages, parties mainly served as a mechanism for aggregation and articulation of interests. In East Asia, whilst political parties also perform such functions, they are not their main ones; their most important role in that region is to create a modern form of the state. Actually, in all late-developing countries, political parties not only serve as institutions for political participation and tools for political leaders to share power; more importantly, they are tools for state building, economic development and social transformation.

That the state was created by political parties does not mean that the state did not exist in China before the coming of the concept of political parties from the West. China's dynastic states existed for thousands of years. Nevertheless, the traditional state was radically different from modern states developed in the West. With the expansion of Western imperialism, the traditional state had to be replaced with Western forms of state. Whilst political elites in China decided to give up their traditional forms of state, they had to do so because Western forms of state were more advanced and effective.

The idea of modern political parties was alien to the Chinese; it was spread to China during the long process of the breakdown of the imperial system and the intrusion of Western imperialism. Factions or cliques (*pengdang* in Chinese) existed in all dynasties, and factional strife could become overwhelming from time to time. But factions or cliques did not have any ideological legitimacy and were not developed into political parties in a modern sense. Modern political parties were introduced to bring down the imperial system and resist Western forces. During the process, Chinese political elites found that the issue was not whether China should 'import' parties and party systems, but what model China should follow. Political leaders realised that parties had to stand in the centre of power in their struggle against the imperial state and foreign imperialism. Sun Yat-sen and his followers 'imported' parties and party systems that had been developed in Western democratic states. In their early days as revolutionaries, Sun Yat-sen and the others believed that a republican government, based on the Western European and North American multiparty model, would enable China to build a strong modern state; the aim of creating such a strong democratic state was, however, not helped by the 1911 Revolution which Sun Yat-sen initiated. New democratic political arrangements 'failed to bring unity and order, not to mention legitimacy. Representative government degenerated rapidly into an autocracy hostile to popular participation and ineffective in foreign policy' (Hunt 1993: 68). Though the multiparty system was in line with democracy, partisan conflicts made it difficult to develop a sound institutional foundation for China's state. Sun realised that without strong political institutions, any type of democratic regime would not be stable and China would not become a strong state. Sun thus turned to the organisational side of state building. His strategy became 'state building through party organisation', which he learned from the Russian revolution. It is worthwhile to cite Sun at length regarding the party transformation. He argued:

> Why has our party not engaged in organized, systematic, and disciplined struggle before? It was because we lacked the model and the precedent ... The Russian Revolution took place six years later than in our country, and yet after one revolution the Russians have been able to apply their principles thoroughly; moreover, since the revolution the revolutionary government has rapidly become more stable. Both are revolutions: Why have they succeeded in Russia, and why have we not in China? It is because the Russian Revolution owed its success to the struggle of the Party member: on the one hand the Party members struggled, and on the other hand they were aided by military forces, and so they were able to succeed. Therefore, if we wish our revolution to succeed, we must learn the methods, organization, and training of the Russians; then there can be hope of success.
>
> (Teng and Fairbank 1979: 256)

According to Sun, the Russians placed the party above the state; the Russian model was more appropriate to China's modernisation and state making than the Western European and American models. China, therefore, should follow the strategy of 'governing the state through the party' and the priority would be to establish a new state structure. 'We do not have a state to be ruled. What we need to do is to construct a state. After the construction of the state, we can govern it' (Sun 1986: 103). Only after a strong and highly organised party had been built could China begin to make a strong state. Only a strong state could lead to a working democracy. This was probably the most important factor that underlined Sun's efforts in 1924 to reorganise the party that he had founded: the Kuomintang of

China (KMT). The reorganisation actually transformed the KMT from a premature Western-style party to a Leninist party. As a consequence of this reformation, the KMT became highly organised and centralised, and Sun's successor Chiang Kai-shek stuck to that course. During the 1926–28 'Northern Expedition', China was finally recentralised under the KMT party regime. However, during the Civil War between followers of the CCP and those of the KMT (1945–49), the KMT was defeated by the CCP. The KMT retreated to Taiwan, and the CCP established its own version of the state – the People's Republic. While the CCP moved away from the KMT in terms of their ideologies, the two parties inherited the same Leninist structure – Party dominance of the state.

Party leaders in China had dual mandates: they were expected to create a viable state, and to ensure economic development. To create a viable and orderly state, they had to, at least, establish effective control over a territory and, at best, establish a legitimate state perceived to be both sovereign and responsive to its citizens' needs. Further, to achieve economic development, they had to, at least, initiate economic growth and, at best, reconcile growth with distributive concerns. To achieve all these goals, party leaders had to depend on political parties, and in this sense, the CCP is the most effective tool that political leaders could employ to achieve their goals.

Historical discontinuity, the importation of the Leninist state, and the role of parties in creating the new state and promoting socio-economic transformation: all of these factors differentiate political parties in China from those in the West. Whilst parties came after the state in the West, the order is reversed in China. This reversal changes the nature of parties and party systems. In the West, political parties are mere institutions of the state. But in China, the CCP is considered as separate from the state itself. Whilst the CCP created the state, it was able to stand above it, and behave like an emperor in the old days, lording over bureaucratic organisations. In other words, the party is the personification of a modern emperor. It is a highly organised emperorship which attempts to exercise total control over the state and society (Schurmann 1968).

Furthermore, when individual leaders create the party, they are able to stand above the party machinery and behave like an emperor who perceives the state as his personal belonging. In other words, individual leaders tend to use political parties as a tool to maximise their power and interests. The personalisation of power strengthens political leaders' personal power, but often weakens the capacity of political parties in leading or coping with democratic transition. The following simple formula outlines the relationship between party capacity, institutionalisation, and personalisation:

$$\text{Party Capacity} = \text{Institutionalisation} / \text{Personalisation}$$

Here, 'personalisation' refers to the rule of man, meaning that the party is governed by individual leaders (their charisma, personality, etc.), while 'institutionalisation' refers to the rule of law, meaning that it is governed by established rules. 'Party capacity' refers to a given ruling party's ability to sustain itself while engaging in socio-economic transformation. The formula attempts to show that there is a positive linkage between institutionalisation and party capacity, while the linkage between personalisation and party capacity is a negative one.

The personalisation of the ruling party leads to many consequences. Amongst others, three are notable. First, strong leaders are often associated with a weak CCP. The CCP is highly personalised, meaning that its top leaders behave like emperors and build their parties as an emperorship. The personalisation of the political party has not only resulted in highly centralised political power, but also rendered it difficult for the party to institutionalise itself. While party leaders are strong, the party itself is quite weak. To a great degree, the party is often a personal tool for individual leaders to organise and perpetuate personal power. When individual leaders fall, the party is necessarily weakened.

Second, a strong party is often associated with a weak state. If the party is weak in the midst of strong individual leaders, the state is even weaker than the party. Political parties were actually the creators of the new states. After the new state was established, it would be very difficult to separate parties from the state. The ruling party is often not only in charge of policy formation, but also policy administration and implementation. The party actually serves as the first level of government, and the state becomes the second level of government; although the party and state are two separate organisations, the latter is actually subordinate to the former. State capacity waxes and wanes in accordance with party capacity. The situation worsens if the strength of the party is the result of the power of individual leaders, as their fall often results in the weakening, or even the downfall, of the party, which in turn leads to the weakening of the state.

Third, and also ironically, while the party attempts to perform as creator of a modern Chinese state, the dominance of the party has actually slowed down state modernisation in China, which is far from being accomplished, despite many attempts at it. China is still 'a civilisation, which pretended to be a state', as American political scientist Lucian Pye (1990) has described it. Since the CCP has been the most important pillar supporting a seemingly modern state (Schurmann 1968), the state is largely incapable of performing the regulatory function entrusted to it. China lacks the defining characteristic of a modern state: the rule of law. Without the rule of law, the Chinese state can hardly become a modern regulatory state; but with the dominance of the party over the state, China is facing insurmountable difficulties in building a system of the rule of law (Zheng 1999).

The CCP in transformation

I have so far discussed the nature of the CCP at length, in order to show why it cannot simply be regarded as a political party in a western sense (Zheng 2006). The discussion also shows the strengths and weaknesses of the CCP in engaging in socio-economic development and self-transformation. So, to answer the question of whether CCP rule is sustainable involves looking at what actions the CCP is taking in order to ensure its own sustainability amidst rapid socio-economic transformation in China.

Rapid economic development in the past quarter of a century has created a new socio-economic environment for Chinese politics. With its economy growing at an annual rate of more than 9 per cent, China's per capita GDP in 2004 had reached US$1,200, approaching the level of mid-income countries. An increasingly open economy has created conditions for the development of a more open society: by 2003, China had surpassed the USA as the world's largest telephone market. By early 2006 China's registered Internet users exceeded 1,200 million to form the world's second largest 'web population' after the USA. To survive this new environment, the CCP has to reorder its relations with various actors in society, and in the following sections, I discuss how the CCP has made efforts to sustain itself by adjusting to such a changing socio-economic environment.

Becoming a catch-all party?

Whilst the CCP remains dominant and enjoys a monopoly of politics in the country, it has been gradually transforming itself into a 'catch-all' party in the past decade. To a degree, the CCP can be defined as a process of politics, opening up – slowly and gradually – to accommodate different social actors. Such a process is reflected in changes in the composition of the CCP.

The CCP today remains the world's single largest political party, its membership having surged past 70.8 million in the year 2005 (see Figure 10.1). It has been undergoing a drastic transformation from a peasantry- and workers-based

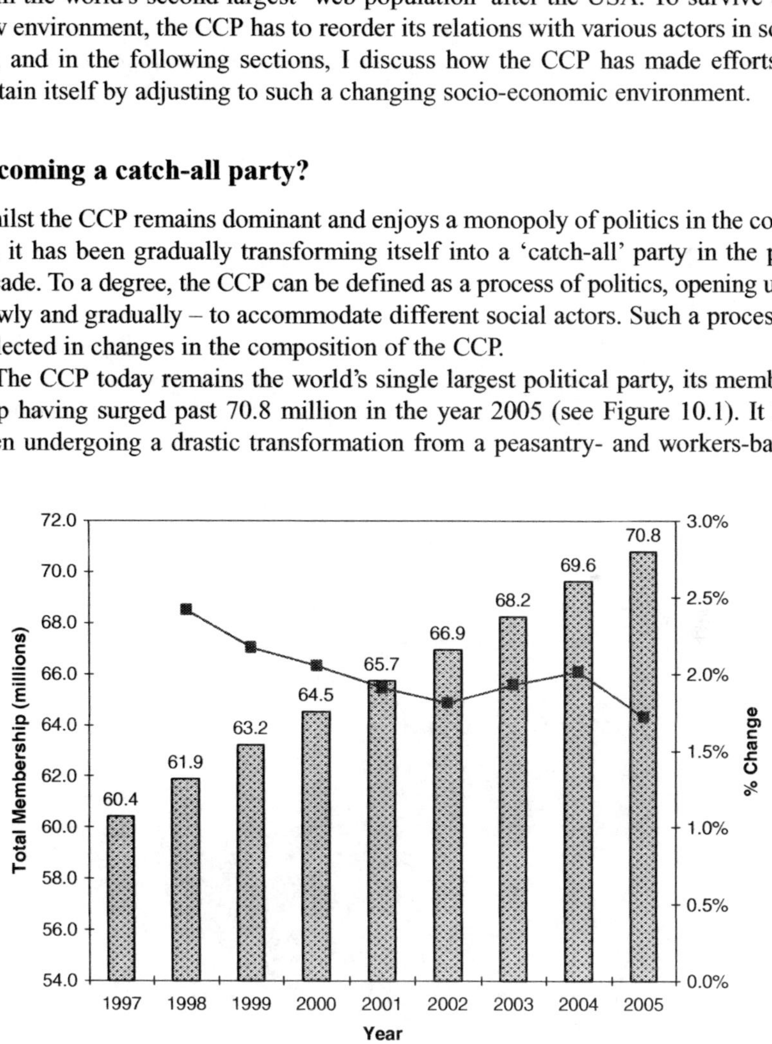

Figure 10.1 CCP's membership since 1997.
Source: Xinhua News Agency, www.xinhuanet.com. (Accessed on 22 February, 2007.)

party to a 'catch-all' one. During Mao's era, the CCP was a revolutionary party that was dominated by workers and peasants; in 1956, the two groups made up 83 per cent of the membership. When Deng came to power, he initiated a so-called 'technocratic movement', replacing workers and peasants with technocrats. Since then, the representation of workers and peasants has dwindled from 64 per cent in 1981 to 48 per cent in 1994, a figure that continued to decline to 29 per cent in 2005 (see Figure 10.2).

Following the radical change to officially admit private entrepreneurs into the party membership in July 2001, the numbers of the once-shadowy group of CCP cadres swelled. Its actual numbers are not officially available, but based on 2005 figures (see Figure 10.2), this group is deemed to spread across various job categories from managers and professionals (23 per cent), to self-employed and free-lance workers (1.4 per cent), to unknown numbers of peasants-turned-private entrepreneurs who remained categorised under their previous profession (19.9 per cent). Given that the contributions of private enterprises to the Chinese economy were not officially recognised by the State Constitution until 1999, this change of faith to allow their owners into the party represents a quantum leap in the CCP's transformation.

Other than these private entrepreneurs, CCP cadres who are current students experienced a big jump in their numbers as well. The 2005 numbers stood at 29.7 per cent almost one-third of the CCP's total membership. Whilst this figure reflects the demographical changes to educational proficiency in China, it also shows the CCP's general move towards building a younger and more educated core of cadres – 23 per cent, or 16.3 million, of the 2005 membership was under the age of 35, and almost 30 per cent of the total had attained, at least, a college degree.

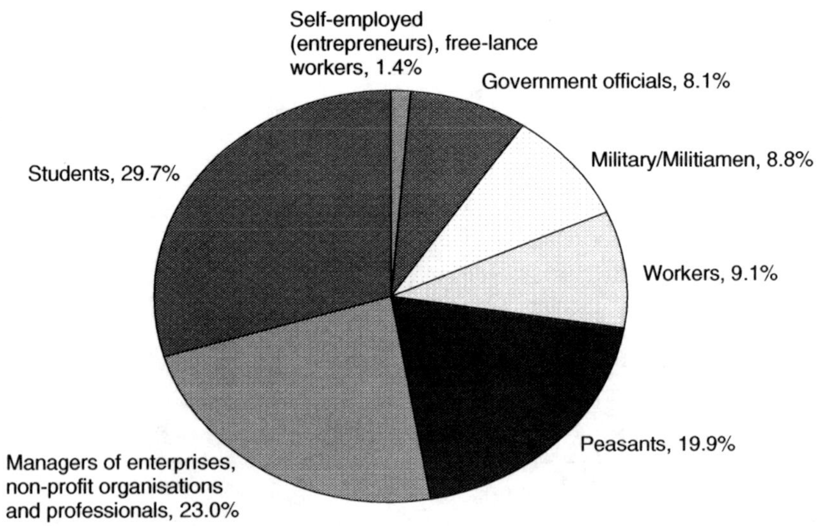

Figure 10.2 Professions of CCP members, 2005.
Source: Xinhua News Agency, www.xinhuanet.com. (Accessed on 22 February, 2007.)

The shift to accommodating the newly-rising social classes and professionals does not mean that the CCP will become a party for these selective social groups. I have argued, early on, that the CCP is likely to become a party for all, not for some, as a matter of self-preservation (Zheng 2004). The CCP has learnt the most important lesson from the fall of the KMT in the mainland. During its rule in China, the KMT was a party for only some, namely, bureaucrats, capitalists, and bureaucratic capitalists; the interests of the majority of the people, mainly workers and peasants, were not represented in the political process. This provided the CCP with an opportunity to engage in a revolution from below by mobilising underprivileged social classes. Furthermore, the party has also learned from its own experience. As mentioned above, the CCP under Mao was also a party for only some, namely, workers and peasants; capitalists and other propertied classes were under attack. The party has learnt from its almost three decades of economic reform that it has to depend on capitalists and other entrepreneurial social groups to promote economic development; that it has to accommodate these newly-rising social groups. This was the rationale behind the 'Three Represents' theory developed under Jiang Zemin. The 'Three Represents' theory implies that the CCP represents the most productive force, the most advanced culture, and the interests of the majority of the people. Nevertheless, to accommodate the newly-rising social classes does not mean that the interests of workers and peasants can be ignored. After the Hu-Wen leadership came into power, the CCP tried to balance the interests of the social groups, both the newly-rising and the traditional ones, such as workers and peasants; this task is a major one for the CCP as long as it remains the only party, with differing emphases being placed by different leaders on the choice of particular groups.

Organisational and ideological changes

The CCP's most powerful instrument is a system called 'the party [CCP] management of cadres' (*dangguan ganbu*), more commonly known as the nomenklatura system.[7] It is the most important organisational principle, giving the CCP a dominant say over personnel decisions.[8] The current practice is 'two-levels-down', that is, each level of the party structure is responsible for political appointments that are two levels below. For example, all positions above vice-ministerial level (such as State President, Vice-State President, Premier, Vice-Premiers, State Counsellors and others) fall under the jurisdiction of the Political Bureau of the Central Committee of the CCP (more specifically the Standing Committee). In this case, the Political Bureau first selects the candidates, then passes the nominations to the National People's Congress (NPC) – China's Parliament – for approval.

The 'party management of cadres' system is also the most effective means for the CCP to control 'localism' in the country. The Political Bureau and its Department of Organisation keeps a tight rein over the selection and appointment of provincial party secretaries and governors, and to prevent them from becoming deeply rooted in locally-vested interests, the CCP exercises the so-called 'cadre exchange system'. This system allows the CCP to curtail localism through regular exchanges of appointments between key cadres of different localities.

In the post-Mao Zedong era, the party ideology has successfully shifted from that of class struggle to one of economic development. This would not be possible without the nomenklatura system. During the early stages of reform, resistance to changes was strong. To counter that, the reformist CCP leadership resorted to the nomenklatura system to retire, or even forcefully remove, those who resisted. The system also allows the CCP to select the 'right types' of cadres and government officials to implement its reformist policies (Burns 2006); hence, the CCP has served as an important facilitator for the state administration to carry these out.

Besides cadre management, the CCP also helps the state administration to mobilise the resources required for the country's transition. This presents a typified 'weak state/strong party' phenomenon, and is a dilemma for China. On the one hand, continuing one-party rule stifles the development of strong state mechanisms – a prerequisite for a modern state; on the other hand, without the party and its apparatus, the state administration is incapable of moving ahead with anything at all, much less its reformist agenda. For the moment at least, the CCP is indispensable to China's modernisation efforts.

In recent years, the nomenklatura mechanisms have also undergone profound changes. Although the party has retained its Leninist structure, intra-party democracy (*dangnei minzhu*) is slowly transforming the ways the CCP works. Experimentations on democratic reforms are being carried out in the ongoing local leadership reshufflings. More democratic and transparent nomination and selection systems are encouraged at the local levels. In the election of the Party committees at the local levels, it is now becoming increasingly common to see more candidates running than there are seats that need to be filled. Sometimes these candidates have first been screened by party cadres and local legislators – as was the case in Jiangsu province in recent years – before public feedback was sought.

The party's rank and file are slowly feeling the heat from the state's turn towards the rule of law. As the CCP's Leninist structure makes its membership highly susceptible to rent-seeking activities, the rule of law fills in for the lack of institutionalised societal supervision; indictments for breaches of the law became pretexts for party disciplinary actions, more commonly 'double restrictions' (*shuanggui*) or 'double expulsion' (*shuankai*). It was reported that in the year 2006, some 97,260 CCP members were disciplined by the party on corruption charges alone. Amongst them were seven government officials at the ministerial level and above. They included high-profile cases such as that of Qiu Xiaohua, China's former Director of the State Bureau of Statistics, and Liu Zhihua, Beijing's former Vice-Mayor, but arguably, none caught the public attention more than the sacking of Chen Liangyu, former member of the Political Bureau and Party Secretary of Shanghai, and the highest-ranking CCP member to be disciplined in a decade, in September 2006. More recently, the Party has been planning to set up a special body for corruption prevention at the central level. The central leadership will directly control that body, independently from local governments.

Corresponding changes have also happened in the ideological dimension. The CCP's dogmatic stance, associated with its Marxist roots, took an abrupt turn in 1978 when the late Deng Xiaoping embarked on his 'open door' and 'four modernizations' policies. Where ideology was applied as a means for class struggle during the Mao era, Deng transformed the whole meaning of ideology to become something that can be applied as a means for development. Deng operated under the principle of 'get-rich-first'. The state of the poor became a secondary priority in Deng's plans, embodied by the slogan, 'to get rich is glorious'. Then Jiang pushed Deng's directives to an extreme, as the Chinese state evolved to become what the scholarly community called a 'developmental state': a state that plays a key role in pushing economic development. It was under Jiang that GDP growth became the single most important performance indicator for local government officials. The capitalists were invited to the CCP party membership; and private properties were granted constitutional protection.

Under Jiang, there were frequent efforts to return to ideology, since the party leadership had found that ideology could play an important role in organising politics.[9] Nevertheless, the prevailing ideology was economism, since it was in the interest of the CCP to reduce people's interest in politics by encouraging them to turn their attention to economic development. It took about two decades after the reform began for the CCP to transform China from an ideology-based society to an interest-based one.[10]

Today, with the passing of Jiang's legacy, ideology plays yet another role. China's current batch of top leaders, headed by Hu, now play the ideological card to justify policies towards building a 'harmonious society' (*hexie shehui*) based on social justice, which is becoming a new core of the CCP ideology. It calls for a drastic reorientation from the development-first strategies implemented by Deng and Jiang, to a return of people-centred policies aimed at addressing the mounting social problems that China faces today. After more than a decade of the ruthless, single-minded pursuit of GDP growth, the Chinese leadership is finding it necessary to step back from its previous mode of economic development. Undesirable consequences, such as income disparities and environmental degradation, are today affecting not only economic growth itself, but also social stability.

Hu began to turn the wheels of China's economic growth in a different direction when he first rose to power. Evidence of this change is the subtle ideological replacement of Jiang's 'building a well-off society' (*xiaokang shehui*) with Hu's aim to 'build a harmonious society'. The present aim of the so-called 'scientific development' approach is to 'strike a balance' in Beijing's various policies. More specifically, it raises the importance of social justice in the pursuit of China's long-term development, in terms of more even distribution of economic, legal and political rights between different regions and social groups. Ideologically, the CCP is progressively moving from its puritan Maoist roots to one that marries socialism with free market principles.

Changing party/state relations

The country's successful transition to modern, effective governance is still very much dependent on significant changes in party/state relations. Since the

CCP/state relations together form the single most important political-institutional infrastructure in China, they are central to all political activities. The outlook at the moment appears favourable for further political liberalisation and democratisation: both the CCP and the state now have broader social bases and are accommodating more participatory elements.

The drastic socio-economic transition has created a new environment for the CCP and the state. Such a new environment requires the CCP to adjust its relations with the state so that effective and sustainable governance is possible. True enough, in recent years, the CCP leadership has repeatedly emphasised the need to strengthen its capacity to govern an increasingly complex society. The CCP has actively pursued this objective by introducing reforms to strengthen state mechanisms.

In the 1980s, a consensus was reached amidst heated debates on China's political reforms. Under Deng Xiaoping and Zhao Ziyang, the party leadership sought to separate the party from the government (*dangzheng fenkai*). Until this policy turnaround, the party was all-pervasive in China's political and administrative life, to the extent that party organisations at times displaced state organisations. According to Deng, the state had to have a degree of autonomy from the party in administering the country.

This consensus, however, was never brought to fruition in real life. Zhao Ziyang's reforms spurred political openness and the rise of social forces. After the crackdown on the pro-democracy movement in 1989, political conservatism loomed, and all talks about reforming the party/state relations faded away from political discussions.

Nevertheless, from the early 1990s, the CCP began the process of institutionalising party/state relations, which was achieved through organisational rationalisation. Amongst others, the office of the State President and the Chairmanship of the Central Military Commission are tied to the position of the Party Secretary-General, who today acts in the name of the State President, especially in China's international affairs. Prior to Jiang Zemin's accession to the post of State President in 1993, the office was insignificant and was usually filled by a retired revolutionary. Previous office holders included Madam Sun Yat-sen (Soong Ch'ing-ling), Li Xiannian and Yang Shangkun.

In an attempt to institutionalise party/state relations, both the State Presidency and the State Vice-Presidency have now become the most important positions in the Chinese leadership; the posts are currently occupied by Hu Jintao and Xi Jinping respectively. Institutionalisation has not only brought about some level of 'division of functions' between important public offices, it also has the benefit of legitimating the Party's command over the military. While the basic principle, 'the Party commands the gun' remains largely unchanged, this power is now vested in a formal office, which acts on behalf of the party.

Another important aspect of changing party/state relations is more space for professionalism. Ideological reliability is slowly giving way, allowing for more professionalism in the ranks of government officials. To boost effective governance the CCP, since the mid 1990s, has begun to loosen its grip on state appointments to give professionals more autonomy in the day-to-day running of the country. The most visible signs are those within the State Council (China's executive branch). The Council has, over the years, become a body of economic and social management by professionals. The posts of Premier, Vice Premier, State Councillor, and of ministers and vice-ministers are now filled by professionals; this is especially the case for positions at the ministerial and vice-ministerial levels. The rise of professionalism largely reflects the increasing need for special expertise in dealing with the complexities of new social and economic issues.

Professionalism has also been injected into both the NPC and the local People's Congresses. The NPC is largely an inefficient platform due to its massive size, which hovers around 3,000. It convenes for only a very short period annually, with a conference that usually spans about 10–14 days. Moreover, the structure of its meeting, which is made up of full-day plenary sessions, is not suited to lengthy deliberations; to overcome these shortcomings, since the early 1990s NPC reforms have focused on expanding the Standing Committee and establishing special committees.

Over the years, the Standing Committee has been expanded to its present strength of 176 members, and now functions as a 'miniature-NPC' – its small size allows more frequent and efficient consultations as compared to the NPC, yet it is large enough to accommodate different social and political bases, particularly those who are non-CCP members. The expansion of this group of 'first-among-equals' serves to raise the quality of motions tabled during annual NPC conferences, and allows follow-up on NPC decisions when the need arises.

Currently, the NPC has nine special committees in the areas of Foreign Affairs, Finance, Education, Minorities, and Agricultural and Rural Affairs, and the number is likely to increase in the future. Special committees usually draw their members from two sources: government officials who had previously served in various state organisations, and specialists in particular fields. These special committees provide expertise and public office experience both in the law-making process and in supervision of the daily functioning of the government (the State Council and its various ministries). Professionalisation has altered the role of the NPC from that of a 'rubber stamp', to one that is capable of overseeing governmental operations.

Under China's one-party system, it is unrealistic to expect a clear-cut separation of the CCP from the state. Thus the issue is not whether, but how, the CCP will exercise control over the state. The CCP has devoted a great deal of its reform efforts to adjust – through institutionalisation and rationalisation – its relations with the state. The only difference is that, while the CCP took front stage in the early days, now there is a tendency for the party to operate behind the scenes.

The CCP makes effective use of party/state mechanisms to achieve the adjustment of party/state relations. The State Council, the NPC, and other key state organisations all have their own internal party groups (*dang zu*). These are 'leading groups' which usually convene to solicit consensus between major interests, prior to important policy decisions. To a certain degree, the *dang zu* in the NPC performs a function that is parallel to the parliamentary grouping in western democracies, except that the former is more powerful due to the nature of the one-party system in China.

At local levels, the party is dominant in a similar way. At the provincial level, the CCP dictates local politics through the provincial party secretary, who is at the same time the Chairman of the Provincial People's Congress, something which was previously not the case, as the Chairman's role used to be filled by a powerless retired cadre or government official. The new tie-in has led to the belief that the CCP can now exercise direct control over Provincial People's Congresses, but there is also little doubt that provincial party secretaries, as representatives of the central leadership, now come face-to-face with local people's representatives. The provincial party secretaries need to listen to the representatives, and take their opinions into consideration before the provincial party committees can make important decisions. The only institutional gap left to be filled is the establishment of formal mechanisms to underline this new relationship.

Political engagement with social groups

Changes in organisation and ideology and in party/state relations have led to greater space for political engagement by different social groups. The CCP has an aversion to bottom-up initiatives; it is more comfortable with the top-down approach through which it is able to keep developments in check. In recent years, the party has been responsible for continuing tight political control, and crackdowns on budding social movements. Yet there are also moves being taken by the CCP to broaden its social base by proactively engaging with different social groups, particularly new social forces that have emerged in China's changing socio-economic environment. Effective governance requires the CCP to solicit political support from these groups.

I have already argued that changes in the composition of party membership indicate that the CCP has engaged with different social groups to broaden its social support. Furthermore, there are other, more institutional, changes in this regard, such as the development of rural democracy and non-governmental organisations (NGOs). 'Rural democracy' refers to the establishment of the rural election system, which was initially introduced in the late 1980s. The rural reform initiated towards the end of the 1970s was based on the household responsibility system, and the rapid spread of this system soon led to the collapse of the old system of governance, i.e. the production brigade system, and eventually the collapse of the commune system. Central government decided to re-structure the governance system at the basic level, and in 1987, the NPC passed the 'Village Committee Organic Law of the PRC (Experimental)'. According to the law:

> Village committees should be established in China's rural areas in order to safeguard farmers' opportunities and rights of political participation. The control over village cadres by farmers and the level of villagers' self-government will be improved through direct election of the directors, deputy directors and

members of the villagers' committees, thus upgrading the quality of farmers' political participation.

(Jiang 1996)

Since the mid 1990s, the election system has developed rather impressively. According to the Ministry of Civil Affairs, which has been in charge of implementing the election system, by early 1997, more than 80 per cent of China's 930,000 villages had conducted at least one round of relatively democratic elections. This top-down reform was aimed at strengthening the rule of the party in rural areas.[11] But the rapid spread of rural democracy soon created contradictions between the elected body and the party committee in these areas. Whilst the elected village committee can draw its legitimacy from villagers, the party committee often faces challenges in dealing with the former. To solve this contradiction, many provinces have developed a system of 'two-ballot' in which the party secretary in a village is subject to a popular vote (Li 1999).

Since the early twenty-first century, the Chinese government has begun to implement direct elections at the township level – the basic level of administration – on an experimental basis. Whilst township elections have not yet come under the auspices of Chinese law, the leadership has indicated the possibility of legalising them; they have, in fact, been implemented in many Chinese provinces (Li 2002).

The development of NGOs has been a major part of the limited political liberalisation. This is especially true in recent years, after the leadership began to place an emphasis on social reforms. Reforms have not only led to a relaxation of state control over society, but have also seen the state actively creating and sponsoring NGOs in order to transfer to them certain functions which it used to perform itself. Chinese NGOs have increased steadily in number over the years. The statistics of the Ministry of Civil Affairs (MCA), which is in charge of NGO registration, show that before 1978 there were only about 100 national social organisations in China. By the end of 2003 their number had reached 1,736. Meanwhile, the number of local-level social organisations grew from 6,000 to 142,121. The number of private non-enterprise units (PNEUs), which did not exist before the reforms, reached 124,491.

The significance of NGOs in China varies, depending on their nature and functions. In the economic sphere, the government has attempted to reduce its direct management role by establishing intermediary organisations such as trade association and Chambers of Commerce to perform sectoral coordination and regulation functions. In the social welfare sphere, the government wants to foster NGOs, onto which it can offload some of the burden of service provision. In the social development sphere, the government wants NGOs to mobilise societal resources to supplement its own spending.[12] These NGOs will have to perform their role according to the government line, i.e. as a helping hand, and cannot easily play an independent role.

Due to lack of autonomy, the political influences of China's NGOs vary widely across different areas, as well as between different NGOs. In some areas such as poverty reduction, charity and environmental issues, NGOs are encouraged to play a greater role, but in other areas such as religious issues, ethnicity, and human rights, the influence of NGOs is much weaker. Also, some NGOs are more powerful than others. Most commercial organisations are extremely powerful in influencing the government's policy-making process: it is not difficult to find business people sitting in the People's Congress and the Chinese People's Political Consultative Conference at different levels of government, but workers and farmers are not allowed to organise themselves, and thus do not have any effective mechanisms to articulate and aggregate their interests. In fact, the declining numbers of workers and peasants in the total membership of the party implies their weakness in China's political system.

When powerful social groups can organise themselves, they become ever more powerful. There is no effective means for weak social groups such as workers and farmers to push for their own objectives. This is so partly because China is in an early stage of economic development, and development continues to be given higher priority than political participation. Workers and farmers might be able to play a more important role with further economic progress: take trade unions as an example. The government's attitude towards workers' rights is under change. Today, even the hidebound, government-dominated All-China Federation of Trade Unions (ACFTU) has recognised a need to take a more activist approach to workers' rights. China is now facing a rising tide of labour disputes, which could destabilise Chinese society and thus undermine the political legitimacy of the CCP. Therefore, there is a need for employers to better understand and honour their obligations under China's labour laws. In an apparent reflection of this new attitude, at the 2003 annual ACFTU Congress, the federation made a direct appeal to multinational retail corporation Wal-Mart Stores, Inc., to allow its workers to establish trade unions.

Yet all these transformations are mere baby steps along the CCP's long reformist route. As China refocuses its attention on maintaining the sustainability of its economic development, the CCP has to reassess the sustainability of its party rule. The mission is clear: to stay viable, it has to boost its governing capacity (*jiaqiang zhizheng nengli*). Governing capacity, in turn, depends heavily on the CCP's ability to renew itself through the party's mechanisms, to legitimise its predominance in political affairs through connecting with the common people, and to reconnect its ideological base with ongoing social and economic changes. These are daunting tasks, but at least the party appears to be going on the right track, for now.

The CCP and global capitalism

An important factor – which is often easily ignored – in sustaining the CCP rule in China is global capitalism. The open-door policy operated since the late 1970s has created an increasingly high degree of interdependence between China and global capitalism. China's development has also been driven by rapid globalisation. The country has, since the early 1990s, become the world's most favoured destination for foreign direct investment (FDI) in comparison with all other developing countries. Not surprisingly, over 80 per cent of the world's 500 largest companies and its top 100 information technology firms have set up businesses in China.

At early stages of the reforms and the open-door policy, China placed emphasis on 'inviting' (*qing jinlai*) foreign capital, which the reformist leadership hoped would help to drive China's economic development. Meanwhile, China began to reform its own economic system in order to gear (in Chinese '*jiegui*') itself to the world economic system. These practices proved to be successful. Within a relatively short period of time, China had transformed itself to become one of the most successful 'export-oriented' economies in East Asia, emulating the 'economic miracles' of the 'four little dragons', namely, Hong Kong, Taiwan, South Korea, and Singapore. Significant changes have taken place in China's economic policy since the mid 1990s. These changes were relatively obscure at first, but they gradually gained momentum, especially after China joined the World Trade Organization (WTO). Among these, two changes are particularly noteworthy. First, by the turn of the century, China found itself moving away from capital shortage problems, to being in a position to wield enormous capital surplus. At this stage, Chinese capital began to venture into the outside world. In 2001, Hu Jintao, then Vice State President, called for Chinese enterprises to 'go outside' (*zuo chu qu*) when he visited Malaysia. The momentum accelerated after Hu became State President in 2003. China's out-flowing FDI, whilst small relative to that originating from the developed countries, should not be overlooked. In this case, it is not the size, but the force behind it, that matters. The policy to 'go out' has gained a strong impetus, since both the state and non-state sectors have become very proactive in this process. In recent years, Chinese firms began to acquire, and to merge with, foreign firms, giving the world at large a first-hand experience of China's economic power.

China has also become a great trading (commercial) state. Underpinning this change is the important fact that China has become the world's manufacturing centre, not unlike Great Britain when at its peak, in the eighteenth and nineteenth centuries. The seemingly unlimited labour supply makes it possible for China to produce massive volumes of cheap goods for the world market. In this respect, China's economic rise has caused no small apprehension for the rest of the world. A natural question is: 'what do we do, when China makes everything?' As interdependency grows between China and the world's economy, the world market can no longer be shielded from economic activities inside China. A recent example is energy pricing. Any minute changes in either the demand side or the supply side in the colossal China will immediately upset the delicate world market prices.

However, to talk about China as the world's manufacturing centre is only one side of the story. An equally important fact is that China has also become one of the world's most attractive markets. China's consumer market, despite its size and potential, has yet to be fully tapped. While China is still a developing country and its per capita GDP remains small, the size of China's middle class, in absolute terms, represents a notable consumer market. Owing to China's large population, this small proportion of its people, as they become richer, can still generate a huge impact on the world's consumer pattern. This growing, and consuming, middle class is good news for international businesses, as China's middle class has become a major consumer for branded and high-end goods. Many begin to holiday overseas; tourists from China are now the primary target groups in many countries, and wherever Chinese tourists go, they help to drive the local high-end fast consumer goods markets. In this regard, Chinese consumers behave like Japanese consumers did in the early days. It is likely that this demand from China's middle class will continue to grow over the years to come. China's booming economy is today one of the engines for growth of the world's economy, especially the economy of many Asian countries.

In Marxist terms, China is now an important link in the entire chain of global capitalism. Without China's entry into this chain, its rapid economic development would not be possible. However, the significance of global capitalism for the sustainability and transformation of the CCP has yet to be explored. Put simply, the CCP is indispensable for international investors in China, and thus for the functioning of global capitalism.

The CCP has provided all the necessary conditions and elements for global investment to be profitable in China, such as cheap labour and land, and low tax rates. This is not the place to make a detailed analysis, but a brief discussion serves the purpose. Intensive competition among different levels of government in China encourages Chinese communist cadres to provide cheaper land to foreign investors. In the 1980s, the central government established many Special Economic Zones (SEZs) to offer foreign investors cheap and even free land. Since the early 1990s, local governments have played an even greater role in this regard, establishing various forms of industrial and technological parks to compete for foreign investments. In recent years, when central government attempted to tighten control of land supplies, local resistance was extremely strong, and central government did not meet with any success in this regard.

The same applies to cheap labour. Labour rights have been a major issue in China for years; the CCP itself has been known for its serious violations of them. Labour unions have been a tool for the CCP to control labourers, not a tool for workers to protect their rights. Although China has a comprehensive labour law, it is barely enforced at local levels – China does not have a sound legal infrastructure to enforce laws, and also local governments tend to cooperate with foreign investors to violate labour rights. When cheap labour contributes to high local economic performance, and high local economic performance helps the promotion of local government officials, local officials have a high political incentive to play a helpful hand in dealing with labour rights violations in foreign-invested firms in China. In any society, a minimum socio-political order is necessary for foreign investment. In many developing countries, social order is problematic. In China, such a minimum order is provided and guaranteed by the CCP.

Another factor attracting foreign investment in China has been the country's preferential corporate income tax rate for foreign-invested firms. For years, the

Chinese government has imposed dual corporate income tax rates on enterprises in China – one for foreign-invested companies and another for domestic-invested firms. For foreign companies, the nominal rate is 15 per cent and the actual rate is 11 per cent, while for domestic companies, the nominal rate is 33 per cent and the actual rate is 23 per cent – more than double the rate for their foreign counterparts.[13] The actual rate is lower because of preferential tax policies in China. The purpose of such a tax policy is to encourage foreign direct investment (FDI), high technology and qualified personnel.

After years of criticism from Chinese scholars, businessmen, and some government officials, claiming that the corporate income tax policy is unfair for domestic entities, the central government has recently begun to tackle the problem. China's top legislature, the Standing Committee of the National People's Congress, has just started to discuss a bill that would eventually unify corporate income tax rates for domestic and foreign enterprises at 25 per cent. But the procedure has not been progressing smoothly because of the divergence of interests within China. While some governmental departments call for a fairer tax system, others fear that such a policy would cause FDI losses.[14] Due to strong resistance from interest groups including some central governmental departments, many local governments and foreign multi-national corporations (MNCs), this taxation reform procedure has been delayed for about two years. As early as August 2004, the Ministry of Finance and the State Administration of Taxation jointly submitted a proposal to the State Council calling for unification of the two income tax rates. Also, Chinese lawmakers and political consultants submitted several proposals during the NPC and the Chinese People's Political Consultative Conference (CPPCC) session (*lianghui*) in the spring of 2005 expressing similar ideas. However, 54 foreign MNCs jointly submitted a counterproposal to the State Council asking for a deferment of the reform, and the Ministry of Commerce is on their side.[15] The conflicting interests of the Ministry of Finance, the State Administration of Taxation and Chinese domestic enterprises on the one hand, and the Ministry of Commerce, many local governments and foreign MNCs on the other, are the main reason for the delay in the reform of China's unfair income tax rate system. The bill for taxation reform was discussed and eventually passed during the NPC and CPPCC session in the spring of 2007. It seems a compromise was attained amongst the various interest groups in China.

It is worthwhile to emphasis the issue of property rights. As a communist state, for many years China had been criticised for the non-existence of a legal system to ensure the protection of property rights for foreign investment. To attract foreign investment requires a minimum enforcement of property rights. Without a set of well-established regulatory institutions, property rights issues are not solved by China's legal system; more often than not, they are dealt with administratively and politically. The CCP and the state tend to easily violate property rights on the one hand, and are capable of providing administrative and political protection for property rights on the other. In the recent decade, the CCP has begun to make increasingly greater efforts to build a system to protect property rights, be they foreign or domestic. Needless to say, for global capitalists, the most effective protection of property rights must be a sound legal system. This is the rationale behind enormous efforts to help China build an effective legal system which are being made on the part of the West, especially the European Union and the United States. The more recent voices on 'China uncertainty' in the West also reflect the concerns of those associated with global capitalism, regarding the CCP's ability to protect increasingly significant foreign interests in China.

Concluding remarks

For the foreseeable future, the CCP is unlikely to give up the one-party system as long as there are sources supporting it; this implies that the CCP is likely to sustain its rule. In this chapter, I have elaborated various sources legitimating, and thus sustaining, the CCP rule. There are cultural roots of authoritarianism in China, and more than anything else, the CCP is the personification of a modern emperor. Unlike the traditional and highly decentralised emperorship, this modern emperorship is highly centralised. The engagement in socio-economic transformation being made by the CCP justifies the legitimacy of its rule.

The CCP has engaged in socio-economic transformation, which in turn facilitates the transformation of the CCP. To cope with the rapid speed of this transformation, the party has been relentlessly searching for a feasible solution to the problem of rationalisation of its relations with the state and with different social actors. So far, 'rigid flexibility' best describes the overall evolution of the CCP: the overall structure remains intact while its content consistently undergoes changes. It is thus important to see the sustainability of the CCP in the light of these content changes, despite a seemingly unchanged one-party structure.

Global capitalism provides the CCP with another helpful hand for its transformation. Global capitalism has two faces in China. On the one hand, it relies on the CCP to provide necessary conditions and elements for its functioning; in this sense, global capitalism and the CCP have common interests in sustaining the CCP rule. At this level, global capitalism serves as a barrier for the transformation of the CCP in particular, and China's political democratisation in general. On the other hand, global capitalism concerns the long-term sustainability of the CCP. Authoritarian and coercive measures that the CCP has so far adopted are certainly not sustainable and effective in the long run. With growing foreign interests, global capitalism has an increasingly great incentive to push the transformation of the CCP and to lead the CCP in a 'right direction'. A new system which can guarantee the rule of law and protect human rights will be more sustainable and effective. At this level, global capitalism can serve as an important source for the transformation of the CCP. Given an increasingly high degree of interdependence between the CCP and global capitalism, the latter is becoming increasingly capable of facilitating this transformation.

A rigid CCP is not sustainable, but a changing CCP is. China's experience in the past three decades shows that the CCP is open to change, and that despite its slow pace, the CCP has experienced changes. Compared to other Communist parties in the former Soviet Union and Eastern Europe, the CCP has survived rapid socio-economic development. Whether the CCP rule is sustainable depends on whether it can transform itself and how it is transformed. It is an open question not only for the CCP itself, but also for the international community.

Notes

1 'Reframing China Policy': *The Carnegie Debates*, Carnegie Endowment for International Peace, Thursday, 5 October 2006. Available at: http://www.carnegieendowment.org/events/index.cfm?fa=eventDetail&id=916&&prog=zch (accessed on 19, February 2007).
2 *Ibid.*
3 For examples, see Pei (2006); Chang (2001).
4 For examples, see Ramo (2004); Peerenboom (2007).
5 For example, see Bergsten *et al.* (2006).
6 For examples, see Dickson (2003); Wang and Zheng (2003); Brodsgaard and Zheng (2004, 2006).
7 See Burns (1989, 1994); Huang (1996).
8 While the state administration has assumed part of this power since the reform and open-door policy, the party still controls the most important personnel appointments.
9 For a discussion, see Wu (2001).
10 For a detailed discussion of this point, see Zheng (2004), Chapter 4.
11 See Li and O'Brien (2000); Li and O'Brien (1999).
12 See Howell (1997); Wong (1998).
13 *People's Daily Online*, 'Liangshui hebing: neiwaizi qiye chongfan gongping jingzheng' ('The unification of the two tax rates: foreign invested enterprises and domestic invested enterprises are expected to compete fairly again'), 30 October 2006, Available at: http://finance.people.com.cn/GB/4972421.html (accessed on 17 January 2007).
14 *People's Daily Online*, 'China to unify corporate income tax rates for domestic, foreign-funded business at 25 per cent', 25 December 2006, Available at: http://english.people.com.cn/200612/24/eng20061224_335446.html (accessed on 26 December 2006).
15 *People's Daily Online*, 'The unification of the two tax rates'; and *Xinhua*, 'Shuizai zunao qiye suodeshui 'liangshui hebing' ('Who is hindering the "unification of the two tax rates" for corporate income tax?'), 2 September 2005, Available at: http://news.xinhuanet.com/fortune/2005-09/02/content_3432949.htm (accessed on 17 January 2007). One of the main reasons that the Ministry of Commerce and many local governments strongly oppose taxation reform is that they fear that possible losses of FDI would be seen as undermining their achievements to date. The deep and widespread penetration of some foreign interest groups across China's central and local governmental institutions is also a big obstacle for the reform. In addition, some Chinese enterprises registered overseas to become 'fake' foreign companies are also likely to oppose the reform.

References

Bergsten, C. Fred *et al.* (2006) *China: The Balance Sheet – What the World Needs to Know Now about the Emerging Superpower*. New York: Public Affairs.

Binder, Leonard *et al.* (1971) *Crisis and Sequences in Political Development*. Princeton, NJ: Princeton University Press.

Brodsgaard, Kjeld Erik and Zheng, Yongnian (eds) (2004) *Bringing the Party Back In: How China Is Governed*. Singapore: Eastern Universities Press.

Brodsgaard, Kjeld Erik and Zheng, Yongnian (eds) (2006) *The Chinese Communist Party in Reform*. London: Routledge.

Burns, John P. (ed.) (1989) *The Chinese Communist Party's Nomenklatura System*. Armonk, NY: M. E. Sharpe.

Burns, John P. (ed.) (1994) 'Strengthening Central CCP Control of Leadership Selection: The 1990 Nomenklatura', *China Quarterly*, 138: 458–91.

Burns, John P. (ed.) (2006) 'The Chinese Communist Party's Nomenklatura System as a Leadership Selection Mechanism: An Evaluation', in Brodsgaard, Kjeld Erik and Zheng, Yongnian (eds) *The Chinese Communist Party in Reform*, London: Routledge, pp. 33–58.

Chang, Gordon (2001) *The Coming Collapse of China*. New York: Random House.

Dickson, Bruce J. (2003) *Red Capitalists in China: The Party, Private Entrepreneurs, and Prospects for Political Change*. New York: Cambridge University Press.

Downs, Anthony (1957) *An Economic Theory of Democracy*. New York: Harper.

Duverger, Maurice (1964) *Political Parties: Their Organization and Activity in the Modern State*. Methuen & Co. Ltd.

Eckstein, Harry (1968) 'Party Systems', in David L. Sills (ed.) *International Encyclopedia of the Social Sciences*, Vol. 11. New York: The Free Press.

Howell, Jude (1997) 'NGO-State Relations in Post-Mao China', in David Hulme and Michael Edwards (eds) *NGOs, States and Donors: Too Close for Comfort?*. London: Macmillan Press Ltd., pp. 202–15.

Huang, Yasheng (1996) *Inflation and Investment Controls in China: the Political Economy of Central-Local Relations during the Reform Era*. New York: Cambridge University Press.

Hunt, Michael H. (1993) 'Chinese National Identity and the Strong State: the Late Qing-Republican Crisis', in Lowell Dittmer and Samuel S. Kim (eds) *China's Quest for National Identity*. Ithaca, NY: Cornell University Press.

Jiang, Wandi (1996) 'Grassroots Democracy Taking Root', *Beijing Review*, 39 (11), 11–17 March.

LaPalombara, Joseph and Weiner, Myron (eds) (1969) *Political Parties and Political Development*. Princeton, NJ: Princeton University Press.

Li, Lianjiang (1999) 'The Two-Ballot System in Shanxi Province: Subjecting Village Party Secretaries to a Popular Vote', *The China Journal*, No. 42 (July), pp. 103–18.

Li, Lianjiang (2002) 'The Politics of Introducing Direct Township Elections in China', *The China Quarterly*, No. 171 (September), pp. 704–23.

Li, Lianjiang and O'Brien, Kevin (1999) 'The struggle over Village Elections', in Merle Goldman and Roderick MacFarquhar (eds.) *The Paradox of China's Post-Mao Reforms*. Cambridge, MA: Harvard University Press, pp. 129–44.

Li, Lianjiang and O'Brien, Kevin (2000) 'Accommodating 'Democracy' in a One-Party State: Introducing Village Elections in China', *The China Quarterly*, No. 162 (June), pp. 465–89.

MacFarquhar, Roderick (1991) 'The Anatomy of Collapse', *New York Reviews of Books*, 26 September.

Michels, Robert (1962) *Political Parties: A Sociological Study of the Oligarchical Tendencies of Modern Democracy*. New York: Collier.

Peerenboom, Randall (2007) *China Modernizes: Threat to the West or Model for the Rest?*. Oxford: Oxford University Press.

Pei, Minxin (2006) *China's Trapped Transition: The Limits of Developmental Autocracy*. Cambridge: Harvard University Press.

Poggi, G. (1978) *The Development of the Modern State*. Stanford, CA: Stanford University Press.

Pye, Lucian (1990) 'China: Erratic State, Frustrated Society', *Foreign Affairs*,Vol. 69, No. 4 (Fall), pp. 56–74.

Ramo, Joshua Cooper (2004) *The Beijing Consensus*. London: The Foreign Policy Centre.

Sartori, Giovanni (1976) *Parties and Party Systems*. New York: Cambridge University Press.

Schlesinger, Joseph A. (1968) 'Party Units', in David L. Sills (ed.) *International Encyclopedia of the Social Sciences*, Vol. 11. New York: The Free Press.

Schumpeter, Joseph A. (1975) *Capitalism, Socialism and Democracy*. New York: Harper.

Schurmann, Franz (1968) *Ideology and Organization in Communist China*. Berkeley, CA: University of California Press.

Sun Yat-sen (1986) *Sun Zhongshan quanji* (*Collected Works of Sun Yat-sen*), Vol. 9. Beijing: Zhonghua shuju.

Teng, Ssu-yu and John King Fairbank (1979) *China's Response to the West: A Documentary Survey, 1839-1923*. Cambridge, MA: Harvard University Press.

Wang, Gungwu and Zheng Yongnian (2003) (eds) *Damage Control: The Chinese Communist Party in the Jiang Zemin Era*. Singapore: Eastern Universities Press.

Weber, Max (1958) 'Politics as a Vocation', in Hans Gerth and C. Wight Mills (eds) *From Max Weber: Essays in Sociology*. New York: Oxford University Press.

Wong, Linda (1998) *Marginalization and Social Welfare in China*. London and New York: Routledge.

Wu, Guoguang (2001) 'The Return of Ideology? Struggling to Organize Politics during Socio-Economic Transition', in John Wong and Zheng Yongnian (eds) *The Nanxun Legacy and China's Development in the Post-Deng Era*. Singapore and London: Singapore University Press and World Scientific, pp. 221–48.

Zheng, Yongnian (2006) 'China's Party-State Relations in a New Political Environment', The UK House of Commons Foreign Affairs Select Committee, Seventh Report, 8 March 2006, Vol. II (HC 860-II), 19 July.

Zheng, Yongnian (2004) *Hu wen xinzheng (The New Deal under Hu Jintao and Wen Jiabao)*. Singapore: Global Publishing.

Zheng, Yongnian (2004) *Globalization and State Transformation in China*. Cambridge: Cambridge University Press.

Zheng, Yongnian (1999) 'From Rule by Law to Rule of Law? A Realistic View of China's Legal Development', *China Perspective*, No. 25, pp. 31–43.

Index

absorptive capacity 57, 65–6
accountability 110–13
adaptive capacity 180
Africa, China and 156
African Union 154, 156
Afro-Asian Conference 154
agenda setting 157, 162
aggregation levels 53–4
agricultural sector, economic exploitation 131
agricultural tax 179
aid diplomacy 155
air pollution 140–1
All-China Federation of Trade Unions (ACFTU) 202
antidumping cases 125, 172
aristocrats 188
arms control 157
ASEAN 154, 155, 156
ASEAN + 1 172
ASEAN + 3 172
'Asian brown cloud' 84
asset management corporations (AMCs) 88
Australia, FTA negotiations 155

Bangladesh 84
Bank of China 88
Beijing, sandstorms 85
Beijing Consensus 154, 163
Belgium
  debt-GDP ratio 87
  revenue-GDP ratio 88
Big Four 88, 98
black carbon emissions 84–5
Bo Xilai 159
Bohau/Yellow Sea Subregion 175
bribery 173
'business revolution' 59
buying power 161

cadre exchange system 195
cadre responsibility system 174
Canada
  debt-GDP ratio 87
  revenue-GDP ratio 88
canals 83–4
capital adequacy ratio (CAR) 88
capital input 34
  forecast growth 40
Carnegie Endowment for International Peace 186
catch up effect 35
CCP *see* Communist Party of China
Central Television Station (CCTV) 153
CEPA 177
Chambers of Commerce 201
Chen Lai 83
Chen Liangyu 196
Chiang Kai-shek 191
China Construction Bank 88
China Daily 153
'China threat' 47, 160
Chinese People's Political Consultative Conference (CPPCC) 149–50, 202, 205
civil disorder 80
Civil War (China) 191
civilization, practice of 16
class structure 182
climate change 84–5, 157
codified knowledge 55, 57
  foreign presence and 62–4
coercive diplomacy 163
Cold War 181
collective memories
  of Communist Party of China 18–20
  of Great China 27
commodification 178

Communist Party of China (CCP/CPC) 186–207
  Central Committee, 6th Plenum (2006) 75
  Civil War with KMT 191
  collective memory 18–20
  and democratization 81
  and global capitalism 202–6
  institutional adaptability 174
  internal reform 15
  International Department 150
  leadership 171
  membership 193–4
  nature 187–92
  as personalised 192
  'rigid flexibility' 206
  in transformation 192–202
    becoming catch-all party 193–5
    changing party/state relations 197–200
    ideological changes 196–7
    organisational changes 195–6
    political engagement with social groups 200–2
community care 178
competence 56
Confucianism 13
  attacks on 17
  ideology based on 16
Confucius Institutes 153
Consular Protection Centre 152
Consulates General, Chinese 151–2
consumer market, in China 203–4
contingent liabilities 86, 87
contract diplomacy 155
corporate income tax 91, 138, 143, 204–5, 207
corporatization 178
corruption 79, 80, 173, 196
CPC *see* Communist Party of China
CPPCC 149–50, 202, 205
'cracked' society 15
cross-border connections 170, 175, 176
crowding-out effects 58, 64–5
Cultural Revolution 181
culture, politics of 16
currency, depreciation 136–7

Daguo Jueqi 12
dang zu 199–200
dangguan ganbu 195–6
Dangjiangkou Dam 83
dangnei minzhu 196
dangzheng fenkai 198
debt-GDP ratio 86–8
  by country 94–5
  China 87–8, 89
  evolution 89
  steady-state 89–90
decentralization 102, 111
delegation, hierarchical 111
democracy 79–81, 188–9
  elections and 188, 189
  intra-party 196
  plebiscitarian 188, 189
  rural 200–1
democratization 188
demographic time bomb 91
Deng Xiaoping 76, 160, 186, 197
  foreign policy 161, 162
  separation of party from government 198
  technocratic movement initiation 194
Denmark
  debt-GDP ratio 87, 88
  revenue-GDP ratio 88
desertification 82–3
developing countries
  China and 154, 155
  globalization and 129–30
developmental state 197
diplomacy 146–7
  China
    as hard power 149–53
    with MNCs 159–60
    as soft power 153–4
    as structural power 155–7
  quality of 147–8
    China 157–62
diplomacy power
  China
    assessment 149–57
    future 162–3
    limits 160–2
diplomatic missions 151–2
disparities
  horizontal imbalances 104–5
  income per capita 100
  vertical imbalances 105–6
disposable income 120
documentaries 17, 18–22
domestic markets, protective measures 125
double expulsion 196
double restrictions 196
Duanwu festival 24
dynastic states 189

economic construction 76–7
economic growth
  challenge 182
  rate 193

economic mechanism, breakdown 77
economic power
absolute 33
China
future trend 39–43
growth sources 34–6
impact on rest of world 43–4
rise 31, 34–6
USA vs 34
definition 33
measurement
exchange rate method 33–4, 40–1, 43
Purchasing Power Parity (PPP) method 33, 34, 41, 43
relative 33
economic reform 132–7
economic sustainability, and political viability 86
economism 197
economy
imbalances 141–2
limits 77
education 106–7, 113
exclusive benefits 132
higher 178, 194
institutions for foreign studies 153
student enrolments 132
see also rural compulsory education
Education Law 106
Eight Values and Eight Shames 16
elections, democracy and 188, 189
Eleventh Five Year Plan 100, 107
Embassies, Chinese 151
embezzlement 79
emperorship 191, 192
energy diplomacy 161
energy pricing 203
energy security 149
entrepreneurs, private 194
entrepreneurship 57, 66
environmental cooperation 170
environmental degradation 140–1
environmental protection, need 81–5, 92
error terms 94, 98
ETDZs 138, 139
EU, research and development expenditure 39
Euro-Zone, Growth and Stability Pact 86
European Union (EU)
China and 156, 206
and WTO 172
exchange rate, government intervention 125
expectations, rising 92
explicit knowledge *see* codified knowledge
export dependency, index of 121–3
exports
country concentration 127–8
by enterprise types 137
goods concentration 126–7
growth 120–1, 139
high-technology 61
planning 133–4
share 122–4
structure 125
subsidies 125
by trading forms 126
extra-budgetary activities 106
extractive capacity 180
'extrovert' economy 175–6

factor endowment, structure 125–6
FDI *see* foreign direct investment
festive state 27
films 21–2
financial capacity, central government 109–10
fiscal decentralization 173–4
fiscal decline 101–3
legacies 104–7
fiscal efficiency 86
fiscal recovery 104
fiscal reform
history 101–4
need 112
fiscal resources
by province 105
disparities 104–5
fiscal revenue, increase 120
fiscal sustainability 85–91
fiscal weakness 7
Five Principles of Peaceful Co-existence 154
floods 83
folk custom, nationalization 23–6
foreign actors 65
foreign companies, wholly owned 62, 64
foreign direct investment (FDI)
attraction 132, 203
dependency on 159
growth 38, 138
out-flowing from China 203
preferential policies of attracting 137–40
foreign enclaves 62
foreign invested enterprises 133, 137
foreign policy system 158–9
see also diplomacy
foreign reserve 125
foreign trade *see* international trade
four modernizations policy 197

France
GDP, ratio to world total 34–5
revenue-GDP ratio 90
free trade agreements (FTAs) 155
Fu Ying 158
Fujian 175, 177

G8 156
Gangneung Danoje 24
ganwei zerenzhi 174
GDP growth
by country 32–3
China
forecasts 39–40, 42
marginal contribution 43–4
NETDZs contribution 139
past 119–20
GDP share, China 122–4
General Bureau of Radio and Television 14
Germany
GDP
growth 31–2
ratio to world total 34–5
industrial output growth 32
revenue-GDP ratio 90
science and technology indicators 46
Social Democratic Party 187–8
global capitalism, Communist Party of China and 202–6
global information, capacity to use 36
globalization
of Chinese economy 59, 122, 180–2
inbound 63
outbound 63
and developing countries 129–30
effects 129
and governance modes 169–70
response to 27–8
GNI per capita, China 42
governance
downward shift 169–70, 173–5
flaw in 77
improvement need 78–81
outward shift 170, 177–80
polycentric 169, 170
sideway shift 170, 175–7
upward shift 169, 170–3
governance deficit 14
governing capacity 202
Great China, imagination of 12, 22
Great Famine 131
Great Nation, rise of 22–3
Greater Mekong Subregion 175
Greater Southeast China Subregion 175
Greater Tumen Subregion 175
Greece
debt-GDP ratio 87
revenue-GDP ratio 88
Group of 20 (G20) 157
Guangdong 175, 176, 177

Han Empire 21
Hanjiang River 84
hard power 149–53
hardware failure 3, 77, 78
highest probability 78
harmonious society
as cultural agenda 16
as democratic society under rule of law 79
Harmonious Society Program (HSP) 75–8, 81, 93, 107–9, 197
cost estimates 111
initial experiences 108–9
objectives 107
programs 107–8, 110
health care 107–9
exclusive benefits 132
expenditures 107
rural 179
hegemonic struggle 182
Hero (*Yingxiong*) 21, 26
high-technology industries 59–61
definition 69
foreign-invested firms in 60–1
historical relics 15
Hong Kong
British surrender of rule 20
and commodity chains 175–6
democratic development 79
economic success 181
integration with China 177
labour productivity in industry 136
trade deficit with China 128
Hong Kong-Guangdong Cooperation Joint Conference 176
household businesses 133
Houtu, Empress 25
HSP *see* Harmonious Society Program
Hu Jintao 76–7, 78, 155, 156, 203
and harmonious society 76–7, 78, 178–9, 197
as State President 198, 203
Huli 138
human development index (HDI), China 42–3, 107
human services, commodification 178

Hungary
  debt-GDP ratio 87, 88
  revenue-GDP ratio 88

identities 175
imagined community 12
IMF 155, 156
imperialism 189–90
import tariff, reduction 137
imports
  country concentration 127–9
  growth 120–1, 122, 139
  planning 133–4
  structure 125–6
income tax 91, 138, 143, 204–5, 207
India
  diplomacy 154
  FTA negotiations 155
  GDP
    forecasts 42
    ratio to world total 34–5
  international intervention 161
  minimum wage rates 131
  and water diversion 84
indigenous actors 65
Indonesia, diplomacy 154
industrial output, growth by country 32
industrial production
  China 59–60, 160
  codification, digitalization, and modularization 59, 62
industrialisation 131
information base, weak 112
infrastructural services, urban-rural differences 107
innovation 56, 140
institutional effect 36
institutional environment 57, 66
institutionalisation 191–2, 198
International Department 150
International Development Association 155
International Monetary Fund (IMF) 155, 156
international political economy (IPE) 148
international studies 153
international trade
  China
    balance 123–4, 141–2
    ranking 42
    reform measures 133
  see also exports; imports; trade power
Internet users, China 193
inter-regional institutions, China's memberships 156
intervention, international 161–2
IT revolution 59
Italy
  debt-GDP ratio 87
  revenue-GDP ratio 88, 90

Japan
  debt-GDP ratio 87
  economic success 181
  FTA negotiations 155
  GDP
    forecasts 42, 44
    growth 31–2
    ratio to world total 34–5
  industrial output growth 32
  labour productivity in industry 136
  research and development expenditure 39, 47
  revenue-GDP ratio 88, 90
  science and technology power 37, 46
    China vs 38
  trade surplus with China 128
  and WTO 172
Jia Zhangke 26
Jiang Zemin 195, 197, 198
Jiangsu 196
jiaqiang zhizheng nengli 202
joint ventures (JVs) 62, 64

KMT 18, 19–20, 190–1, 195
knowledge
  distribution, indigenous vs. foreign companies 57
  know-how type 55
  production 55–6, 69
  see also codified knowledge; tacit knowledge
knowledge-based economy 47
knowledge filters 57–8, 64
knowledge industrialization 66
Korea, Republic of
  debt-GDP ratio 87
  economic success 181
  FTA negotiations 155
  labour productivity in industry 136
  revenue-GDP ratio 88
  trade surplus with China 128
Kunshan 176
Kuomintang of China *see* KMT

labour force, absorption rate 130
labour productivity, in industrial sector 133, 136
labour rights 204

labour supply 130, 140
late-development advantage 40
law, rule of 192, 196
learning, parallel 64
learning-economy 47
legal system 171, 206
legitimacy capacity 181
Leninist party-state 181–2
Li Peng 176
Li Shimin 21
Li Xiannian 198
life expectancy 107
Liu Zhihua 196
local state corporatism 173–4
localism 174, 175, 195
locality, nationalization of 24–5
Luding Bridge 19

Macao 177
MacFarquhar, Roderick 186
macroeconomic control 160
Malaysia, labour productivity in industry 136
manufacturing goods 203
  exports 121, 125
  imports 122, 125
Mao Zedong 153, 160
  class struggle 197
  Communist Party of China under 194, 195
  three canals proposal 83
Market Exchange Rate (MER) basis
  economic power 33–4, 40–1, 43
  Purchasing Power Parity (PPP) basis vs 54
  research and development expenditure 48, 49
marketization policy 178, 179
mass media, control 14
mass media politics 17
May Fourth Movement 11
Mazu 25
memories, collective 14
Mexico, minimum wage rates 131
MFA 150, 158
military power 146
  national wealth vs 22
Minimum Living Standard Assistance (MLSA) 79
minimum wage rates 130–1
Ministry of Civil Affairs (MCA) 201
Ministry of Commerce 205, 207
Ministry of Education (MOE) 112
Ministry of Finance (MOF) 112, 205
Ministry of Foreign Affairs (MFA) 150, 158
Ministry of Higher Education 153
Ministry of Railways 159
missions
  Chinese
    diplomatic 151–2
    to international organizations 152
'My Long March' 18–19

nanotechnology 49
Nathan, Andrew 186
nation-state 169, 181
  see also governance
national debt
  comparative perspective 94–5
  see also debt-GDP ratio
national emotion 8, 12, 13–14
  background 14–17
  producing 18–22
national lesson 146
National People's Congress (NPC) 150, 195, 199, 205
  Standing Committee 199, 205
National Science and Technology Conference (NSTC) 38
national study 26
national wealth, military power vs 22
nationalistic violence 28–9
NATO 156
negotiation, in diplomacy 157–8, 162, 163
neo-liberalism 170, 177
NETDZs 139
Netherlands
  debt-GDP ratio 88
  revenue-GDP ratio 88
  trade deficit with China 128
New Cooperative Medical Scheme (NCMS) 108–9, 110–11
New Deal policy 179
new diplomacy 159
'New Socialist Countryside' 107, 110
new technological regime 59
New Zealand, FTA negotiations 155
NGOs 201–2
Ninghua Battalion 19
nomenklatura system 195–6
non-interference 154, 158, 161, 163
North Korea, nuclear program 16
NPC *see* National People's Congress

occidentalism, Chinese version 20–1
OECD countries, fiscal situation 86–8, 94–5
Olympic Games 26, 153

open door policy 58, 197, 202–3
open-up effect 35
'opening up' 119, 182
Opium War 20, 22
Organization of American States (OAS) 156
overseas Chinese 132
ownership reform 133

Pakistan, FTA negotiations 155
Pan-PRD project 177
Pan Yue 92
parallel learning 64
party capacity 191–2
party groups 199–200
party management of cadres 195–6
Party Secretary-General 198
party/state relations, changing 197–200
patent applications 37, 51–2
  by foreign companies 63
Patent Cooperation Treaty (PCT) 51
patent system 37
patriotism education 15
peacekeeping 157
pensions 179
People's Bank of China 88
People's Liberation Army (PLA) 146–7, 150
personal quality, development 17
personal responsibility 113
personal services 178
personalisation 191–2
'petit nationalism' 2, 28
Philippines, minimum wage rates 131
physical power 147
PLA 146–7, 150
planning economic system 131
  see also economic reform
policy implementation capability 110–13
Political Bureau 195
political engagement, by social groups 200–2
political parties 187–92
  in China 189–92
    see also Communist Party of China (CCP/CPC); KMT
  in East Asia 189
  in West 187–9, 191
political restructuring 182
political viability, economic sustainability and 86
politics
  of culture 16
  of events 27
  television 23
pollution 82, 140–1
poverty, growth of 159
poverty rate 92
poverty relief 154
power 148
power supply failure 3, 77, 78
  highest probability 78
Premier 199
price liberalisation 133
primary goods
  exports 121, 125
  imports 122, 125
private enterprises 133
private non-enterprise units (PNEUs) 201
privatization policy 178
production, industrial *see* industrial production
professionalism 198–9
property rights 205–6
protectionism 28
provincial party secretaries 200
Provincial People's Congress 200
public diplomacy 150
public emotion *see* national emotion
public expenditure, management reform 104
public sector, commercialization 106
public services
  accountability of providers 112
  urban-rural gap 107
Purchasing Power Parity (PPP) basis
  economic power 33, 34, 41, 43
  Market Exchange Rate (MER) basis vs 54
  research and development expenditure 48, 49

Qin Empire 21
Qiu Xiaohua 196

random walks 94, 98
Red Army 18–19
'Red Memories' 18
reforestation 84
Reform and Opening-up Policy 15
reforms, resistance to 93
regional institutions, China's memberships 156
relational power 148–9
  China's diplomacy as 154–5
research and development expenditure
  China 39, 47
    growth 39, 48
    indigenous vs. foreign firms 62–3

research and development expenditure—
cont'd
international comparison 48–9
Market Exchange Rate (MER) basis 48, 49
Purchasing Power Parity (PPP) basis 48, 49
research and development location, China as 64–5
research fields 48–9, 50
research institutes 153
resistance, arts of 13
respiratory illnesses 140–1
revenue-GDP ratio 88, 90–1
by country 94–5
China 88, 90–1, 95
revenues
central government
discretionary 102–3
as share of GDP 102
Rise of a Great Nation 11
'rising up' 182
River Elegy 11, 23
RMB, depreciation 136–7
rural compulsory education 100, 108, 110
costs 111
difficulties 106–7, 109, 112
rural democracy 200–1
rural *dibao* (minimum living stipend) 100, 107, 108, 110–11
rural out-migration 110–11
Russia 190

S&T *see* science and technology
sandstorms 83, 84, 97
science and technology power
aggregation considerations 53–4
building process 64–6
China
forecasts 42–3
fundamental issues 55
growth driving forces 38
Japan vs 38
re-evaluation 58–66
review of indicators 48–54
rise 37–9
USA vs 38
definition 36
'GDP-type' perspective 69
'GNP-type' perspective 69
indicators 36–7, 46
new conceptual framework 55–8
'scientific development' approach 197
scientific innovative capacity 36
scientific publications 48, 50
quality 54
SCM Agreement 142–3
self-employed individuals 133
self-interest, enlightened 94
'self-raised funds' 106
separatism 175
SEZs 138, 144, 177, 204
Shanghai 82
Shanghai Cooperation Organization (SCO) 157, 172
Shantou 138
Shenzhen 138
shoes 175
Singapore
economic success 181
labour productivity in industry 136
sinking 82
SITC codes 125, 126, 127
SOBs *see* state-owned banks
social disintegration 28
social disorder 78, 80
social elites 188–9
social insurance 178
social justice 197
social programs, expenditure on 91
social welfare, socialization 178
socialist countryside 178–9
socialist market economy 76
socialist spiritual civilization 16–17, 23
socialization 178
SOEs 90, 113, 178
profits 101
soft power 148, 149, 153–4
software failure 3, 77, 78
highest probability 78
soil erosion 83
Soong Ch'ing-ling 198
South Korea, *see* Korea, Republic of
sovereignty 154, 161
Special Administrative Region (SAR) 177
special economic zones (SEZs) 138, 144, 177, 204
spillover effects 56, 58, 64–5, 140
sports 26
Standard International Trade Classification (SITC) codes 125, 126, 127
Standing Committee 199, 205
state, creation 190–1
State Administration of Taxation 205
State Council 199, 205
State Councillor 199
State Environmental Protection Agency 141
state-firm relationship 159

State Forestry Administration 83
state-owned banks (SOBs)
budget constraint 91
privatisation of units 91, 93
recapitalisation 87, 88, 90, 91
state power 180
State Presidency 198
state revenue, raising 90, 93
state-society relationships 12–13
Confucian frame 17
State Vice-Presidency 198
Still Life 26
Strategic Economic Dialogue (SED) 160
'strength' 147
structural effect 35
structural power 148–9
China's diplomacy as 155–7
students, in Communist Party of China 194
sub-regional institutions, China's memberships 156
subsidies 142–3
actionable 142
prohibited 142
Subsidies and Countervailing Measures (SCM) Agreement 142–3
substate institutions 169–70, 173–5
Summer Palace 20
Sun Yat-sen 190
suprastate organizations 169, 170–3
sustainable development 92
Sweden
debt-GDP ratio 88
revenue-GDP ratio 88

tacit knowledge 55, 57
foreign presence and 58–62
Taiwan
and commodity chains 175–6
democratic development 79
economic success 181
intervention into 161
KMT retreat to 191
trade surplus with China 128
Taiyuan 82
Tang Empire 21–2
tax rebates 102–3
Tax Sharing System (TSS) 102, 104, 174, 180
technical innovative capacity 36
technocratic movement 194
technology
assimilation 66, 67
as economic growth pivotal factor 47
import 38, 66, 67
new, capacity to apply 36
see also science and technology power
technology catch-up effect 36
telephone market 193
television
history dramas 17, 18–20, 26
see also documentaries
television politics 23
temple festivals 25
TFP *see* total factor productivity
Thailand
labour productivity in industry 136
minimum wage rates 131
think tanks 173
Third World, China as belonging to 160
Three Gorges Dam 83
'Three Represents' theory 195
Tianjin 82
tianxia 2, 21
Tibet 161
total factor productivity (TFP) 34, 40
by industrial sectors 133, 134–5
tourism 204
township elections 201
toys 175–6
trade associations 201
trade planning, reform 133–4
Trade Policy Review Body 169
Trade Policy Staff Committee (TPSC) 171
trade power, China
challenges 140–3
factors contributing 130–40
see also international trade
Trade Related Investment Measures (TRIMS) Agreement 142
trade rights 133
trade unions 202
transborder links 170, 175, 176
transfers, discretionary 103
Transition Monitoring Mechanism (TRM) 171–2
trapped transition 93–4
Treaty of Amity and Cooperation (TAC) 154
TRIMS Agreement 142
TSS *see* Tax Sharing System
'two-ballot' 201

UK
GDP
growth 31–2
ratio to world total 34–5
industrial output growth 32
revenue-GDP ratio 90
science and technology power 37

UN *see* United Nations
under-central diplomacy 160
UNESCO 24–5
United Nations
  Peace Building Commission (PBC) 157
  system reform 162
universities, student numbers 51, 53
urban-rural gap, public services 107
USA
  and Chinese legal system 206
  economic power, China vs 34
  GDP
    forecasts 42, 44
    growth 31–2
    ratio to world total 34–5
  industrial output growth 32
  New Deal policy 179
  North Korean nuclear program and 162
  research and development expenditure 39, 47
  revenue-GDP ratio 88, 90
  and rise of China 182
  science and technology power 37, 46
    China vs 38
  Strategic Economic Dialogue (SED) 160
  taxes 90
  trade deficit with China 128
  and WTO 171, 172
Uzbekistan 172

value-added tax (VAT) 91, 104
values-based diplomacy 161, 162
'values-free' diplomacy 161
Vice Premier 199
village committees 200–1
village investment funds 110–11

Wal-Mart Stores 202
Wang Longde 100
'war on the internet' 2, 28
water
  conservation 84
  shortage 78, 82–5
water pollution 82, 140–1
Wen Jiabao 76–7, 79, 100, 178–9
Western Europe, GDP, forecasts 42
Westernization movement (*yangwu yundong*) 11
World Bank (WB) 155
World Non-material Cultural Heritage Chapter 24–5
World Trade Organization *see* WTO
Woxin Xiangtan 21
WTO 170
  antidumping cases 125, 172
  Chinese entry to 155, 170
  Chinese membership of 170–2
  Dispute Settlement Mechanism 171
  obligations to 142–3, 171
  Trade Policy Review Body 169
  Transition Monitoring Mechanism (TRM) 171–2
WTO Agreement 171
WTO Implementation Coordination Committee 171

Xiamen 138
Xiang River, battle of 19
xiaokang shehui 197

Yang, Old Sister 19
Yang Jiechi 158
Yang Shangkun 198
Yangtze River 84
Yao Ming 148
Ye Xuanping 176
Yellow River 82, 83
Yingxiong 21, 26
Yixian 25
Yuanmingyuan 20–1

Zeng Qinghong 198
Zhang Yimou 21, 26
Zhao Ziyang 96, 198
Zhenguanzichi 21
zhonghua minzu 15, 28
Zhou Enlai 146, 153
Zhuhai 138, 177
zones, types 177
Zouping 173